NAVY DAREDEVIL

I came to Vietnam to fight communists, but I thought of them as armed Viet Cong and NVA regulars. I never once thought I might be moving against a fellow American. It went against the grain. Despite all the training and indoctrination they'd put me through, I wasn't able to just accept that it was our duty, and therefore right for us to do. It was the way the enemy themselves would do it. Once we went in that room, once we laid hands on him, there was no turning back . . . .

COVERT ACTIONS

Also by James R. Reeves
Published by Ballantine Books:

MEKONG!

COVERT ACTIONS

JAMES R. REEVES
AND JAMES C. TAYLOR

BALLANTINE BOOKS • NEW YORK

Library of Congress Catalog Card Number: 86-91589

ISBN 0-345-33136-2

Manufactured in the United States of America

First Edition: April 1987

*This book is dedicated to all who,
however reluctantly,
served their country when called,
and to those who now stand ready.*

PREFACE

This story, like its predecessor, *Mekong!*, is based on the actual experiences of James C. Taylor, a former SEAL and Vietnam veteran. Like *Mekong!*, it is fictionalized, although to a lesser extent. The reader will discern five episodes, any one of which could be expanded to book length if extensively fictionalized. All five episodes took place during Mr. Taylor's first, and only, tour in Vietnam. The second tour is completely fictitious. Many of the characters are modeled on the men with whom Mr. Taylor served, although some are totally creations of our imaginations. The names of all characters are totally fictitious.

CHAPTER 1

We had the layout, and we knew his room number, so once we got into the corridor, it was simple enough to find his stateroom. We only had to worry about someone coming into the corridor and seeing us. We moved quietly. Bob lightly brushed with his fingertips the door of each room as he passed along one side, counting silently. I did the same on the other side, and with my free hand took out the syringe I carried on a cord looped around my neck. Bob came to the door, gave me a little wave, and flattened against the bulkhead while I moved up. Our bare feet made no noise on the metal deck.

I flattened against the opposite wall and looked both ways down the corridor before I checked the number on the door. It was his room all right. Hell, they even had his name on a little plastic plaque on the door. I wasn't supposed to know his name, but I couldn't help but read it, and it registered in my memory. I knew Bob had read it too. I looked over at him and our eyes met for a minute. The usual wicked glint was gone, and his forehead had little worry creases in it. He was bothered by this mission, just like I was. It was one thing to snatch a gook, or assassinate a VC cadre, but an American officer?

Well, we had come this far. I nodded at him. "Let's go do it!" I whispered.

He reached for his syringe, popped the cap on it, and held it up in his right hand, like a doctor. Then he reached for the doorknob with his left hand, and slowly began to turn it.

I moved across the corridor and waited tensely by the door. My job was to slip in, put a hand over the guy's mouth so he couldn't cry out, and position his head so Bob could stick the needle in his neck. The beds were all on one side of the room, but a man could sleep with his head toward either the aft or the forward bulkhead, and I had to determine which way his head was turned in no more time than it would take me to cross the room. Unless he was afraid of the dark and slept with a night-light, there would be only the dim glow of the watch light over his door to see by. I wished I had a flashlight, even a little penlight, in case the shadows were darker than we had anticipated.

If I made a mistake and grabbed his feet, he'd yell and bring the sentries running. What would we do then? Take him anyway? Leave him, with him warned now that NISO was onto him? Kill him? Could we get away without having to kill a sentry or them killing one of us? What if he woke up when the door opened? Suppose the hinges squeaked. Suppose . . .

"Goddamn!" Bob whispered. "It's locked!"

I looked at his hand and saw it slipping on the knob as he tried to turn it. I looked at his eyes again. His forehead was furrowed, and big beads of sweat trickled from wrinkle to wrinkle. He shook his head, indicating he couldn't open the door. I glanced back at it as he released his grip. There was a keyhole. It was possible the colonel had a habit of locking his door. But I had to try it myself. I couldn't believe we'd come all this way just to find the damned door locked.

Then I noticed that the crack along the doorjamb was wider at the bottom than at the knob, or above it. In fact, the door appeared to have a slight curve to it, as if it had to bend slightly in order to latch. Of course! The bulkhead was warped. There was probably a change of stress in the hull because the ship was virtually empty of fuel. The door might be jammed closed instead of locked.

I grasped the knob with both hands, and pulled as I turned it. My palms were sweaty and slipped, so I automatically rubbed them on my chest. The wetsuit hadn't dried out, though, and it did no good. Bob grinned and reached inside his wetsuit for the olive drab scarf he'd brought along in case we needed a blindfold. I wiped my hands on it and tried again. It began to turn. I pulled and turned *very* slowly, so it wouldn't click loudly when the latchbolt cleared the facing.

The click was very faint. I held the door closed with the knob turned fully, so that the latchbolt remained completely retracted, and looked over at Bob. There were fewer worry-wrinkles around his eyes now. He nodded slightly to signal that he was ready to go. I took the plunger end of my syringe between two fingers of my left hand, so that it would be ready if I needed it. I looked at my watch. About fifteen minutes had elapsed since we'd first come aboard.

We hadn't been seen yet, but a sentry might step into the corridor at any moment.

I took a deep breath and exhaled slowly. My heart was pounding so hard it was almost shaking my body with each beat, but not from fear. It was adrenaline pumping.

When I opened that door, I would go into the stateroom of an American officer to kidnap him and turn him over to NISO interrogators for questioning. It might be the end of his career. It might be the end of his life. I had come to Vietnam to fight communists— armed Vietcong and NVA regulars. I'd never once thought I might be moving against a fellow American. It went against the grain. Despite all the training and indoctrination they'd put us through, it just didn't seem right. It was more like something the enemy would do. Once we went in that room, once we laid hands on him, there was no turning back. We were committed to a course of action, and we'd have to live with the memory of it for the rest of our lives. If I was going to back out, it would have to be now. How the hell had I gotten myself into this situation?

Not many who know me would believe it, but I was raised in a real churchy family. When I was a kid I went to church every Sunday and read my Bible for Sunday school, too, but not much of it took. I was aware of the book of Job back then, but I never paid much attention to it. I was young, and full of piss and vinegar, and figured none of that kind of thing was going to happen to me.

Lately, though, I've been thinking that maybe old Job and me have a lot more in common than I realized back then. Of course, he was a godly man, and he didn't do anything to bring on all his bad luck. It seems like God and Satan had a little bet going about whether Job could bear up if times were hard, and God let Satan dump on Job. Kind of shitty business, if you ask me. I mean, wasn't Job making all those sacrifices and crap in the first place just so God would look after him?

Anyway, I made some sacrifices too: four years of my life, and some blood, and the hearing in my left ear, not to mention going through a lot of fearsome and worrisome times. I did that for the people of the United States, because it was their government that said they needed me to do it. I expected a few things from them in return, like getting my life started again, and some help with my medical bills, maybe a break getting a job. Instead, they dumped on me. They made me a scapegoat for the war, and turned their backs on me when it came to getting a job or even trying to tell them why I was unhappy.

Old Job, he sat in the dirt and tore his clothes and threw ashes over his head when he got uptight. I sit here in my living room and stare at the fire and drink Scotch. If I turn on the television, there's that god-damned Jane Fonda in another movie making millions off the notoriety she got from supporting our enemies. Pisses me off.

At least Job's friends came around to see him sometimes, even if they only sat there with long faces and drank his wine and told him he ought to just curse God and get put out of his misery. My friends don't come by very often, and when they do, they don't want to talk about what's happened to me. They want to drink my beer and whiskey and talk about almost anything else. It makes them uncomfortable to talk about the war, because they weren't in it. They were safe over here, getting set up in careers and having families and fucking their neighbors' wives and all the time raking in the money, while I was over there in the mud and rain with those damned little devils trying to blow off a chunk of my ass.

Well, so be it. I'll sit here in front of the fire and sip my Scotch until the sun comes up and the time for nightmares is over. The fire reminds me of the camp we hit with flamethrowers, and that starts me thinking again. Thinking about the things I did and the people I killed in the name of duty and honor and country.

I was in some firefights in 'Nam, a lot of them, and I killed a lot of Viet Cong and North Vietnamese soldiers. Sometimes I think about the girl with the bomb strapped to her back, or some of the others. I shot them or blew them up or broke their necks or cut their throats, but they were fighters—they'd have done the same to me. The girl, too. I don't regret killing them. Their ghosts don't haunt me. If I'd been just a little slower, or noisier, or more careless, they might be thinking about me now, and I wouldn't haunt them, either.

It's other ghosts that bother me. Some that didn't die in combat. American ghosts.

When I left Vietnam that first time I thought I'd seen the last of that godforsaken place. I was happy as hell to be coming back alive, even if I did have a hole in my head where my left eardrum was supposed to be. Things didn't go well for me, though.

First off, in the airport in San Diego a runty little MP told me I had to take off my black beret, because it wasn't recognized in the States. I guess it bothered

the peaceniks and little old ladies—of both sexes—
who didn't like to be reminded about Vietnam.

Then the stateside doctors decided my wound—the
damaged eardrum—wasn't severe enough to warrant
a discharge. If the entire eardrum had been missing it
would have been a total disability, but in the inter-
vening weeks some scar tissue had patched things together in there. I had partial hearing that would come
and go. It was bad enough I couldn't dive anymore.
Oh, ten or twelve feet in a swimming pool didn't
bother me, but the pain got pretty severe if I tried to
go deeper. So I lost my diver rating.

I still had two years of active duty to go before my
enlistment was up. The Navy would reassign me to
something for that time. They even tried to get me to
go back to 'Nam, in the riverboat Navy. They must
have thought that explosion scrambled my brains.

I'd brought some problems back with me. There
were things that bothered me that had happened over
there. There were times I fucked up, and got my men
killed because of it. There was one guy, named Billy,
whose death bothered me really bad. Some people
seem to think that to be in Special Forces you have
to be some sort of unfeeling superman. We're not.
We have feelings just like everybody else.

It had been months since Billy died, and I still
thought about it all the time. Billy had placed his trust
in me. He was forever telling his wife about me, and
how well we got along. I guess the reason I took him
under my wing was because he was one of the few
guys that really had a lot going for him. He loved his
family very much and they loved him a lot too. He
always got letters and tapes from home, telling him

how much they missed him and how proud they were
of what he was trying to do in 'Nam.

Not very many guys got letters like that. I didn't.
His wife would always say hi and tell me to take care
of myself, or something like that, when she sent a
tape. I talked a little to his wife and his dad, once,
on the tape recorder. They recorded a little message
back. His dad said, "It sounds like Billy's got a good
friend." Not once did I ever hear them say that the
war was a lot of bullshit. Not once did they ever write
it. They were behind him all the way. They were
strong and proud people, and I guess I wanted to be
part of that. He had everything going for him, and I
wanted him to have it. That's why I tried to keep him
from seeing a lot of action.

In the last tape he got, his wife told him that in five
more months his name was going to be changed to
Daddy. That really made Billy light up. He had been
in 'Nam a little over three months, and he was looking forward to being a father. She went on to say how
much she loved him and how much she cared. She
ended the tape, "You and Jay take care of each other,
and the baby and I will do the same."

The guys were forever telling me about their problems at home, or with each other, wondering what to
do. Billy just told me about how great everything was
at home. He knew I didn't get any mail from back
there. When he was around, I had someone to listen
to *me* for a change, and I could get all the shit out of
my head. He couldn't offer any advice; he'd never
had to make a life-or-death decision with someone
else's life, so he couldn't fully understand the hurt
and the guilt that you're left with. But he really cared,
and that was good enough.

Then we walked into an ambush. They got around us on three sides and were really pouring it into us. I thought I'd get Billy out of it, and I sent him back for help. They got him before he could get very far. We fought our way out of the ambush, and it was a running fight all the way back to the river. I carried his body out. The ironic thing is, the rest of us only got flesh wounds.

That was months before I was shipped stateside, and when I got back, I still couldn't close my eyes without seeing the back of his head fly off, or feeling the stickiness of the blood as I held him in my arms. I was still haunted by his wife's words on that last tape: "You and Jay take care of each other. . . ." I tried. I tried.

I wrote a report on how it happened, and they sent it with the telegram informing his family of his death. I haven't heard from his family since it happened. I think they blamed me, and rightly so.

But there were some other things, too. . . .

I had nightmares and flashbacks before I left 'Nam, but not so bad as I had them when I got back to the States. I didn't sleep as soundly in Vietnam. A lot of the times, I took Dexedrine to keep me alert. On patrols, I didn't sleep at all, unless they lasted several days, and then I only slept lightly. If I had a nightmare it woke me. When I got back to the States I slept more soundly, and sometimes I wouldn't wake up when I had a nightmare. I would be up, moving around, and still be having the nightmare. It was like sleepwalking. It scared me. I was afraid I would hurt someone while I was dreaming.

The flashbacks were like nightmares, but they came when I was awake. They'd come when I was tired, or had been drinking, or had somehow let my guard down. It was like I had this little sentry in my mind keeping the flashbacks away, and they'd get in when he was tired, or intoxicated, or had been distracted by something. In 'Nam, the nervous tension of being on patrol, the fear of being ambushed and killed, kept the sentry alert. Back at the barge, I was with people that could handle it if I flashed back. I wasn't worried that I would flash back and strangle Bob or shoot him; he could take care of himself. But in the States, I worried about hurting somebody.

The newspapers didn't help either. They made a big deal out of it every time something happened: "VIETNAM VET GOES NUTS, SHOOTS MOTHER" or some such garbage. That just made me worry more.

Sometimes the nightmares would be scenes—things I had seen, horrible things that make you lose respect for your fellow man and start thinking of him as an animal. Like that time in Bac Lieu Province.

It was one of those villages you encountered sometimes that was really neutral. They had their own armed guards there to protect them, and some of them were mean as hell. A real rough bunch. They were probably smugglers and pirates, but that was their village and they didn't want the Saigon government or the Viet Cong coming in there telling them what to do. They weren't from the Delta originally; they had been moved down from I Corps—Quang Tri Province—by the Marines as part of a resettlement program. The village they'd been in before had occupied a key position, and they'd been caught in crossfire pretty often. They didn't like the Delta much, but I guess the land was good for rice, and there wasn't the constant fighting there had been up north. They were short of housing. There were only four or five buildings in the village, and each was occupied by three or four families, with five or six people to the family.

There were a bunch of elderly people there, and some very young ones, but not many young adults. Most of them had either taken up with one side or the other and left the village to fight, or had been killed by the Viet Cong or arrested by the government.

We went in on a mercy mission, carrying food and medicine, and made friends with them, after a fashion. We couldn't talk to them, because they didn't know English, but we treated their sores and injuries, and fed their kids. And we'd check in on them every once in a while to make sure they were all right. We'd help them with their boats and things.

Then an NVA regiment slipped into the area and started building up. A patrol ran into them and took four or five casualties. Then a Vietnamese Marine patrol went into this village for a couple of weeks and muddled around the paddies, but came back reporting no contact. We were sent in to see if we could locate the NVA so the Army could bring an air cav outfit in and drive them out.

Bac Lieu Province was flat and mostly covered by rice paddies, with lots of little villages scattered here and there. Near the coast the rice paddies gave way to marshes and mangrove swamps, and there were a few little wooded areas scattered around. That's where the Viet Cong and the NVA would hide out. There were a few rubber plantations and banana plantations in there too. Most of the villages were either near the coast or along streams, because most of the transportation was by boat. There were damned few roads, and only a few trails.

This NVA outfit practiced psychological warfare.

They would go into a village and warn the people that the Americans and the ARVNs would torture them and kill them. These NVA had some ARVN uniforms and a white man working with them. He might have been a Frenchman or a Russian. Or an American. They'd dress up in the uniforms and go into the village several days later and interrogate people, torture them, maybe kill some. The white guy would go in with them, and he'd "order" the murders and the torture. That way they discredited both Americans and South Vietnamese.

We went into the village with a interpreter and told them what the situation was. They believed us. Maybe it had happened to them before, up in Quang Tri Province. Anyway, they told us the NVA had been there several days before and had "warned" them. They told us which way they'd gone. It was a cold trail, leading out into the open paddies and marshes, and we didn't follow it. We figured they might have set booby traps on their back trail, or doubled back and ambushed it. And we didn't think they'd go far across the paddies anyway. We struck out instead to where we thought they'd most likely be, and didn't find anything.

Coming back out, we thought we'd swing back by the village and just check on them. As soon as we caught sight of it we knew Charlie had doubled back on us, and it hadn't been too long since they'd left. Some of the houses had been burned down and were still smoking.

A few villagers had survived. Some were unhurt, some were just alive, and some were mercifully dead. Some had been burned, and some had been mutilated. They had lost fingers, toes, noses, and ears. Some had been strung up between two trees, with their genitals cut off and stuffed in their mouths. One old man had his tongue cut out and the stump tied off to keep him from bleeding to death. He was damned near dead from shock anyway. The younger men, the guards who had fought back against the NVA's attack, had been tied hand and foot and then the big artery in their thighs had been punctured so they would slowly bleed to death. There were big puddles of blood around them. Some of the others had been shot in the kneecaps, to cripple them for life. Others had their arms broken at the elbows, compound fractures with the sharp splinters of the bones sticking out through the flesh. Some of the women had been impaled on bamboo stakes, with the stakes rammed into their crotches and coming out their chests or their mouths. Some had had their breasts removed. Their babies were just lying there. They hadn't had anything to eat or drink in a day. Other babies had been beheaded or cut into pieces. There were little kids crawling around crying who had been bayoneted or shot. One woman had her breasts slit—not cut off, just split in two. She had to hold them together with her hands. If she let go, they started bleeding again.

Some of the older people had gotten out of it without being mutilated. But not many.

It was the worst incident of this kind I'd ever seen, or even heard about. Some guys who had been in Vietnam several tours said it was the worst they knew about too.

Of course, we did all we could to help them, but we didn't carry that much in the way of medical supplies. We called in for medivacs and a team of medics, and tried to staunch the flow of blood from the worst wounds until they got there. It was just a finger in the dike compared to what they needed. The medics came on the first chopper, and they just walked around in a daze for several minutes, looking at the carnage.

It was a vile thing to do. Those people didn't want to be involved with either side. They didn't want the Americans around, or the South Vietnamese, or the North Vietnamese. They just wanted to be left alone. They'd learned to adapt to the war and survive the war on their own, without help from either side. To die the way they died, to be punished for surviving, just wasn't warranted. They were decent people. They didn't deserve that.

We were stunned by it. And we would get sick thinking about it for days and weeks afterward.

I had a lot of animosity toward the enemy after that.

Before, when we'd capture a VC or NVA, if he was just an enlisted man and unlikely to have much information of value, we'd try to psych them out by being nice to them. We'd feed 'em, fix up their wounds, even bathe them and delouse them. We'd put our black berets on them, pat them on the back, and talk to them about baseball. They liked baseball. We'd tell them about football, and about movies. They liked westerns. Then we'd tell them, ''We don't want to kill your people. We'll kill those that are shooting at us, but we're not here just to kill people. We're going to let you go. You go back and tell your people we're not here just to kill them. Now, go on.'' And they'd run off. Others would walk away, looking back every once in a while like they didn't believe it.

We weren't likely to do that anymore. We'd cut on them or just kill them instead of letting them go. I didn't care. After Bac Lieu, I never felt any compassion for them.

I had nightmares about Bac Lieu in 'Nam, and when I got back to the States. Especially when I got back here. I tried to make people understand why, but they didn't want to hear about it. A lot of them didn't want to believe it. Uncle Ho could do no wrong in their eyes.

Sometimes the nightmares would be what I called the Escape Dream, with me trying to escape and Charlie coming after me. This dream also came out of something that really happened.

It wasn't long after the massacre at Bac Lieu that we went in for a recon patrol up the coast in Ba Xuyen Province. We landed just inside one of the mouths of the Mekong called the Cua Tranh De, intending to walk about ten kilometers overland to a village. We planned to observe for several days. Command suspected supplies were being landed there by boat from North Vietnam.

We went in about 0600, and it was raining. Goddamn, it was pouring down, and it was muddy. The mud was over your ankles and sometimes up to your knees. Everything was either mud or under water. The boats dropped us off on a little sandbar right at the mouth of the river, and that was the last firm ground we saw. We moved directly into some jungle. There was jungle along the river for quite a ways there.

I took the point, and I was the one who spotted the gooks. I don't know how many there were, but they had encased us. We weren't that far from the beach, but the boats were already gone. They had our backs to the water.

Bob was on my right flank and Tony on my left. The bush was thick, and we were moving in close order to stay in sight of each other so we wouldn't miss any hand signals. We hadn't gone very far inland when I spotted two NVA moving in a zigzag path toward me. I raised my hand to signal a halt and glanced quickly around at the team to make sure they saw me. When I looked back to the front I saw another one on the left, also moving in. Looking around, I saw two more, behind the first two I'd spotted, also moving up.

The bush had thinned out right where we'd encountered them, and I was afraid I'd give our position away if I moved, but the gooks appeared to be getting more numerous. They must have heard the PBR throttle down to land us, or else an observer on the bank had radioed back a warning. They knew we were coming in, and they were moving into position to hit us. They were moving fast and knew what they were doing. It was time to act.

I pressed the button on my hand radio. "Five Hotel Charlies on the point and moving in. Reply?" "Hotel Charlie" was the code for "hardcore" and was less of a mouthful than "November Victor Alfa" for NVA.

"Three on the right flank." That was Bob.

"One on the left," Tony said.

"Okay, stand by to rock 'n' roll. On my lead," I answered. There wasn't time to say much more.

I let the radio swing back down by my side and switched my rifle to fully automatic. More enemy had come into sight. When they were about thirty feet away I opened fire. The others followed. It sounded like Chinese New Year and the Fourth of July all at once.

"Back it up! Move! *Move! Move!*" I yelled. I was moving backwards, firing with my rifle held high, between my hip and my shoulder.

Bob was shouting, "Go! Go! *Go!* Damn it! *Go!*"

And the gooks were shouting to each other just like we were. There was a hell of a racket out there.

I had backed away about forty feet and had emptied one clip and reloaded when *pop!* I was knocked forward and down, face-first into the mud. I was in a very small clearing, about the size of a bathroom, and the mud there had come halfway up my shins. I dropped my rifle when I went down, and pain started shooting through my head.

I tried to get up. I got my knees under me and could support my weight with my left arm, but when I tried to stand up I fell to the right. I couldn't hold my head up, and my vision was blurred. I tried once again, but that time I couldn't even get my head off the ground. I couldn't move my right leg or my right arm, and every once in a while my body would jerk.

"Goddamn, I'm hit!" I yelled. I could still hear the team shooting, and shouting to each other, but my own words sounded distant and echoed in my head. "They've blown my head off, Bob!"

"Damn you, Jay! You son of a bitch!" he shouted back. He didn't want to leave me, but he knew he had to. He was shouting to the team to move back when a couple of NVAs ran past me. Two more entered the clearing and stopped to look down at me. I heard Bob yell "Let's go!" one more time, and that was the last English I heard.

I could feel something warm running down the nape of my neck. I thought the gooks might shoot me if I moved, but I had to know how bad it was, so I felt the back of my head with my left hand. I could feel a large knot and a cut, but nothing that felt like jelly. I wasn't losing any brains, anyway. If I had been shot, it wasn't bad. There hadn't been an explosion, so I was sure it wasn't a grenade or a mine. I probably tripped a deadfall or Malay sling, and a pole or some part of it had hit me a glancing blow on the head. It had knocked the hell out of me.

My vision was starting to clear, but the pain was still throbbing through my head. I could hear shots fired somewhere in the distance, and I instinctively felt for my rifle. I couldn't find it anywhere.

Several more NVA had come into the clearing. They just stood there and looked down at me. Finally, one rolled me over and stuck the muzzle of his rifle in my chest and started jabbering at me. I didn't know what he was saying, so I just lay there and looked at him. Then he reached down and ripped my shirt open. That seemed to be a signal to the others, who started pulling my boots off and ripping my pockets to get everything out of them.

One of them found my beret. He walked over to me, shouting, and kicked me in the nuts. The pain took my breath away, and I had to struggle for air. They rolled me over and stuck my face down in the mud. I knew I'd had it then. I just knew I'd had the big Green Weenie. He held me by the hair and put his entire weight into pushing my head down. If I struggled, I just burrowed my face deeper in the mud. I tried to hold my breath, but I hadn't had a chance to catch a deep breath when they rolled me over, and soon my lungs were demanding air. I clamped my lips together, but very soon an involuntary gasp filled my nostrils with mud. I struggled harder, twisting and wriggling my body to throw him off, but one of them kicked me in the groin again. The sharp pain forced another gasp past my clamped lips, and my mouth filled with foul slime.

They rolled me over to twist my arms up behind my back and tie my wrists together. I vomited, and cleared most of the mud from my mouth. They didn't cross my wrists. They made a loop around one wrist and then around the other, and jerked them so that my palms were together. They tied off the loops, then went around three or four more times and tied another knot in the middle. They used something like a strip of leather about half an inch wide. It wasn't rope.

When they tightened my hands down behind my back I felt a warmth surge through my body, like someone had injected hot coffee into my veins. I thought for a second, "I'm dying now, they've suffocated me. In a moment everything will go black." But it didn't. That was when I realized they were tying my hands. Feeling was returning to them, but too late. They already had several turns of leather on my wrist.

Then they kicked me in the groin again and rolled me over on my back. I was hurting too much from the kick to fight, but at least I could breathe. I sucked in a deep breath—still tasting the foul gray mud, but it didn't matter right then.

I expected they would take my diving watch, but they overlooked it or something. It was on a black band and had been in the mud. Possibly they hadn't seen it. I wore it on the inside of my wrist, and it was partly covered by the bonds.

They worked on tying my feet while I gasped for breath, and then they started kicking and stomping on my legs. It surprised and confused me at first, then I blacked out for a while. They really worked me over. When I did come around, I realized they did it to make my legs swell so it would be harder to get the bonds off, and to make it hard for me to escape if I did get loose.

When I realized again what was going on, they were

dragging me off into the bush. I couldn't see any familiar surroundings or anything. One of my eyes wouldn't open all the way. It didn't feel swollen. I just couldn't lift the lid more than a tiny slit. Even with the other eye open, I couldn't see anything but the undergrowth they were dragging me through. They were dragging me face down, by my arms, and limbs and leaves kept slapping me in the face. I was worried that a broken limb or thorn might jab me in the eye, and I tried to keep my face turned back and to the side.

Then I'd think, "Shit! Don't worry about getting an eye gouged out! They're going to do it anyway!"

I passed out several times while they were dragging me.

While I was out I had nightmares about Bac Lieu. I had visions of the men that had their genitals severed and stuffed in their mouths, and I was one of them. I guess the pain in my groin and the shitty taste of the mud in my mouth contributed to that.

Then I woke up. They'd stopped dragging me. They'd taken me to the edge of their camp, but they didn't take me on in. I guess I was too much of a load for them and they got tired. There were three of them around me. They had me on my side, and one guy had hold of my forearm. When I tried to straighten up, he lifted up on my forearm and it would hurt through the shoulders.

I could hear voices and shouting and laughter. It sounded to me like a village full of cannibals carrying on over the missionary in the pot, hollering and whooping it up over the big kill they'd just made—or were going to make.

CHAPTER 2

The people from the camp kept coming over and looking at me. It was annoying. It made me feel like a goddamned monkey in a cage. They'd come over and they'd look down at me, and some of them would kick me in the nuts with their insteps. It wasn't a hard kick, just enough to hurt without making them numb. It gave me belly cramps, and it hurt way up into my chest. Every now and then one of them would kick me in the back. The unexpected, sharp pain would make my back arch. Then they would kick me in the groin again and make me double up the other way.

They just wanted to keep me down. I was so much bigger than they were, I think they were afraid I might get loose and take after them.

After a while, the pain from getting kicked in the

groin just became part of a general overall pain. It still hurt to get kicked, but the intensity was less. My body would jerk, but the pain just didn't register in my mind like it had before.

It was tough to judge what time of day it was, but the rain had stopped, and the sun broke through the clouds. It got hot fast with the sun beating down, and the wet ground started steaming. The sun in my eyes made my head hurt worse, and the drying mud on my face gave me a peculiar feeling of tightening.

I was lying on my back with my arms under me, and I noticed a lump in my back where my left wrist was. I moved my arms and the lump moved also. That was when I first realized they had overlooked my diving watch. It had a compass attached.

One of them came up with a bamboo pole. It wasn't a thick one, just an inch or so around. They were yacking at each other, and they'd poke me with the damned pole, in the face or in the belly or in the groin—especially in the groin. They seemed to get their kicks out of that. When I stopped reacting to the kicks enough to satisfy them, they began to whack me with the pole. They hit me on the shins, causing big welts that began to throb. Then they began to hit me on the ends of my toes, and it hurt like the devil, like jamming your finger. It made the joints swell and stiffen.

They just kept on and on like that, whacking me with the pole and kicking me in the groin every once in a while. The pain was like when you got a whipping. They'd hit or kick and then wait a second or so to let the blood come back, and then hit or kick again. Then they'd wait, and hit or kick, wait, and hit or kick . . .

They'd say things to me in Vietnamese, but of course I couldn't understand what they were saying. They

weren't cursing me or spitting on me or anything like
that. I think it was just the usual military questions:
"How many of you were there? Where were you supposed to rendezvous? What was your mission?" But
they didn't torture me to get information, because I
couldn't understand their questions and they didn't seem
to have anyone there who spoke English.

With all that, they didn't cut on me or anything.
They must have known I was Special Forces, and
they were holding off on that shit until I was questioned by someone who spoke English. I'd been
wounded in the head already, and they'd probably get
their asses chewed out if they did something to me
that killed me before they could interrogate me.

Finally, I was too dazed to react at all anymore, and
I closed my eyes and thought, "To hell with it. I'm just
going to sleep and end it all." That was when they left
me alone. When I realized they were gone, I tried to
open my eyes. My left eye still wouldn't open all the
way, and I couldn't get clear vision through it. Pain
shot through my head with every pulse-beat, and my
body throbbed all over from the beating. My toes felt
like they'd been broken, and the bonds on my wrists
and ankles were cutting off the circulation to my hands
and feet and making them swell and throb. I thought,
"Jesus, I wish I had an aspirin."

Then I got mad. Mad as hell.

When I did get my eyes open and focused, I was
looking at a thicket of bush about ten feet away. There
wasn't anything else in my line of sight, but I could
hear sounds around me as if there was a camp. I tried
looking over my shoulder, and no one hit me or
kicked me, so I rolled onto my back and then onto
my other side, to look around. The nearest gooks were

thirty or forty feet away. Several of them were squatting by a fire. One of them turned his head and glanced at me. I thought, "Oh shit, here they come again," but he just turned back to the fire.

There were other groups sitting here and there under little thatched roofs that kept the rain off their cooking fires. It wasn't a big area, just a sort of park about thirty yards across, with grass six or eight inches high, and bush and trees scattered around. A couple of Americans were sitting propped against a tree about twenty yards from me, and scattered around the area were other prisoners lying face down, or on their sides. They were all tied like I was, but the gooks didn't have us in a group, and that confused me. I thought they'd want to have us all together so if something happened they could machine-gun us all at once.

One thing I realized for sure: since this wasn't a prisoner-of-war camp, but rather a temporary camp, they were going to take me somewhere else to be interrogated.

I knew what that meant: more beatings, more kicking, water torture, bamboo slivers under the fingernails. Days on end of it. A cage too short to stand in and too cramped to sit down in. Rice and maggots to eat. Or they might decide to make an example of me to convince someone else to talk. In that case, they would really come up with something fiendish: bamboo slivers in the nostrils and ears, even in the anus and the penis. A barbed stick rammed up the anus so the intestine would tear itself to pieces trying to eliminate it. Or the old favorite—skinning alive.

I had to get out of there before they could start.

I didn't have anything to lose by trying to get away. There was a slim chance I could make it, but a slim chance was better than no chance at all. I stopped thinking about giving up and dying and started planning a way to get the hell out.

There was activity all around, people coming and going all the time. There were fifteen to eighteen gooks in sight, and it seemed as if there were more out in the bush, but I couldn't be certain.

One of the gooks squatting nearby was muttering. Every now and then he would repeat the same words, and you could see some of them shake their heads. I don't know if that meant the same thing to them as it did to me, but it looked like something was wrong. I imagined they were waiting for someone in charge and wondering why he hadn't arrived.

A couple of hours went by without my being kicked or beaten any more, and my head started clearing some. Every five or ten minutes one of the gooks would come over and poke at me a little bit, just to harass me and check on me.

The sun had gone behind the clouds again, and it wasn't bright enough to see very far but it was light enough to see the other prisoners and the enemy soldiers. It seemed to be getting somewhat darker, as if it was getting later in the afternoon. That's when I began to believe I could actually escape. I said to myself, "I can get out of here." Then I asked myself, "How?" as if I were two people carrying on a conversation. I answered back, "Just do it. Just cut the hell out. If I can get the feeling back in my legs and feet . . ." They tingled because circulation to them had been cut off by the shrinking leather strap.

I just had to get over to that damned thicket of bush and get into it. I didn't know where I would go once

I got there, but I knew damned good and well it would conceal me until I could get my hands and feet loose.

Of course, if they saw me escaping they might shoot me. Not likely if my hands and feet were still tied, but if I got them loose . . . More likely, they would just catch me and beat me some more. I surely didn't have anything to lose, so I wasn't scared. I was just determined to get away.

I thought, "If I'm going to do it, I need to go now, but it's too light. If the damned sun would just set! I wish there was a pull-chain I could yank and turn that cocksucker out!" It got darker and soon started to rain. That worried me, because my sense of time, based on the dimming sunlight, might be off by several hours. If the sun came out again after I'd made my move there'd be no way I could hide from them.

The rain began to soften the caked mud on my face and body. I rolled over on my side. My diving watch was still on my arm, and I thought, "I've got to keep that. I need to roll over on my back and keep that watch in the mud. If the rain washes all the mud off they'll see it and take it." So I rolled over on my back, even though it was uncomfortable to lie on my arms, and let the rain wash the mud off my face.

The gooks kept coming over to check on me every few minutes, and I pretended to be in a daze.

There was movement going on all around me, even on the other side of the thicket of brush I wanted to get to, but suddenly everything got quiet. The normal jungle noises stopped. The gooks stopped their muttering and chattering, and a couple of them came over to stand beside me, their weapons in their hands. I saw others go do the same with other prisoners. One took his foot and pushed over the two Americans propped against the tree. It didn't take much imagination to guess why: someone was in the area. An American or South Vietnamese patrol? Or the people they were waiting for? The torture might be just beginning, or they might be about to end my worries with a bullet.

The two gooks watching me suddenly took off into the bush at a run. I relaxed a little. I wasn't going to be shot right away, at least, but there was a patrol out there. If it was one of ours, it might mean a rescue. But these gooks would put a bullet in my head if it looked like I was about to be rescued. If I wasn't killed by a grenade or a stray bullet first. "God," I prayed, "don't let this be a rescue attempt. I've got a better chance of getting away on my own!"

About thirty minutes later, I guess—it seemed longer—I heard gunfire. There was one shot, and then a few seconds later I heard six or seven shots over toward the other side of the camp. All the other gooks I could see had their attention turned that way.

It was time to go.

I used my feet and my shoulders as much as I could, and I rolled and rolled and rolled. It seemed like I'd never get to the bush. Every move sent pain searing through my bruised muscles and strained tendons. Each time I rolled over, my head seemed like it was going to split apart.

Once I was in that clump of brush, I started pushing with my feet and inch-worming with my body, or rolling from side to side and pulling myself along on my back with my shoulders. I kept crawling and pushing and crawling and pushing and crawling until I got to an area where the bush was thicker. I managed to crawl under where it was the thickest. I hadn't gone that far—probably thirty or forty yards. Maybe it was only half that far, and it just seemed farther.

I was tired, so I just lay there a while to get my breath and think things out. Where the hell was I going to go? Here I was, my hands and feet tied, lying under a bush in a remote part of the Mekong Delta. There probably wasn't another white man within twenty miles, except for that patrol, and they were in contact with Charlie. I wasn't going to be able to go to anyone for help. Most likely the villagers around here would turn me in to the NVA, even if they didn't favor the communists, just to avoid trouble later.

I was going to have to save myself.

A slight breeze brought a whiff of salt air and an idea: if I could just get to the water, I might be able to hide there until a patrol boat came by. This area was patrolled regularly. I had a mental image of myself hiding under overhanging foliage along a steep bank while Charlie searched the bank, until a PBR sped by. The water was my element, and I convinced myself if I could just get to it, I'd be safe. My captors were probably all soldiers. I hadn't seen any diving gear in the camp. Probably they couldn't even swim, at least not well. I was sure they'd never find me.

I lay there fifteen or twenty minutes, resting and thinking. Just about the time I was getting ready to move on again, I heard movement in the bush. They were out there hunting me. Instead of moving on, I had to crawl farther into the bush and hide. I listened and could tell from the sounds that they were coming closer. I closed my eyes and tried to convince myself I was invisible. "They can't see me," I thought. "They can look right at me and not see me." I was psyching myself up to lie there without moving. I pictured myself lying there in the bushes, and then made the image of my body fade out so the bushes could be seen right through me. Then I concentrated on that picture while they searched all around me.

There were sounds of movement everywhere. Twigs snapped, branches scratched against cloth, boots squished in the mud. I could hear one of the searchers breathing from the exertion of walking in that goop. "He must be awfully close," I thought, and tried to control my own breathing while concentrating on that mental image. Brush rustled somewhere near my head.

Then a heavy weight suddenly mashed my foot into the mud! He'd stepped on my foot! I stifled a gasp of surprise and pain, but my body stiffened in anticipation of a kick or a bullet. Disappointment at failing to escape and the certainty that I would be beaten and kicked again filled my guts. And anger. I was angry at God, at the gooks, at everything. "Oh, fuck, this is it! I've had it now," I thought. "God, couldn't you be on my side just this once?" Then I thought, "Hell, I don't give a shit. Might as well get it over with." I was trying to convince myself.

I lay there waiting for what seemed like hours. It couldn't really have been more than a couple of minutes before I realized he was moving on, slowly, still searching every bush. The mud was so deep and soft my feet had just sunk in under his weight. He probably thought he'd stepped on a rotten limb or something.

"God," I said silently, "I'm sorry I got mad at You. Thank You. I know You're on my side now."

After the gook was gone, I listened until the sounds of their search moved away. Then I took off, crawling.

I went another forty or fifty feet, I guess, and then stopped again. I didn't hear any more movement.

By now I could move a lot more freely. I had worked some of the stiffness and soreness out of my bruised muscles. I started thinking about getting my hands free. I crawled into a little area that was open enough for me to move around, and I started working on getting them free.

Just as I got started, I heard the gooks coming back. I went ahead anyway.

When I was a kid, I used to "turn cattails." That means you hold onto a bar or a limb and work your legs up between your arms. Some call it "skinning a cat." I got over on my side, and I started trying to work my hands down. With my long legs and my long arms, and the way I was tied, it was awfully hard to bring my arms down and put my feet back through them. I kept working and working at it. And I kept rustling the brushes and making other noises. I was sure they would bring the gooks over to find me. The bruises on my arms and legs made them ache from the strain and stretching I was putting them through. Worse was the shooting pain in my testicles. They were swollen from the beatings too, and they were being mashed between my thighs as I tried to force my legs through my arms above the bonds. Every once in a while I would have to stop to listen and rest a little, and then start up again.

I finally got one foot through, but I couldn't work the other one up high enough. My legs hurt bad. Forcing my wrists apart as far as they could go put an extra twist in the thong that bound them and cut off the circulation to my hands. Even though my fingers were tingling and swollen, I could move them, and I was finally able to grab my pant leg and squeeze it and pull my leg up. I worked at it about thirty minutes before I got it up and through.

All this time the gooks were out there. I could hear them moving around, hunting for me, and I had to be careful not to make noise while I worked. Fortunately, they never got as close as they had been on their first sweep through the area.

After I got my hands in front of me, I waited and listened a little while. Then I started trying to untie my feet. They had taken my knife, or I would have just pulled it out and cut the bonds. I could reach the knot but it was tied awfully goddamn tight, and when I tried to pull on the knot to loosen it, my hands wouldn't grip the wet leather. They were too hurt and swollen. Neither could I bend over and pull my feet up enough to reach the knot with my teeth—that would have been hard enough anyway, and I was too sore from the beating and kicking to bend very far. The knot between my wrists was on the wrong side, and I couldn't get to that with my teeth either, so I tried working my hands to loosen the leather. That only made the bonds tighter and caused my wrists to hurt worse.

I was going to have to get by with my feet and hands tied.

Finally, I decided I'd try to stand up and see if I could get along better by hopping. I rolled over and got up onto my knees and slowly stood up from that position. Balancing was difficult. My legs were weak and tingling, and my feet were tingling and asleep. I could hop, but it jarred me. With every hop, my nuts would bounce. That hurt. I could stand up, but I couldn't move as fast as I could by crawling.

I could get to the cover on my watch, and I pulled

that off with my teeth and looked at the compass. I knew I had to go south to get to the coast and east to get to the river. Any other direction would just lead me farther into the paddies.

It was 2030—8:30 P.M., civilian time.

I got back down and started crawling southeast. I could make better time if I could grab something or hook an elbow against something and pull. I could move my legs better than I could earlier too. I stayed in the thickets, because there I had better cover and I could hook an arm around a bush or put a foot against a root and help myself along.

I could hear the VC around me, beating the bush for me. They knew I was in there, but they never did come close. I just crawled on and on.

When I got to the shoreline, I figured I had crawled about half a mile from the camp.

When I got close to the shoreline, I could smell the water and hear the sloshing of the waves on the beach. Then I wondered about the time, and I suddenly thought, "The fuckin' tide's going out! And it'll be after midnight before it starts coming back in!" That would mean a hundred feet or so of open ground to cross before I could get to the water.

When I came to the final treeline, I lay there and looked at the opening and thought, "The only thing left between me and escape is crossing that damned opening and getting to the water." There might be places where the gap between the bush and the water was narrower, or where some driftwood had piled up all the way across it, but there wasn't any as far as I could see up or down the shoreline. I would cross right here.

I figured once I got to the water I could get out far enough so that I couldn't be seen when I surfaced for air. If I had to, I could work myself along the bank, hold myself in shallow water near the shoreline, and lie in water about three feet deep and just push myself up for breaths. I didn't want to get out into deep water. If I stayed in the water long enough, the tide would come in and that would take me out to the channel anyway, but by then it would be near dawn and getting light, and I had a chance of being picked up by a passing boat. This part of the river was heavily patrolled, and the chances of a boat passing near enough to see me were pretty good. So I lay there and listened for sounds of people moving through the bush, and thought about how I could cross that area quickly. My head had cleared up quite a bit by this time.

I heard a boat run by. I couldn't see it, but I heard it. It was probably way out in the middle of the channel.

There were no sounds of anyone beating the bushes nearby, so I started. I worked my way down to the high-tide line. I couldn't crawl fast, and I knew the damned VC were still around there looking for me, even if I couldn't hear them at the moment. I knew I'd leave a trail they would easily spot and could follow, where I went in, but there was no helping it.

When I reached the open area I swung my body around parallel to the water and started rolling over and over. The bottom was fine silt and mud, which made rolling difficult. My elbows and feet slipped, and I got coated with the shit again. I hoped it would wash off when I got into the river, or it would really weigh me down. Then I rolled into the water. For the first few feet it was more hindrance than help, but when I reached a depth of four inches or so I was able to lie on my back and push myself along with my feet and get out into greater depth.

I tell you, when I hit that water I was really relieved.

I stayed in the shallow water, four or five feet deep, along the edge so I could stand on the bottom and stick my head above the surface to breathe. I had to fight the current from upriver and the tide coming in from the other direction to hold my position. The river was dumping out into the sea and the tide was bringing the sea in, and the water backed up where the two met. The water kept getting deeper and forcing me in toward the shore.

The moon was rising, and I could see that the clouds were low and broken. Sometimes the moon would be obscured and I could breathe easy, but sometimes the clouds would open up and the moonlight seemed as bright as day to me. The closer I was forced toward the shore the better chance the gooks had to spot me, so I stayed out where the waves would just barely break over my head.

There was nothing to do out there but think.

First I thought about the patrol. I wondered how many had been killed, and how many had been shot up, or if they'd all gotten away. Had any of the others been captured? I didn't think so: I probably would have seen them. Several of them could have been shot up. I hoped Bob was all right, although why I should be concerned about that hard-nosed bastard I couldn't begin to explain.

I thought about the other prisoners back at the camp. Had any of them tried to escape? Did the gooks beat on them when they found me gone? Probably, though I hoped not.

I thought about my mother and my brother. I used to worry that Mom might just fall apart if I was killed.

Now I knew better. I knew she'd adjust. She'd cry awhile, but then she'd go back to work. She'd go on. My brother, too. I wasn't indispensable.

I stood out there up to my neck in the Mekong River and thought about drinking bouts and bar fights, and how I came to be in the Navy in the first place, and what I was going to do next, or when dawn came. I tried to decide what I would do if the gooks came along the beach and found the trail where I entered the water and sent a boat out to look for me.

I was out there maybe an hour or so before they came. One man appeared on the muddy strip between the water and the jungle and worked his way down-stream. Just as he came to the tracks, the clouds parted and let the moon shine through, so of course he saw them. He looked out toward the river for a few minutes, then disappeared into the jungle. Five minutes later he was back with five or six others. They saw where I went in, and four of them even got out into the water and started looking around. I caught my breath and sank to the bottom and rested there until I needed another breath. Then I'd pop up for a quick breath and sink down again.

It was still night, but I could see. I could see them every time I popped up for air. I really lucked out. A night with a full fucking moon.

I could hear them talking and splashing in the water around me. They weren't close, but if they kept wading around out there they were going to find me. Each time I'd sink back down after surfacing for air, I thought the next time I popped back up they'd be standing there and they'd see me. They couldn't wade out to where I was, but they were working out to where the water was maybe chest deep, looking and kicking at the water. When I was under water I could hear the splashes.

At first I had been sticking my whole head up to breathe, but now I just let my nose and face break the surface, gulped in some air, and went back down. I did that repeatedly, until about 0130 or 0200, when the tide started to recede. The gooks stayed right there, working farther from the shoreline as the tide went out.

Persistent little bastards.

That's when I decided it wasn't any good staying there any longer. I had to get the fuck out. If I got into that goddamned channel I'd have a chance—a remote chance, maybe, but a chance. So I started swimming.

In the Navy, they teach you what we called the "worm swim." You can worm your body, that is, move it like a worm, and you can actually swim, even with your hands and feet tied. I had my hands in front of me to help me too. I wasn't worried about the current. I just wanted to get away from the VC and stay alive. So I'd go down and worm-swim toward the channel just below the surface, and worm my way to the top for a breath. Just before I broke the surface I'd roll over on my side, and by turning my head, I'd let my nose and mouth break the surface for a quick breath. Every other time or so, I'd just float there for a while and get several breaths, and then I'd glance back. It seemed like the shoreline just stayed at the same distance. I could see the gooks only faintly because of the darkness, but they were still there, still looking.

I didn't think much while I was out there. I was too busy thinking about catching my next breath and about the gooks on the beach to worry about anything else. After a while, I noticed the beach and the gooks were farther away. I was out where the current was sweeping me toward the sea. I could hear the roar of the breakers when I was submerged. For some reason it reminded me of an old hymn that I used to hear when I was a kid and went to church regularly, something about Crossing the Bar. The refrain ran through my mind again and again as I surfaced for a breath and sank back, floated for a while, then surfaced for a breath and sank back . . . and all the time was swept farther out to sea: "Let there be no moaning of the bar, when I put out to sea."

It was a relief to be out of their sight, but at the same time I was a little scared. I had escaped from the gooks, but now I was depending on a boat to come along and rescue me before I got exhausted and drowned.

The water began to get salty, and soon I was able to float with less effort. I surfaced and rolled over on my back to float for a time, to let my exhausted muscles rest.

I couldn't keep it up endlessly, of course. It still required a certain amount of effort, and the kick I had to do with my feet tied wasn't a good one, and pulled things in my groin. After a while, it was back to the routine of surface and breathe, hold your breath and relax, let yourself float just at or below the surface until you have to breathe again, and repeat it again . . . and again . . . and again.

I was exhausted from the effort of the escape, and from the swimming, and from the beating. Every muscle ached, and every bruise throbbed. My head pounded, back where I'd been hit. If only I could just lie still for a time, close my eyes, and let sleep take over! It was like those long hours on sentry duty, or when you're sitting on an ambush and nothing is happening, but you're awake, and you start to remember something that happened or some girl that you liked, then suddenly you awake with a start as your head starts to sink toward your chest. I had to fight to keep from dozing off, even though I was holding my breath and then struggling to the surface to breathe. Sleep became a very real threat to me. If I dozed off, I'd drown. It might seem impossible to someone who has never been that tired, but a couple of times I was startled awake when I almost opened my mouth to breathe while I was still under the water.

It quit raining, and the visibility got better. About 0915 I heard a boat coming. I heard him coming when he was still miles away, even over the growling of the breakers. I knew it was a PBR or a Swift boat because of the moan of the engines and the high-speed propellers. For a long time it seemed as if he wasn't getting any closer, but then suddenly he was right on top of me. Then I got a little scared that he might run right over me, but they passed about twenty yards away. I kicked to the surface and broke the water with my head and shoulders and raised my hands over my head. They saw me and circled back. The coxswain cut the engines and they coasted up beside me. The twin-fifty on the bow was pointed right down at me, and some of the crew had rifles pointed at me as well. I didn't care at that point.

"Get me outa this water," I croaked.

"He's an American!" somebody yelled, and the guns swiveled away. Three crewmen came to the rail and reached down and pulled me up. It was a Coastal River Squadron boat.

They didn't bother to untie me: one sailor got out his knife and they cut that shit off me. Then it really hurt! It was like when you mash your thumb and when the blood returns to it it throbs. They rubbed my hands and feet to help the circulation, and, oh my God, it hurt!

I looked down at my diving watch, still on my wrist, and thought, "Thank God they overlooked it!" Then I leaned back and took a deep breath, and thought, "Well, you made it, you old son of a bitch."

I told them what had happened to me. And I told them, "They've got more prisoners in there. Somebody ought to get 'em out."

"Well, where's it at?" they wanted to know.

"I'll lead ye back in there. I want to kick some gook ass."

"Fuck that. You're in no shape to lead us anywhere. Tell us where it is and we'll call it in to Command."

I told them the coordinates as best I could. I told them how far I had come out, and how far I thought I had crawled. Hell, I was on my damned belly and crawling five or six hours. Then I was in the water another ten or twelve, something like that.

They radioed in, and somebody got on the stick and sent the air cav. An hour later they arrived and went in. They did a good job, too. They hit the camp fast and pinned the gooks with their backs against the water. They really kicked ass. The coordinates I gave got them within about fifty yards of the place. They got there just in time, too, because the enemy had three or four sampans in there and had loaded some of the prisoners up. They rescued twenty-one prisoners altogether, but they only got twelve or fourteen kills. The rest of the gooks got away, but they didn't take any of the prisoners with them. One of the prisoners said they'd had him three or four days. Some of them were South Vietnamese—I just hadn't seen them—and some of them may have been civilians.

I asked the corpsman about my head, and he said, "You've got a pockmark back there: it's busted, but it won't do any good to put stitches in it. It's not that deep."

The NVA were starting to build back up in the area. There had been a major battle there back in 1967, and it had been patrolled pretty heavily until the Americans started pulling out. When the patrols slacked off, Charlie infiltrated. The villagers had dug tunnels for air-raid shelters and hideouts, and the NVA took them over.

The guys, they didn't have much to say, except Bob, who told me, "We were going back in there. We'd told Command that we'd lost you and we were going in to get you out."

I was the only one captured. Several of the guys were hit, in the leg or the arm or the side—fatty-tissue wounds, nothing serious. No bones broken. They were able to maneuver around, and they got out. Of course, when the gooks got me and started hollering, the patrol knew about it.

I hadn't done anything heroic. I had just wanted to get the hell out of there. I was just trying to survive.

CHAPTER 3

I get frustrated when I think about being captured, and I especially resent getting my ass whipped. I swore I was never going to let them get me in that position again, that *nobody* was ever going to get me down and stomp my ass like that. As long as I could get a finger on the trigger, I'd take as many of them as I could with me, and save the last round for myself. If I lost my rifle again, I'd pull the pin on a frag and lie on the son of a bitch before I'd let them get their fucking hands on me.

Sometimes I dream about swimming with my hands and feet tied. They tell me that I lie on my side and move my hands together in a swim stroke as though they were tied. Sometimes I just swim and swim and swim, and it gets harder and harder to break the surface for a breath, and the boat never comes. Sometimes I'm swimming to get away from the enemy and one of them is swimming after me, or they're coming after me in a boat, holding torches over the water.

When I got back from 'Nam, before they'd let me furlough home, I had to go see this shrink and tell him about all the bad shit I did over there. I went in every day and talked to that son of a bitch for an hour, but it only took me about ten minutes to figure out that he wasn't hearing a word I was saying. I could tell from the stupid questions he'd ask that he hadn't been listening. Every time I'd stop talking for a while he asked some question to get me started again. He wasn't listening to the answer, he was only hearing the sound of my voice.

That pissed me off. He was a doctor, and he was supposed to help the veterans who came there to adjust to life in the Land of the Big PX after they'd been through all that murder and mayhem over in 'Nam. He was getting paid for it. He probably charged the goddamned taxpayers fifty bucks an hour to sit there and draw dirty pictures on his little notepad. But he couldn't be bothered with listening. How the fuck would he know if you had a problem?

I started saying all sorts of shit, saying the ABCs, describing how I'd fucked his wife the night before, telling him how I was going to rearrange his face . . . he didn't hear any of it. He never reacted to anything except his nurse ringing to remind him the session was over, or when I quit talking. I tried just not saying anything, but the son of a bitch would repeat his stupid questions over and over and over like a broken record until I started talking again. Then I could start reciting, "Mary had a little lamb . . ." and the dumb fucker would start scribbling on his pad like he was taking notes.

Finally, about the third session, or maybe the fourth, I stood up and walked out the fucking door, still talking. I don't think he ever noticed.

His nurse squawked, "Where are you going? The session isn't over!"

I told her, "Yes it is, lady. It was over three days ago."

I didn't go back. I went on my furlough home.

That lasted about three days too. I listened to how everybody's crops were, and how their kids were doing in school, and who was still married and who was divorced, and after a while I realized I didn't care, so I got drunk and stayed drunk. Then I had to listen to their complaining about my drinking. Finally, I got on the plane back to San Diego and spent the rest of my two weeks partying around. I even made the jail in Tijuana.

There was some trouble there. I don't remember much about it, but I woke up in the back of a van with a hell of a hangover and my hands and feet manacled. The SPs had got me out of jail and were taking me back to base. Uncle Sam had paid my fines and docked my paycheck for the next six months to get the money back. When they saw I wasn't violent, the SPs took the manacles off and took me with them into a cafe. Over coffee they laughed about me getting picked up. They said it was just a Drunk-and-Disorderly until I resisted the Mexican police, and that it took half the police force to lock me up. I told 'em if I hadn't been drunk it would've taken the Mexican army. It could be all bullshit for all I could remember, but I had a knot on my head with some ugly-looking stitches in it and blood caked in my hair, and my ribs were bruised like someone had kicked me there.

Shit, wouldn't you know it: when I reported back to base they reassigned me to the damned Shore Patrol. After the ass-chewing, of course.

I screwed around in the Shore Patrol for a couple of months. The first few days were okay. I was doing something different. But I just couldn't keep up my enthusiasm for picking up drunks and AWOL sailors. I sympathized with them too much. After all, I had been in their shoes too many times. Sometimes there would be a scuffle with a drunk, but for excitement it didn't measure up to the months I'd just lived through. It got dull pretty fast.

Then, one night out on a jeep patrol with my partner, Bill Something-or-another, we came across a car with its hood up on a residential street. A sticker on the door said "Chaplain." There were two women in it, and they seemed really happy to see us for some reason. When we pulled up behind them, they got out of their car and came back toward the jeep to tell us what was wrong. They were none too steady on their feet, and they slurred their words and giggled when they talked. It turned out one was an Episcopal chaplain's wife and the other was her sister. They'd gone out for an evening off-base and developed "car trouble" on the way back. They'd killed the engine and flooded it when they tried to start it.

I got in the car and started it with no problem. When Bill put the hood down, I told him, "Follow me in the jeep. I'd better drive these broads home . . . before they show their asses. *Our* asses would be in trouble for not picking them up if they did, and if we take them in, the Chief'll send 'em home and chew our asses out for embarrassing the chaplain.''

They couldn't agree about where they were going, and kept arguing about where to turn or if I should go straight. I finally got tired of it, grabbed the chaplain's wife's purse, and hunted through it until I found her driver's license. The name on it was McFee. Patricia McFee. The address was nearby. When I pulled into the driveway, the younger one squinted near-sightedly at the door and said, "Oh, there it is! Stop here!''

"If I didn't, we'd be parked in the living room," I told her.

"That sounds like a good idea,'' Mrs. McFee said.

I killed the engine and took the keys, and went around to the other side to open the door. "Come on, ladies, let's go in the house,'' I told them. I helped them out of the car and steadied them each by the arm until Bill came over and took the youngest one's arm. We led them to the front door, where I tried the keys one by one until I got the door open.

Inside, Mrs. McFee flopped down on the couch and propped her feet on the coffee table. She wasn't very careful about her skirt. As she slouched back against the pillows it rode up over her knees and showed lots of thigh. The younger lady tripped coming through the door, and Bill had to catch her with both hands. She smiled at him and put her arm around his neck as he led her to a chair and sat her down.

I'd switched on the lights when we came in, and got a good look at them for the first time. The younger one was really a good-looking broad, and the chaplain's wife, who couldn't have been more than thirty, wasn't bad either. Not at all what I would've expected. As she lay back on the couch with her skirt pulled up, and grinning a lopsided, drunken grin, it would have been easy to forget she was somebody's wife.

"Where's the chaplain?" I asked, thinking I'd better get in touch with him and get him home. These two might decide to go out somewhere else after we left and get in trouble.

"He's out at sea," she said, almost gaily.

It was unlikely that he'd be coming in that night, so I asked the other one about her husband.

"He's left my ass! Run away to Canada! He's a draft dodger." She giggled.

"Your old men are gone, so you went out for the evening and kicked up your heels, huh?"

"You got it, sailor!"

"Give the man a prize!"

I looked at Bill and shrugged. So much for that effort. We'd have to try something else.

"How about if I fix you some coffee?" I asked them.

"I don't want coffee." Mrs. McFee sounded determined. She'd probably lock her jaw shut and refuse to drink it.

"You ladies have had your fun this evening. You need to sober up a little so we can leave and know you won't get in any trouble."

"Aw-w-w-w," the younger girl pouted, "are you goin' to leave us?"

"Don't want to get sober," Mrs. McFee insisted.

"Now, look, Mrs. McFee, this isn't a good situation for an officer's wife to be in, and a chaplain's wife especially. It could be a real embarrassment to your husband if you got into any trouble tonight, not to mention that Bill and me would get our butts chewed out—pardon my French, ma'am—for not headin' you off.''

"Have you ever been 'headed off'?'' Mrs. McFee said to her sister.

"No! How do we do it?''

"Mrs. McFee, your husband's career . . .''

"Fuck his career!''

Bill turned his head away to hide a snicker. "Lady, you sure don't talk like a chaplain's wife,'' he said.

"I talk like I damn well please,'' she told him. "I'm tired of bein' Miz Goody-goody all the goddamn time. Can't say bad words, might upset th' admiral's wife! Can't have but one drink at a party, the off'cirs wives might gossip! Can't wear shorts, somebody might not like it! Can't swim in my bikini, somebody might see me! Shit! It's like livin' in a glass jar!''

I didn't blame her for feeling that way, but it wasn't solving my problem.

"Is there somebody we could call for you?''

"Somebody to hold my hand, you mean? What's wrong with you, sailor? Can't you hold it?''

"Maybe he likes guys!'' her little sister butted in.

"Somebody to sober me up is what you mean,'' she went on, "somebody to babysit. Keep me outa trouble. No, nobody you can call. You'll have to handle th' job yourself. Make me a drink, sailor.''

"That sounds like an order from an officer,'' I told her.

"Iss an order from an officer's wife,'' she said, slurring her words just a little.

"Me too. Make me one too, honey,'' the younger girl said to Bill.

I looked over at Bill and shrugged.

"Well, what do you want?"

"Culabibra . . . cula . . . cubra . . . oh, hell! Rum 'n' coke," the younger one giggled.

"Scotch 'n' soda. In the pantry," added her sister. Bill and I went into the kitchen.

"You're not going to give 'em more to drink!" he said.

"What the hell," I told him. "If their husbands are gone, what're we going to do with 'em? Maybe they'll get enough to drink and they'll pass out. Anyway, they want us to stay around: they said so. Let's see what they've got in mind." I was looking him in the eye, and saw his pupils enlarge as he understood what I was thinking.

"That's trouble with a capital T, man."

"Hand me that Scotch."

"You're not going to drink with them? You're on duty!"

"I ain't that crazy!"

"Couldn't prove it by me."

"You jist go out to the jeep and call in. Tell 'em we brought them home and now we're gettin' 'em quiet. I'll take care of things in here."

The women didn't sip their drinks, they gulped them. I sat down on one end of the couch, and Bill sat down on the arm of the chair where little sister was sitting. They tried to get us to drink with them but we told them no, we were on duty.

"Is being married to a chaplain worse than being married to a minister?" I asked Mrs. McFee.

"No . . ." she said, letting her voice trail off as if she were thinking about it.

"Well, if you're damned unhappy, why'd you marry him?"

"He wasn't a chaplain when we married. We were in college. And he liked to party as much as anyone."

"When did he get religion?"

"When his student de-fer-ment ran out." She said the word deferment very carefully.

"You mean, he became a minister so he wouldn't have to go fight in 'Nam? You have to go to school for that too."

"It's easier to get a deferment for studyin' religion than for business administration. He got drafted anyway, but a chaplain doesn't have to fight. And he gets officer's pay."

"But it's not what you had in mind when you got married."

"No. He was going to be a banker. A rich fuckin' banker. We were goin'a live in a goddamned big house and drive a fuckin' Cadillac. Now look at this *dump!* And that piece of shit I'm drivin'!"

The house really wasn't very nice for an officer's quarters, but it beat a fucking bunker in a firebase, or a bunk in a barrack. The old Ford she drove had a lot of miles on it, but lots of people drove worse. I couldn't see she had so much to complain about.

"Well, be glad he's smart enough to stay out of it. It ain't no place I'd send my worst enemy."

"He isn't that smart, he was just desperate. He doesn't have any balls." I realized she didn't give a shit about the guy. She'd married him for the money, or the money she thought he was going to have, and she felt cheated when he switched from banking to religion.

She'd turned and was sitting with one leg thrown

up on the cushion of the couch. Her dress had worked up even more as she wiggled her butt into a comfortable position, and she didn't bother to pull it down. A little bit of her panties was showing. If she wasn't on the make, no woman had ever been.

"Were you over there?" she was asking me.

"Yeah! Yeah." I had to get my mind off what was in those panties. "I was over there. I'd still be there except I was wounded."

"What ship were you on?"

"I wasn't on a ship. I was with the SEAL teams."

"Oh, I know who they are. They like to raise hell a lot. And they have balls. You must have had balls."

"Yeah, and I still got 'em," I said, thinking how close I'd come to losing them.

"I'll bet you know what they're good for, too?"

I did.

Bill took the little sister into one of the bedrooms. Pat—that's what she said I should call her—started undressing right there in the living room.

"I wanta do it on the front lawn with the porch light on," she told me. I talked her out of it.

Well, I was worried there might be some problems. We were late calling in, and I thought the neighbors might call the main gate and ask what was going on at the chaplain's house, but nothing came of it.

As long as her husband was at sea, I'd meet her for a few drinks and a roll in the hay. Rarely would I go over there, only when it was already past midnight, and then I'd leave before dawn. She seemed to get her kicks from being indiscreet, though. She despised her husband, or what he'd chosen to be, and instead of leaving him, she was out to hurt him. I don't think she was attracted to me especially. She'd made up her mind to cheat on him, and I was a young, horny sailor who was damned fool enough to screw around with an officer's wife.

Bill and I brought in a drunk one weekend, a brown water sailor who'd been back from 'Nam just a few weeks, and he got a little wild when we started to lock him up. He broke loose from Bill, who made a grab at him. The guy caught Bill flush on the chin with a right that backed him up against the bars and glazed his eyes. Then he tried to kick me in the balls. I got my knee up and partly turned, so that he just got me with a glancing blow. He lunged right past me and down the corridor between the cells. He was heading for the front door, but he didn't get far. The CPO on watch heard the ruckus and came to see what was going on. When he stepped into the corridor the guy hesitated for a second, and I caught up with him. I grabbed him by the hair and threw him up against the bars, banged his head against them a couple of times, then let him have my nightstick in the kidneys once or twice. I lost it for a minute. The CPO had to stop me.

Later, after he complained all night about his side hurting, they took him to the hospital. They thought at first his kidney might be ruptured, but it was only bruised.

It might have blown over with just an ass-chewing, but just after that Pat called. She wanted me to come over after I got off duty. Like a fool, I did.

Then, when they took the sailor in to the hospital, the CPO on watch wanted to get hold of me. I wasn't in, so he called Bill. Bill was sleepy and tired, and probably still a little dazed from the crack on the chin.

The Chief got the number from him, and called, and Pat answered the phone.

She answered, still half asleep, "McFee residence."

After that, the shit hit the fan. Needless to say, it was the end of our relationship.

Sometimes I'd meet a girl in a bar, or on the beach, and we'd be getting along just fine until she asked what I did. When I told her I was a sailor, that was usually enough for her to lose interest. To some of them, just serving your country instead of yourself was enough to mark a man as a damned fool. If she stuck around after that, she would probably want to know what I did in the Navy. That meant she had a brother in the service, or relatives, maybe even her father—or her husband. But when I told her I had been with the Teams, she'd find some reason she needed to be somewhere else.

There was the rare one that it didn't bother. One spent an entire evening with me after she found out I was a SEAL. It wasn't until we got to her apartment that I found out she'd been a biker's girl. She had "Harley Davidson" tattooed on her butt and "If you can read this stick out your tongue" right above her pubic hair. The others were about as rough. Most of them were looking for somebody to knock them around a little, rough them up, maybe make them do some kinky sex.

Not even the toughest ones stuck around after I had a nightmare or a flashback when I spent the night. When I was flashing back, they weren't in control anymore. I wasn't playing by the rules, and it scared them. So they'd leave, or kick me out of their place.

I began to think I would never have a normal relationship with a woman again. And this after just a couple of months.

I didn't understand the people I met in San Diego, so I went to L.A. and Frisco. There they were even worse. Flower children with their values all warped. I knew from my furlough that it wasn't any better back in Arkansas, just different. People back there had their tidy little lives, and there wasn't room for me anymore. I had changed, and so had they. Even though we grew up together and shared the same background and culture, our values were just as different as mine were from the flower children and the other fruits.

So I was confused, and lost, and uncomfortable even around my own people.

I began to get angry.

When I got angry, I drank. When I drank, I got drunk and angry and got into fights. When there was trouble on the job, like when a sailor tried to fight us when we picked him up, I went into a bar after I got off duty and drank, and heaven help anybody that even looked at me the wrong way.

They were usually short fights, and nobody got hurt really bad. Either I was too drunk to fight and got my ass waxed, or I was sober and they didn't stand a chance. Some of the bartenders got to where they didn't like to see me coming around.

I'd go down to where the SEALs hung out, in Coronado. They were more friendly. I was one of them, even if I wasn't part of their immediate team. I didn't enjoy it that much. It made me feel washed up. A has-been.

Over in this bar in Coronado where the SEAL teams

hung out, I'd run into their commander. He'd heard
from some of them I had been in the Teams and had
had a tour in 'Nam. He introduced himself and we
had a few drinks. I guess I had more than a few,
because he told me, in a friendly way, I shouldn't
drink so damned much. "Stay off the damned rum,"
he said. "It'll rot your liver, if it doesn't get your
brain first."

I started telling him what a rough time I was having
getting adjusted to shore duty here in the States. He
asked me why I had transferred to the Shore Patrol,
and I told him. Then I told him I didn't like it at all.
He listened. He actually, honest-to-God listened, and
he heard what I said.

Then he told me his own story, and it sounded a
lot like mine. He'd come back from duty with the
Teams in 'Nam and gone through the same sort of
adjustment. For him, it resulted in a divorce. She'd
waited for him while he was in combat, but she
couldn't stand him when he got back. He started
drinking a lot, and even got into a fight with another
officer at a party. He damned near lost his rank before
a friend, a CPO with one of the Teams, straightened
him out.

"How'd he do that?" I'd wanted to know.

"He got me interested in soccer," he said, straight-
faced.

"Wha-a-at?"

"He went to the Admiral and told him he thought
he could help me, but the Admiral had to back him
up—in other words, make me cooperate. Then he
came to me and told me his son was on a city league
team, and they needed a coach, and I was him. Of
course, I told him to fuck off. He just called the Ad-

miral and handed me the phone. The Admiral told me to do it or I'd lose my commission and spend some time in the brig drying out. It was the brig time that bothered me.''

"They wouldn't do that to a gold striper.''

"They had *me* convinced. Anyway, I took it on. Thought I could fiddle around out there for a few weeks and they'd finally give up on me.''

"So what happened?''

"I got interested. They were a great bunch of kids. They had lots of spirit, they just didn't know much about the game. But they were eager, and that made it easy to teach them. The first thing I knew, I really cared whether the little fuckers won or lost. It got to the point where I couldn't wait to get off duty so I could go down there and work with those kids. I quit drinking so much—I had to, to measure up as a coach—and straightened my life up. What it took was a real interest in something.''

"I don't think that would work for me.''

"Sure it would. You just have to find something you're real interested in. Something you want to do.''

"Well, sports ain't it.''

"So build model airplanes or something. Decide on something you like to do, and don't think about all this other crap.''

"I like to drink,'' I'd told him with a grin.

When the commander of the SP detachment there called me in and told me, "Tyler, we're going to have to ship your ass out of here or get you help. Would you prefer the Philippines or the shrink?'', I thought of the SEAL commander. I told the SP commander I wanted to talk to someone before I answered.

"You want legal counsel?" He sounded like he doubted he should let me.

"I want to talk to someone," I insisted.

He wanted to know who. I didn't want to say. I figured he might stop me somehow.

"You should go back to the psychiatrist," he said, but he let me call the SEAL commander.

I arranged to meet him in the bar after duty hours. He wasn't all that sympathetic.

"I told you what to do," he said.

"Model airplanes and Little League soccer are just too . . . trivial. I couldn't spend any time on that shit. Get me back on the Teams until my enlistment's up. I'm bored with this Shore Patrollin'."

"You said you couldn't dive anymore."

"I can't dive deep. I can still dive twenty, thirty feet."

He looked away for a while. He might have been thinking, but I thought he just didn't want to look at a has-been.

"I can still jump, and all that other stuff. Let me teach some of the tadpoles about booby traps, or sneak 'n' peek patrols," I insisted. "I'm good at that covert shit."

He looked at me then, for several minutes. I knew he was thinking really hard about something, because he scratched between the first two knuckles of his right hand with the index fingernail of his left, and I'd seen him do it before.

"Would you consider intelligence work?" he asked.

"You mean, like spy 'n' counterspy, an' all that?"

"Something like that, yeah."

"I did a lot of recon over in 'Nam."

"Well, this would go beyond just recon. You might have to go up into North Vietnam, maybe even China."

"Do I look like I'm that crazy?"

"I guess we'll see what the shrink says about that. If you keep getting your ass in trouble you'll be back to see him. In a hospital. One of those with the ten-foot chain-link fence around it to keep you from jumping ship."

"Don't I have no other choice?"

"Not that I know of."

"I guess I could go to the Philippines."

"You'd just get in trouble there. Do you think Subic would be any better than San Diego?"

I wasn't really warm on the idea of going to sunny, stinking Subic. I'd been there once, and that was one time too many.

"Would it be *real* spy shit?" I asked. "I don't speak any foreign language, just 'come here' and 'put your hands on your head' and 'lie down' in Vietnamese."

"COMPHIBPAC has put together a roster of second-tour and third-tour SEALs for special 'over the fence' operations in North Vietnam. The CIA and DIA need combat veterans that are good at 'sneaky Pete' operations to escort their agents through combat areas. Marine Recon and the Green Berets have rosters too, by the way. COMPHIBPAC wants to do more than that: they want to put together a team specializing in that kind of operation, a team that isn't just haphazardly put together from the personnel available at the time. That kind of team would get better and better with each mission.

"After the war, the Army and the Air Force will

be fighting with the Navy over a share of the defense budget, a budget that will certainly be cut back by the anti-military forces in Congress. The SEAL teams will be competing with the fleet Navy for a share of the Navy budget. There'll be pressure to cut back to one team, or do away with the SEALs entirely. Admiral Jameson thinks the Teams have something unique to offer the country in a cold war as well as in a shooting war, and it won't hurt to have friends in the CIA and DIA when the budgets are decided. That's the politics behind this special team idea.

"Some of the missions may involve diving, but I imagine that most of them won't, because the agents would have to be trained as divers. The agents would do the 'real spy stuff.' Your job would be to get them there alive and back out again, and to supply some firepower. There might be more recon missions, like you did on your last tour, but up north."

"I don't think I'm interested. I don't want to go back to that damned Vietnam. That place sucks."

"You might get sent somewhere else. The Canal Zone, Central America, the Caribbean, South Africa, the Middle East . . . they're all possible trouble spots. It could even be somewhere in Europe. But it would probably be 'Nam. Or you could get sent to the Philippines."

"Olangopo smells like shit and dead fish," I said, remembering.

"If you stay with the Shore Patrol, you'll probably get sent there anyway."

He was right. To Subic or a psychiatric ward. What a fuckin' choice. "What do I have to do?" I asked.

"I'll check on it. Put in your chit for Intelligence

School anyway, and if there's anything beyond that, I'll let you know."

The bar maid came by to see if we wanted another round, and I shook my head. The Commander waved her away and grinned at me.

Intelligence School wasn't too tough. Like most military schools, there was a lot of review of what had gone before, and I'd done all right in that part of SEAL training. Mostly, it was common sense.

I also had to get back into shape and refresh myself on some basic skills. I started out with a beginning BUDS class until I was fit, then I stayed that way with several hours of PT and running the beaches every day. The instructors worked me in with the UDT and SEAL trainees so I could refresh myself on certain skills I hadn't used much, like parachute jumps. Then I had three to four hours classroom time a day. That's hard on an old country boy who never did like schooling that much anyway.

My evenings were free, except when I had some assigned reading or problems. I still spent a lot of them in the bars around Coronado. I kept a close watch on how much booze I was taking in, though. I still was unhappy, but Intelligence School had given me something to concentrate on. The Commander had been right about that. When I thought about the lessons, I could block the rest of it out of my mind. The physical activity of PT and retraining helped too. During those weeks with the Shore Patrol I'd missed being in situations where I was tested physically and mentally.

There was something still missing, though. I didn't know then what it was. All I knew was that life still seemed pretty stale and flat. It wasn't until I got back to Vietnam and heard the snap of AK rounds cutting the air close to my head that I realized what it was that was missing: danger, and the excitement that goes with it. It's like a drug. Once you've known it, once you've conquered your fear and felt the adrenaline pumping, you're hooked. You get high on besting the other guy, on killing him when you know that if you let down your guard for a minute he can kill you. Elephant hunting or tiger hunting must have been like that in the old days, before modern guns gave man the edge. And like quitting a drug, you get withdrawal symptoms when you go back to a humdrum life.

I felt there was something missing, I just didn't know what.

Sometimes I wondered what had happened to Pat, if she and her husband were still on base, or if she'd finally divorced him. I never tried to call.

One night I picked up a broad that I had seen hanging around in the bar before. She wasn't turned off when she found out I was a SEAL. In fact, she seemed turned on by it. She was a real fire-breather. Thought we ought to nuke Hanoi, and got right friendly when I told her I was probably going back.

A couple of weeks later we were married.

As the Intelligence School neared its end, we started running exercises. At first they weren't anything special. We'd just go a ways up or down the coast and insert a four- or eight-man team and make our way to some assigned destination with the instructors there on the shore looking for us. Then the exercises got a little tougher. They might bring some guy in and tell us to insert with him somewhere near Encinitas and get to Escondido by dawn. Then they'd get some Marines out of Camp Pendleton and offer a weekend pass to whatever outfit caught us. Or we'd have to get onto San Clemente Island to find some guy and get him off, with the area being patrolled by boats and helicopters.

Then one day they told us to get ready to go "out of town" for a week or more. The next morning we loaded up a C-130 and flew off, and none of us knew where in hell we were going. It turned out to be an extended exercise. There were several of us from the Intelligence School and a bunch of newly graduated SEALs and UDTs (underwater demolition teams). First, we staged into this base in Central America— that's all they'd tell us. We ran several exercises, and then went by sub on down to the Falkland Islands for some exercises there.

After finishing the school, I got my new security rating and my new assignment.

I looked at the little ID card they gave me and said, "These damned letters and numbers don't mean a thing to me. Did I pass?"

The instructor looked at me and shook his head. "Goddamn, Tyler, you got a 'Q' clearance. That's about the highest they give out. About the only people that have better ones are the President and the Joint Chiefs. Hell, you could go anywhere you wanted to in the Pentagon."

"Well, I'll be damned. The Pentagon, huh?" Shit, the East Coast wouldn't be a bad assignment.

Then I looked at my new assignment.

Vietnam.

CHAPTER 4

I was running away when I went back to 'Nam, running away from rejection, and from nightmares, to a nightmare world. Somehow I felt safer among my known enemies over there than among my supposed friends on the other side of the Pacific. And there was something I must have been running back to also. Call it brotherhood, if you like: a shared sense of purpose, a shared identity, a feeling of belonging to a tight, close-knit group. Those things were missing in the States. I didn't feel like I belonged there at all.

In a way, it wasn't as bad going back for the second time as it was the first when it was all a big unknown to me: what the country was like, what the people were like, what war was like. Now I dreaded what I knew about instead of what I didn't know.

I spent the night before I left carousing with my new wife. Just before dawn, I showered and cleaned up—I knew it was going to be a long plane ride—and then she took me to the airport where I caught an early commuter to L.A. It was like a business trip, except that I carried a seabag instead of a briefcase. She kissed me goodbye at the gate and reminded me that I hadn't turned in the GI life insurance form. I was making her the beneficiary in case I was killed. I showed her it was in an envelope in my pocket, and told her I'd mail it in L.A. I caught the Saigon Special in L.A. and was on my way. I forgot to mail the envelope.

There were lots of soldiers and Marines and a few sailors on the plane. It had a full load, and the stewardesses were kept busy serving drinks and slapping hands off their asses. I slept all the way to Honolulu, because I hadn't slept any the night before.

There was a layover in Honolulu, and I found myself in a bar with an Army sergeant. He was going back for his third tour. I thought at first he was a glutton for punishment until he told me he was a supply sergeant. He said his outfit had been rocketed once, but other than that, the toughest action he'd seen was trying to keep the Saigon Commandos from stealing everything in the warehouse. He thought it was funny how so many people back in the States envisioned 'Nam as being such a dangerous place. "You're in more danger in downtown Chicago!" he said.

He sure as hell hadn't been in the same 'Nam I'd been in.

That got him to talking about his old lady. He'd met her and married her just before he went over the first time. He thought then he was going to be in danger every minute. He said he figured the only reason he married her was to have somebody to think about him, somebody who gave a flying fuck if he came back alive or not. They kept up a regular correspondence for a while, until he began to write her that being in the rear in Vietnam was no more dangerous than being on a post stateside. Then, after a bit, her letters got to be more infrequent, and their tone changed. He wrote a buddy to go by and check on her to see if anything was wrong. Something was wrong, all right: she was shacked up with a guy.

The sergeant got her on the telephone from Saigon and had it out with her. She told him he'd married her under false pretenses: he'd told her he might be killed in 'Nam, and now he was saying he wasn't in any danger after all! He told her to get the divorce papers started. She had the brass to ask if she would still be the beneficiary of his insurance!

"That was all she wanted, the insurance," he said. "She thought she had a sure thing: she could sleep with me for a few weeks, and I'd go off and get killed, and she'd get the check. A lot better than fifty bucks a trick! And she'd be able to take right up with her old boyfriend." He chuckled and shook his head. "I guess there's a lot of her kind around."

I told him I reckoned there was. After a while I went to the men's head and took out that envelope with the insurance form. I looked at it a long time, and thought about her, and the way she'd been the only one that really seemed interested in me. Then I thought about the sergeant and his ex-wife. I thought about my widowed mother back in Arkansas. I started to tear it up. I even tore the edge of it a little bit.

Then I changed my mind and started to go mail it. Finally, I just said, "Fuck it!" and stuck the damned thing back into my pocket.

I reported to Special Forces Command Headquarters in Saigon, to a Navy Captain in NISO, Naval Intelligence Special Operations. He kept me waiting for fifteen minutes to show me I wasn't anyone special and then had me come into his office. After he introduced himself, he waved at a chair and told me to sit down, and then started telling me why I was there. His name was Gartley.

He was a tall blond man with short, very curly hair that gave him an unmilitary look. He seemed more likely to be boozing it up in a college frat house than commanding special forces in a war zone. His uniform was very neat, though, and he was erect as a flagpole. I think he might have been a schoolteacher in civilian life, because he talked like he was delivering a lecture, even though I was the only one in the room with him.

"You are aware, Tyler, that we do a considerable amount of clandestine intelligence gathering in North Vietnam, Laos, and Cambodia. This is normally carried out by agents inside the countries. Some are natives that, for one reason or another, agree to provide us with information. Some are foreign nationals. Some work for money, some for ideology, some because their government wants them to. Some are Americans."

I sat and listened to his bullshit, thinking, "Man, this son of a bitch is proud of his work!" He was strutting back and forth in front of his desk like a rooster that had just gotten off a hen.

"Americans can get into a country in a number of

ways," he went on. "Diplomatic staff, for example. Businessmen. Even reporters. Despite the press's apparent hostility toward the government, some reporters are individually cooperative, even to the point of spying for us. Usually, they just keep their eyes and ears open for anything of military or political significance—they're trained for that, and they do it very well.

"Since we don't have diplomatic relations with North Vietnam, the avenue of employing spies on the embassy staff is closed to us in this case. We have to depend on businessmen and reporters, and on foreign nationals we can pay off. There are many foreign nationals in Hanoi. The French, for example. Many of them are still smarting from the loss of their colony. They may even have personal grudges against the Viet Minh. So they can be bought, or persuaded to collect information for us. We often insert our own people disguised as French citizens. Or Japanese, or Chinese. But that method takes some time, because they are closely checked and watched at first. It takes a while before surveillance slackens and they learn their way around enough to slip away.

"Frequently, however, we must use a trained agent. Perhaps it's a highly technical job that needs to be done quickly. An agent inserted by the usual means wouldn't be able to get started fast enough. In those cases, we insert our agents surreptitiously.

"But North Vietnam is a war zone. Not to the extent that the South is, but a war zone nonetheless."

"No shit!" I thought.

"There are frequent exercises for troops in training, and frequent patrols out looking for pilots and crews of planes that have been shot down. There are antiaircraft batteries along the roads and railroads, and garrison troops around strong-points. There are large numbers of troops being moved south toward the combat area. There are patrols out to interdict Montagnard raids—the 'Yards are conducting their own guerrilla war against the North Viets, with our help. All these things get NVA soldiers out into the countryside, not to mention the peasants who have their own business out there, and that makes it difficult for agents who aren't trained or experienced in that kind of thing to make it to, say, Hanoi, without being observed. And, of course, they know we run operations into their country, and they have patrols out to interdict them.

"The agents need trained and combat-experienced escorts when they insert through the North Vietnamese countryside. NISO has agreed to make SEALs and UDTs with the appropriate experience available to the CIA and DIA for these missions.

"In addition to armed escorts, the intelligence agencies frequently have need of men to conduct snatch operations, assassinations, shoplifting jobs—"

"Shoplifting?" I hadn't heard the term before.

"Snatching a specific hardware item, like a radar set or antenna, or a missile. I'm sure you've heard the rumors that a couple of years ago a SEAL team went into North Vietnam and stole a complete surface-to-air missile. That sort of thing.

"At any rate, we have a lot of specialized reconnaissance missions requiring men of your experience and training. Contacting and exfiltrating defectors. Surveillance jobs, maybe some special photography." He picked up a manila folder and leafed through it. "I see that you had quite a bit of combat experience on your last tour. There shouldn't be much of that on this assignment. If shooting starts, you've probably failed in your mission.''

"Not necessarily, asshole," I thought.

"We don't at this time have a standing force exclusively for this mission, but we do have a roster from which we select the individuals, according to the conditions and specific requirements of each operation. However, we have enough of these special recon missions that we want a quasi-permanent group organized and used to working together, so they can do the job more efficiently.

"The roster contains the names of second- and third-tour veterans with appropriate experience and training. The Army Special Forces and Marine Forces Recon also maintain such a roster and have in the past supplied men for the specially assembled teams. They may also organize special teams. We want to beat them to it.

"Your chain of command will come through NISO from MACV, not COMPHIBPAC. Specifically, through me, as long as I am assigned responsibility for Tacforce.''

"Tacforce?''

"That's what they're calling this outfit, for lack of a better name. Right now, we're it, you and me. Your job will be to select and organize the team, and lead the team you select. If a second team is needed, a second team leader will be recruited and will select his own team from the roster. Once you get the men together, you'll plan and rehearse the operation until you are functioning well together. If there's time.

"You will be operating out of the Quang Tri area.

First priority will be to acquaint yourself and your men with the terrain along the approaches to Hanoi.

"Chief Johnson will show you your temporary quarters."

"Come o-o-on Chief!" I was thinking. "Get me the hell away from this James Bond motherfucker!"

"When you get your gear stored, take an evening on the town," Gartley went on. "I'll brief you some more in the morning, and we'll give you a look at the roster. There should be some names you know on it."

He sure was a windy bastard.

Saigon hadn't changed, of course. It was still crowded, noisy, smelly, and busy. Chief Johnson and I hit a couple of bars and ate some native food—I figured I might as well get diarrhea and get it over with. After a couple of hours the Chief excused himself and went home to the Vietnamese woman he was living with and left me to drink alone or go back to the barracks, as I pleased. I had a few more drinks and then left. I hadn't seen any familiar faces, and the bar girls looked old and worn out.

It wasn't exactly a cheerful "homecoming."

Through the relative quiet of the barracks, I could hear distant explosions. An Arc Light attack somewhere near the city—probably up by Tay Nin.

The diarrhea hit me right after breakfast the next morning. Captain Gartley really didn't have much more to say to me, which was good, because what he did have to say he had to work in between my trips to the head. Finally, in mid-afternoon, my bowels settled down a bit and I got a look at the roster.

It wasn't a long roster. There weren't that many second- and third-tour SEALs in-country. And some of the names I did recognize. Some were guys I'd gone through BUDS with; others were guys I'd met in San Diego or 'Nam. The names were split about evenly between Teams One and Two, but I knew only two or three of the Team Two SEALs. Some of them looked like they'd be pretty good: there was a guy from Colorado who'd spent most of his first two tours on long-range patrols up along the Ho Chi Minh Trail. Of course, I looked for certain names, and in some cases I wasn't disappointed. My old comrade-in-arms Bob Brewster was on the list. Somehow, I knew he would be, because during our first tour we made one of the best recon teams operating in the Delta, and that's a fact. That ain't just bragging. Chief Petty Officer Tahlequah Mackintosh was not on the list. I wondered if he just hadn't come back for another tour, or if Charlie had gotten him in the end. The Chief was a full-blooded Cherokee Indian, and the best scout and tracker in Vietnam. On our side, anyway.

In the end I had a list of names of people I knew that were good and some that looked to be good from their records.

Bob Brewster was several months into his second tour. He'd put in his chit for a second even before his first one was over. Some men might have been changed by the brutality of the war, but not Bob. He'd be the same. Life had already shit on him, until there wasn't a lot that could happen to him worse than what he'd been through already. He was about five-feet-eleven and 220 pounds, all muscle. He had a round face with heavy whiskers that made him look unshaven, and somehow his uniform was always dirty and wrinkled. He sometimes looked like he'd just walked right out of one of those Kentucky coal mines he used to work in. Not only was his uniform dirty, his body and his mind and his mouth were, too. He even embarrassed *me* sometimes. He was a hell of a patroller, though, and you could depend on him in any situation.

Phillip Casburn was a Texan. Not a tall one or a big one, just medium height, kind of slender. He even had small feet and a small head. He wore those high-heeled, pointy-toed cowboy boots and a cowboy hat when he was in civvies, and they were both way too small for me. The only thing big about him was his mouth. Not that he was a bragger. He just talked a lot. He was a good man in the bush.

Anthony Delucchi was from Chicago, and he looked just like you would expect: black-haired and olive-skinned. He tanned real dark in the Vietnamese sun. He wasn't talkative, but he was very good-humored. He kidded around a lot, and kept the other guys in a good humor. He and Bob got on well, and they joked back and forth a lot. During SEAL training he had to bunk next to Bob, and the stink of Bob's farts would sometimes drive him outside. Bob told him the ingredients of his farts were a military secret.

Darren Fitchew was another talker. He was a Connecticut Yankee, and I thought they were supposed to be men of few words, but not Fitchew. He loved to play cards, and spent a lot of his off time gambling. He'd play any card game, but he mostly played Spades for money. I hadn't seen him since we shipped over for the first tour, and that was too often. He got on my nerves when we were in barracks, but he was a good shooter and fighter, and I knew he could be counted on in a pinch.

Another guy I knew from training was "Cajun"

Jerry Quinn, from Shreveport, Louisiana. He had big thick lips and dark curly hair, and I always suspected there was a "nigger in the woodpile" somewhere in his background. He was always grinning and laughing and telling Cajun jokes, and he could talk French to the Viets that understood it. He was about six-foot-three and weighed 190 pounds when he was at fighting trim. He had broad, sloping shoulders, and the little Vietnamese girls practically swooned over him. Before he joined the Navy, he had been a stevedore and a boxer. He and the Chief used to go a round or two.

It was harder to pick men I didn't know. The information in the roster package wasn't all that complete. It gave their name, rank, and serial number, and their current assignment. It gave a little about them personally and physically, and described their previous experience very, very briefly. There were evaluations by their former or current commanders. I picked five other names, more or less at random, relying pretty heavily on the evaluations.

I would make my own evaluations when I got them together and out in the field.

I submitted my list of names to Captain Gartley, and he started making arrangements to get them all together in Quang Tri. I went on up there and got settled into a barracks to wait for them to show up. I knew that most of them would be in the field, and they wouldn't be sent up until they finished their missions. It might be a week or more before they all arrived. In the meantime I had to learn my way around the base there at Quang Tri and find out where to check out equipment and get supplies. It was always a good idea to get to know the petty officers and sergeants in charge of supplies.

I hoped Bob would be one of the first to show up, just so I could see the look of surprise on his face when he saw me again. We could have a reunion— go to the bars and get in a fight or two with the Marines. But the first three to show up were Cajun Quinn and Tony Delucchi, and a Team Two SEAL named Joe Magoun. Quinn came in laughing and back-slapping and telling his latest Cajun joke. Tony was kidding around with him, and Magoun was watching the two of them and grinning like a new kid in school.

Magoun was the smallest of the men picked off the roster, at five-seven and about 165 pounds—that was on his records. I'd say he'd leaned down to 150 from diarrhea and bush rations, but he was wiry and strong. He didn't tan much—he had a ruddy complexion and just got redder. He had a boyish face and a boyish grin, besides being smaller, and it made him look younger than the other two. It was hard for me to believe he was really pushing thirty pretty hard. He was one of those people that mature late and age late. He'd done one hitch in the Navy as a diver before he put in for SEALs, and had gone through all that tough physical training when he was twenty-five. It was hard on me at twenty-one.

I'd thought from the name he might be French or Belgian or of some kind of Eastern European descent. But he was Irish, and he was a scrapper. I found that out very quickly, the first time I saw him. I stepped up to him and stuck out my hand when Quinn introduced me.

"Hello, Joe, how're ya doing? I'm Jay Tyler," I said.

He took my hand, all right, but said, "The name is Joseph, Jay Tyler, like Mary's husband, the step-father of Jesus. Joseph's the name my father gave me, and I'll thank you to call me by it."

So, of course, we called him Joe.

"Hey, Joe," we'd say, "seen Jesus lately? How's he doing?"

Or, "Hey, Joe, had a letter from Mary lately? I heard she was three months pregnant. Let's see, you've been here six months? Must have been another immaculate conception."

"Have your fun, have your laughs," he'd say, "the Lord will pay youse back for your abominations."

He cussed and drank and chased whores just like the rest of us.

He had worked out of Kontum and Pleiku, and all the way over the Laotian border to Thac Hiet, mostly recon missions on the Ho Chi Minh Trail with Army Special Forces—Green Berets and LRRPs. He'd been shot up a few times, but he'd come back for more.

He was a Petty Officer Second Class, and he had more time in service, but I was still in charge of getting them together and selecting the final eight. If he was one of them, he might be selected to lead the team on any one mission, if the team members decided he was the most experienced and competent. In that case, I'd want him to lead. Rank didn't mean a lot in the bush. Even if Captain Gartley came along, the most experienced man would lead the patrol. If that was the Captain, it would work out fine. If not, he could give all the orders he wanted and no one would hear them until we got back to base or into camp. He could make the big decisions, like whether or not the U.S. should nuke Hanoi, but the patrol leader made the important ones, like what tactics to use or whether to move or stay put.

Quinn and Tony had been together down at Can Tho. They'd been working on one of those special missions the Captain was talking about. The Captain, I found out, had been in the bush with them some, and wasn't too bad at it.

"We've been chasing some North Viet dude around down in the Delta," Tony told me. "We've been working with ARVN's Military Security Service down there, with a Major Thi. He's been using every source he could come up with to get a line on this guy, a Colonel Dong—"

"Dong-g-g-g!" interjected Quinn, like a ringing gong.

"But every time we got to a village we found out the Colonel had been there and gone. It got to be a standing joke: every time we got the bad news, somebody would say 'Dong-g-g-g!' Major Thi sure got pissed whenever he heard it."

"What is this Colonel, that they want him so much?"

"Psyops. He goes around from village to village keeping the people in line, making sure they know it's better for them to support the NVA than the government. You know, strings up the local schoolteacher or some hamlet official and cuts him up a piece at a time. The usual bullshit. They think he might have been responsible for that massacre in Bac Lieu. Remember Bac Lieu?"

Did I ever.

"In one ville," Quinn put in, "where they hid their rice from the VC tax collectors, he tortured the village chief's old lady until the chief told them where the rice caches were. Then they dug up all the caches and took *all* the rice, killed the old lady anyway, and made the chief carry the rice away for them.''

"Major Thi had a helicopter load of rice sent out to them, to replace what they'd lost,'' Tony added. "Then we went chasing off to try to catch them. Dong came back, took all the new rice, and had all the village elders castrated. Twenty-four or -five of them.''

"So now, nobody wants to talk,'' Quinn pointed out. "They don't want to say anything about where he is or even if he's been there.''

"I don't blame 'em. How did you find out anything?''

"Somebody always talks. A kid lets something slip, or somebody wants revenge. Thi never lets on who talks to him and who doesn't.''

"Thi's sly,'' Quinn told us. "Sometimes, when he finds out where this Dong might be, we pack up and leave the area, so Thi can send another outfit to sneak up on Dong.''

"But you ain't got him yet.''

"We're gettin' closer. Or were, till we got called up here.''

"We've had one break,'' Tony said. "A helicopter gunship spotted an NVA column in the bush and made a pass at it. Turned out to be Colonel Dong and his crew. They missed Dong, but he tripped over a root or something as he was running away and fell down a bank. Wrenched his hip, or maybe even broke it. He can't walk. They have to carry him around in a litter. Thi got that information from a prisoner we brought in.''

The next day Lusk and Thompson arrived. Thompson had been operating out of Quang Tri, so he was just back in from a patrol. Thompson was about my size, about six-feet-two and 190 pounds, with brown hair and a deep tan. He was outgoing and had very strong likes and dislikes. He was from Tupelo, Mississippi.

Thompson was real competitive, and he liked sports, all kinds. When he had time off he was usually in a baseball game or a football game with the REFs—the Rear-Echelon Fuckoffs. If he was in barracks he was listening to some game broadcast over Armed Forces Radio. He was very self-sufficient in the bush, according to his commander's evaluation, and had a lot of willpower and determination. It seemed to me he liked to be in the spotlight, to be the center of attention around the barrack or on the ball field, and lost his temper too often if things weren't going his way.

He'd spent most of his first tour along the coast between Qui Nhon and Quang Tri. They kept watch on small-boat traffic along the coast and in the inlets and rivers, and called in air or sea strikes when they observed supplies or troops being brought ashore. The population was pretty dense along that coast, but it had been a Viet Minh–controlled area before the country was partitioned, and a lot of the people still had strong loyalties to the communists. He'd operated with a team of three others. On the last patrol of his first tour, two men were seriously wounded and the other two shot up before the boats could get them off.

After R-and-R, he'd put in for a second tour. Since then, he'd been working the Quang Tri area. He came in from his patrol with his camo headscarf tied around his head like a sweatband. His uniform was sweat-soaked and his face smudged where he'd just wiped off the camo paint. He found himself a can of beer and sat down on his bunk and just looked at all of us. Then he belched loudly and lay back on the bunk, muddy boots and all. In seconds he was asleep.

Dwight Lusk came in that afternoon on a C-130 from Saigon. He was a slender blond from McClure, Pennsylvania. He was real quiet, didn't talk much at all unless you spoke directly to him, and stayed kind of aloof from the rest of us. Quinn and Tony would be joking around and the rest of us haw-hawing like a pasture full of jackasses and he'd just smile a quiet little smile and go on with what he was doing. He seemed to be a little suspicious about everyone, as if we were about to pull a dirty trick on him. His commander's evaluation had been that he was very steady and practical, but warned that he would procrastinate and obstruct a mission if he had reservations about it.

The one time he did open up and really talk to us was when Quinn mentioned the French restaurants in Saigon. He and Quinn discussed their relative merits for thirty minutes—the rest of us were sort of left out in the cold—and he seemed to know what he was talking about. They got to arguing about which was better, French cuisine or New Orleans Creole cookery. It got to be obvious that he enjoyed the good life, good food, good wine, good women—but then, who doesn't? Still, I got the definite idea that the Lusks were probably quite well off back in McClure.

Lusk had been working out of Song Be with the South Vietnamese riverboat sailors. One of the tributaries of the Song Be called the Hoyt formed a part of the border with Cambodia, and they ran patrols up and down the river in specially muffled PBRs. He'd worked with the Vietnamese Special Forces up there, watching supply routes off the Ho Chi Minh Trail, and occasionally ambushing supply parties. He said it really got nasty up there. They had contact almost every patrol. VC and NVA regulars paraded through there like it was downtown Hanoi.

He spoke only a little Vietnamese. He'd worked with an interpreter or with Viets that spoke some English. His worst experience was when his interpreter got hit only seconds after they'd made contact. He hadn't gotten off a radio call. The Viet radioman at their base camp didn't understand English, and Lusk couldn't tell him in Vietnamese they needed support. So he got on the radio and called in the clear, in English, until he got a U.S. firebase that had a translator and could relay his call for help in Vietnamese. The firebase was too far away to help with its artillery. I guess he was pretty scared until the helicopters showed up, and even then, because they circled the area a long time before making firing passes. He knew they wanted him to pop smoke, but he couldn't even tell them in Vietnamese which side of the smoke he and his men were on. Finally, one of the Special Forces realized what was going on and came to the radio. They got out all right, but from then on Lusk made sure he went out with no less than three men who spoke English.

Phil Casburn came in two days later, in cowboy boots and hat, with a big red bandanna around his neck.

''Why, howdy, Arkensawyer!'' was the first thing he said, and after that he didn't stop talking for two hours straight, except to light a Camel. He'd been in My Tho with our old outfit, doing recon and setting up ambushes, mostly out in the Plain of Reeds. He had the usual stories of man-eating mud, living on a daily basis with poisonous snakes and alligators—"Some of 'em were around so much we give 'em names!"—and sparrow-size mosquitoes that made dive-bombing attacks. I'd seen all that shit when I was there last tour.

Casburn had come back to 'Nam after taking his furlough in Austin. He hadn't fit in back in the Real World either.

"I just couldn't bear to see them longhairs 'n' other misfits running around the streets like real people that had good sense. Damned unwashed anti-'Mericans. What's the white race coming to? Even the damned Mexes looked cleaner."

He and Bob Brewster had seen each other occasionally in My Tho.

"He's as ornery as ever," Phil said.

"I wish he'd show up," I told him. "I'd like to see the asshole."

All of us went out on a short patrol along the DMZ to get used to working together, and to get me back into the routine. We saw some infiltrators, some November Victor Alfas, or NVA regular troops, but they didn't see us, and we called in an artillery strike.

When we got back, Darren Fitchew and a guy named Mike Olfson were in the barracks. They had been working together down in the Ca Mau, off of a barge called Seafloat. Fitchew said they were glad to be away from the place.

I told him the ground was a lot steeper up here.

"Yeah, and it's a hell of a lot drier, too. I'm sick of mud and mangroves. Even the 'Cong get sick of

that place. I don't know why we don't just give it to
'em.''

Olfson was a big, fair-skinned blond from Minnesota. He was a likable guy, who right away joined
the conversation and seemed to get along with everybody. I soon found out that he was good on ambushes
because he was very patient and self-disciplined, and
he was embarrassed when he did something wrong or
failed to accomplish a task. Fitchew was always trying
to get him into a card game, but Olfson was real
careful with his money. He had a wife and kids in
Minnesota, for one thing, but that was just his way.

They'd found an enemy "hotel" in the U Minh
Forest near Vinh Long, a bunker-and-tunnel complex
Charlie had waterproofed with plastic liner. Where
they got the plastic was anybody's guess. Small
groups of NVA would pass through the area and lay
over there for a day or two before moving on. Fitchew and Olfson and two Biet Hai Rangers had lain
in the mud for two weeks watching the place and
waiting for a large group to come through. Two of
them would pull back far enough to pick up water
and C-rations dropped from a helicopter, and then
they'd wallow back to the camouflaged observation
spot. It was an exhausting crawl, taking all night each
way. The NVA seemed always to move in small
groups. At one point, Fitchew was ready to call in a
strike, but Olfson talked him into waiting a while
longer. Then two groups arrived at the same time,
about eight in one and twelve in the other, coming
from different directions. The smaller group passed
within twenty-five feet of the four watchers but went
on by.

That's when the strike was called in. A-4s off the

USS *Hancock* made the first attack, and then a company of air cav finished the job. There wasn't much fighting. A few gooks tried to escape afterward, but the cav had the place surrounded and cut them down right quick. Those that survived went back into their holes. The troopers went around blasting the bunkers and entrances to the tunnels. They worked through the area with long poles, poking into the muck every foot or so to find tunnels near the surface. They found several and blasted them.

The four watchers stayed where they were the whole time. The troopers never found them. They stayed there that night. No one came out of the complex after the cav left. Two nights later seven NVA came out of the jungle and looked around the place, chattered excitedly, then went away. The watchers pulled back to their LZ during the fourth night. They were satisfied. Not one gook had gotten out of the tunnels alive.

"They probably drowned when the damned tunnels flooded," Olfson concluded.

Bob Dasher flew in from Cam Ranh Bay, where he'd just gotten back from one of these special jobs. He said he'd been up to Haiphong to take pictures of the cargo on some of the ships being unloaded up there. I thought maybe he was talking about radar or missiles or tanks.

"Nope," he said, and kind of hesitated. I thought maybe he was going to keep it to himself, but then he really opened up. "Shit, you wouldn't believe it. Clothes, medicine, boots and shoes, that's what we slipped in to photograph. I thought that CIA guy was nuts or something until I started looking at the stuff. He was photographing the shipping labels on the crates and the labels on some of the stuff. I said, 'What's so important about that shit?' 'It says "Made in the USA," ' he told me. So I took a look at it. It was brand-name stuff, all right. Major companies. Even the clothes. And there were oil drums from a major oil company.''

"You're shittin' us! American companies?''

"Guns?''

"Didn't see any.''

"By clothes, you mean uniforms?''

"Civilian clothes, mostly. But some that could've been uniforms. Like service station attendants wear.''

"Was there any plastic? Like big rolls of it?'' Fitchew wanted to know.

"Plastic? Yeah, now that you mention it.''

"Come on, tell us the names.''

He shook his head. "They made me sign my life away not to tell anybody those names. I must've signed fifteen or twenty papers, and it took three hours to do it. They told me, 'You read it, then sign it!' And I sat there and read every word. What it said was, 'This never really happened, and if you say it did, we'll prove you're a liar.' So I'm not saying anything. I'll remember them, though. I'll never buy anything those bastards make, and my family won't either.''

"Damn it, we've all got security clearances here. You can tell us.''

"Uh uh. They told me not to tell anybody, not even my wife. 'Maybe the President of the United States, if he comes to you and begs you to tell him.' That's what they told me. They said they'd stop those companies from doing that kind of shit, but I bet they don't stop 'em for very long.''

Well, we sat around and thought about that, and we all began to get kind of down about it. American companies trading with the enemy. War materials, yet. It made you wonder what we were fighting for. It reminded me of something my old uncle used to say, the one who was in World War II: "The Russians always said we'd sell them the rope they need to hang us." It looked like he was right.

After a while, Lusk spoke up. "Sometimes I don't think I want to fight this war anymore."

We got Dasher to tell us over some beers that night about his experiences in Cambodia. He'd worked out of Phnom Penh during his first tour, some against the Khmer Rouge, but mostly watching the Ho Chi Minh Trail in eastern Cambodia. He did a lot of recon work in the Parrot's Beak and Fish Hook areas for the joint US-ARVN push into that area in the spring of 1970. His main criticism of the operation was that it moved too slow. By the time the forces converged inside Cambodia, the NVA troops had slipped away.

"They were in there," he said. "I saw them, I saw their big supply dumps and commo bases. And I watched them pack up and leave when the invasion first jumped off. If they'd been a little faster, they would've done a lot more than just destroy supplies and camps."

Brewster finally dragged his ass in about two days later. He was dirty, and his greens looked like he'd slept in them for three days, which he probably had. He had grown a thin black mustache. He dragged his seabag over and threw it under a cot. I walked over and stuck out my hand.

"Hey, Bob! How the hell have ye been?"

"Hey, Tyler," he said. He didn't look at all surprised to see me. He just stood there with his hands on his hips and a smirk on his face. "I think I've got worms again. Do worms make your ass itch?"

Same old Bob. You just didn't want to stand too close to him, or downwind.

"Ain't ye gonna ask me what I'm doin' back, for Christ sakes?"

"Yer jist like a fly, Tyler: ye couldn't stay away from this shit."

"Speakin' of shit—you had to take cover in any more latrines?"

"Why don't you drop it, Tyler, while yer still ahead?"

"Well, fuck you. I'm goin' to get a beer."

"Fine. Bring me one, will ye? I wanta lay down here awhile an' rest."

"Yeah, I'll bring ye one: I'll bring ye a used one, you lazy fucker!"

"Piss on you, too."

I walked out and headed for the EM club down the street where the other guys were getting together. After fifty yards or so I heard footsteps behind me. In just a matter of seconds he'd caught up to me and was walking in step with me.

"So what the hell's all this shit about, Tyler?"

Yep, things were back to normal. Bob was here. The brotherhood was back together. The war could go on now.

CHAPTER 5

Bob was a good man to have around when the shit was flying thick and fast. He might be personally repulsive to a lot of people, including a lot of SEALs, but he was beautiful to me. On patrol, he was my good right arm. Or maybe I should say my good left ear.

After I'd escaped from the little bastards that had captured me, and had been checked out at a hospital in Saigon, they gave me some pills to take, and some shots, and sent me back to the team. When I got back to the barge Bob came up to me and asked, "You going to be all right?"

I told him, "Yeah."

He said, "Well, that's good. I'm glad you're going to be back. I was afraid I might have to take over this son of a bitch as patrol leader. Next time you decide to go AWOL for a couple of days, check with me first, okay? You really don't need to be pulling that kind of shit, Tyler.''

I said, "I understand, you concerned son of a bitch!''

He really was concerned, in his way. He looked at me and shook his head a little, and went over and started bullshitting with some of the other guys. He didn't say anything more about it. It had scared him, and it was unusual for him to worry about anything.

My gonads swelled up, but aside from the pain there wasn't any problem. My toes were sore, and it was hard to walk. It was like trying to walk around after an operation. I was stiff and sore for a long time, and I had to work out to get the soreness out. Bob would say, "Man, better take it easy. Don't overdo it," but's that's all he would say about it. He might bring me a cup of coffee or a beer or a Coke, something he'd never done before. He didn't babysit me or anything, but for a while he wouldn't get too far away from me.

And it was Bob who kept me afloat and got me on board the boat when I was wounded.

For the next couple of weeks the team worked together on minor missions, to get to know each other and how we would work together in the field. At the same time, the South Vietnamese had picked a group of Lin Dei Nugel Ngai, their equivalent of SEALs, for us to work with and get familiar with, so we carried out several joint operations. Not that these were picnics in the woods: we just hadn't got to the heavy stuff yet. These were ambushes and raids, and patrols around the DMZ. Of course, we weren't limited in the territory we could cover.

They'd asked us to test certain weapons under combat conditions. So we'd pick an area that had thick bush and known enemy camps and villages, and we'd go in and hit one. Then we'd come back and report how the weapons performed: the kill factor was so-and-so, or the bullet penetrated a two-inch tree and deviated only so many degrees and still took the target down. After fully automatic fire the barrel cooled down quickly. The kick was light. The accuracy was good, or poor. We had five misfires, the firing pin is faulty. It jammed twice, because the cartridges don't feed into the chamber smoothly. On this one, the forearm broke and the damned barrel fell off. On that one, a little grit jammed the trigger. In cool rainy weather the barrel stayed cooler, but the stock swelled and threw the sights off. The sights caught in the bush. And so on.

Near the end of my first month in-country, Command sent us on a mission in the Central Highlands to check the rate of NVA infiltration down near Kontum. It was right after the big South Vietnamese push into Laos west of Khe Sanh, Operation Lam Son 719, and MACV wanted to know if the offensive had reduced the rate of infiltration south of that point. It had been a routine patrol, with only a few small enemy patrols sighted. They were so small they weren't worth calling in air strikes or artillery fire. We just ambushed them.

By the time we saw them we were sure there weren't any big units around, so we didn't mind giving away our position. We would hit them hard with grenades and small arms, then pull back before they could react. We might kill three or four each time. If they came after us we'd hit them again and withdraw again. If they turned back before they got close to us and went on down the trail, we'd catch up to them and hit them again. We kept picking at them, killing one here and

two there, until there weren't but two or three left. We'd
let those go, for psychological effect. It was the same
tactics they used on our troops.

We were coming back in to our LZ when we heard
a patrol coming. We lay low and waited, but even
before they came in sight we knew they were Americans. We could hear them talking to each other, just
strolling along a damned trail, looking up in the trees
and off at the clouds, bullshitting and playing grab-
ass. They went right by us. Their point man was
slouching along about ten yards ahead with his rifle
at trail, and the first guy behind him had his rifle
across his shoulders with his hands draped over it.

"Sixteen more days and I'm goin' home!" one of
them hollered back at someone in the rear. "Eat your
hearts out, motherfuckers!"

"Sixteen more feet and you're going home in a
baggy," I thought, as he shuffled past the muzzle of
my rifle.

Two came down the trail together, going through the
motions of watching the bush, but one was describing
some woman to the other. Both were looking at the trees
and brush along the trail but they were seeing breasts
and ass. Talking like that takes your concentration away,
even if you're whispering. They weren't. They were
probably distracting the guys around them too.

The entire platoon went by less than five feet from us
and never saw a damned thing. We let them get out of
sight before we moved on. I wished one of us'd had a
camera to take some pictures. It might have done them
some good to see pictures of themselves on patrol taken
when they thought no one was around.

The trail they were following cut our path at about
a 45-degree angle, so we were soon a good half to

three-quarters of a mile from them. That was when we heard the shooting.

I knew right away they'd been hit.

It wasn't unusual to hear gunfire when you were out on patrol. There wasn't a constant roar of battle over there. It was more like deer season. We'd hear three or four shots over on that hill, like a deer just ran past a couple of hunters. Then it might be hours before we heard anything else. Then you might hear *pow!pow!* from another direction, and just a few minutes later another two or three shots from somewhere else. Then you might hear nothing else for the rest of the day.

We heard a short burst of shots, and then a few singles, and a burst of what was obviously M-16s. Then there was a lull with a few more single shots, and another burst of fire from the Americans.

I thought, "What in the hell have they got over there?" There wasn't enough return fire to justify the amount of M-16 ammunition they were putting out. I looked around at the guys, and they just shrugged.

We tried the radio, and sure enough they were on the radio crying for help. We answered, and they said they were taking heavy fire and could we assist. Bob shook his head and said, "Heavy fire? If they are, them gooks must be usin' silencers!" We asked for their location, and they gave us coordinates about half a mile away, so we decided we should go over and give them a hand.

At first I thought we'd flank the gooks and drive them off, but after listening to the panicky officer on the radio I was a little afraid we might get shot up by the Americans if we tried it, so we told them what direction we were coming from and went on in to talk to the platoon leader.

They had followed the damned trail right across a

clearing. The gooks waited until they were all in the open and hit them. They went down on their bellies in the grass, and stayed there, afraid to move, so bunched up they were nearly piled on one another. Those that were shooting were shooting blind, just spraying the trees. They'd hold the goddamned guns over their heads and spray a clip or two, but they weren't firing low enough. They weren't bothering Charlie at all.

I left eight of the guys back at the edge of the clearing, and three of us ran in to talk to the platoon leader, who turned out to be a green Second Lieutenant. He probably hadn't been in 'Nam more than two weeks. We found him on his belly with his head down, pleading into the radio for some air support. We tried to find out from him how many enemy there were, and where they were, but he didn't know. And he didn't know what to do.

We scanned the area quickly and could only pick out five or six enemy shooters. They were sharpshooting, just firing single shots, aimed fire.

"You need to turn their flank," I told him. "Get some men out. My men are back there. I'll send them around that end of the clearing. You send yours around the other way. And pass the word to your other men that we're starting a flanking movement on both sides."

I got on the radio to Bob and told him to take the men out to flank the gooks. I told him how many positions we'd spotted and where they were, and what the soldiers were doing. While I talked, the two men with me took some of the gook positions under fire. By the time I'd finished, the Lieutenant had passed the word to his men and they'd started moving.

They raised up in a bunch and ran for the trees. Right toward one of the gook positions.

Shit! I thought. I should've kept my damned mouth shut! In time, my men could probably have run all the gooks off without any casualties to ourselves.

We took the enemy positions under fire right away, of course, but there were only three of us doing any effective shooting, and that bunch of GIs was between us and the one gook.

"Spread out!" I yelled. "Spread your asses out!" as I shot, but it was all over by then. The bunch were down on their bellies again, with three or four of them hit, and I knew they'd never move again.

I told the Lieutenant, "You need to spread them out. Scatter them out."

He said, "Yeah, go ahead. Put 'em out."

I told him, "This ain't my command, asshole. It's your baby."

"You got any suggestions?" he asked. The fucker was battle-happy.

"Yeah. Get their asses spread out!"

We spread ourselves out so we could get a better angle on the gook positions. We'd move and shoot, shoot and move, in short hops and single shots. I was stepping on bodies, the doggies were so bunched up. "Spread out! Scatter out!" I kept telling them, and a few began to scatter out a little, and to shoot back at the gooks with more determination.

The return fire petered out. Before long, all the shooting was M-16s.

Bob called in to say they'd killed one gook and wounded one, and captured two more running across a clearing. They came in, bringing the enemy and their weapons.

Two scrawny, half-starved peasants. Leftover Viet

Cong. And two weapons, one an AK-47 and the other a U.S. 30 carbine.

The soldiers had a medic with them who started working on the wounded. The others were standing there waiting for their platoon leader to do something. He was just standing there rubbing his face, pushing his helmet back on his head and then pulling it down by the brim, and kicking at the dirt.

Bob went over to him. "You got some wounded here, and some dead. You need a Medivac in here."

"Yeah. Call a Medivac. Radio a Medivac," he said. He went over to the dead gook, and the wounded one, and looked at them awhile. He shook his head and wandered over to look at some of the bodies of his men. I think he wanted to cry, but he wouldn't let himself show any emotion.

The radio man yelled over that HQ wanted to know how many casualties he had. The Lieutenant just looked at us and asked, "How many casualties?"

"*Fuck!* It's your goddamned platoon, numbnuts!" I yelled at him.

A noncom took over and got the wounded and the dead brought to one side of the clearing. There were eight dead and six wounded, two of them pretty severely.

The soldiers were walking around saying, "Jesus Christ!" and started lighting up cigarettes. Some of them refused to look at the dead, even those who were friends. "Looking at them ain't going to do no good," they'd say.

The Lieutenant was a case of nerves. He stood there shaking, and pushing and pulling his helmet back and forth on his head. He didn't know what to do next. His men looked to me for orders.

"What the fuck do we do now?" one of them said.

"Get some men out to watch the perimeter. Make sure Charlie doesn't come back in on you," I told them. It wasn't my place to tell them anything, but somebody had to look out for them. Two or three hardcores could have wiped out the whole fucking platoon. Several of my team had gone out already on their own initiative.

We stayed with them until the Medivac came, but then we pulled out. We had our own mission, after all. And we didn't want to be too close to that outfit. They were a walking liability.

One guy just stood there looking at the corpses waiting for dustoff. They were staring right back at him.

"Close their eyes," I told him.

"They're dead," he said. "Why bother?"

"They've seen enough of this fucking war already," I told him.

Some time in early May they called us in to brief us on a mission. There was a Marine officer present, and he did a lot of the talking. It seems that we were second choice, but the Marine Recons were all tied up, and they wanted some area checked out in a hurry. We were the closest available team.

They called us in and showed us what information they had. There was some NVA activity up north. Air reconnaissance had flown over using infrared detectors to spot enemy troops on the ground, moving around at night. There was a strong buildup about sixty kilometers west-northwest of Quang Tri, tight up against the DMZ. They were probably building up to make an attack after we pulled more troops out and left ARVN on its own. Our people wanted to knock out that buildup, but there were five or six camps in there, and they weren't sure which were real and which were just decoys. They also wanted to find out how supplies were coming in and what kind of defenses had been put up. They'd taken aerial photographs of the area and had made maps from them. They also had some maps captured from North Vietnamese that showed the terrain.

Other patrols had tried to get into the area and had failed.

Charley was smart: he would set up decoy camps and run fake supply trains. He also had cardboard trucks to fool the air photo interpreters. I never saw any, but I knew guys who had. Supply trains might follow two or three different routes into an area, but only one would really be carrying munitions, medicine, or food. We had to know which ones to hit.

When we were planning our route in we looked over the terrain to figure its effect on maneuverability. We wanted the shortest possible route, but we always had two or three optional routes that we could take to get out of an area. Going in we usually had just one. We could look at the maps and aerial photographs and figure out the best way to insert the team. In this case, we chose to go in by para-insertion. They'd drop us off as close to the hit zone as we wanted to get.

We looked at hills, streams, and any rivers that might provide a water supply or a transportation route. We didn't necessarily choose a route with heavy brush for cover, but once we had dropped in, we wanted a covered area nearby where we could hide. We also liked to be close to a supply of fresh water.

We picked one of the smaller camps to check out. To get to where we wanted to go, fast, we made a parachute insertion from a helicopter. We dropped into a very small clearing one night. We had a quick-opening chute, for quick-delivery situations, that you could jump with from 500 to 700 feet up. They took us over in a helicopter, and hovered, and when we went out we pulled the cord.

When we got down, we regrouped and checked to make sure that none of the guys had been hurt or had lost any of their weaponry. I'd made them all carry two pads and pencils apiece, because usually someone would lose one. We also carried two extra weapons, because a strap might come undone, or someone might hit the ground and break a stock or something. We made it okay, so we destroyed the extra stuff, pinpointed our location, got our bearings, and took off.

When we found the supply route, we hid and watched the NVA go by to determine what kind of weapons they were carrying. It was all small arms, nothing heavy, so we knew this wasn't the main route. We *did* find out where the weapons were coming from. We logged it and called in, and they flew in and picked us up. We were out two or three days.

When we got back we reported to Intelligence, and they sent us right back in. They dropped us off in a thick area about two or three miles from the enemy camp. We jumped from a C-130, which was flying at a higher altitude than the helicopter had been. To conceal the sound of our aircraft, and to confuse them, we had four or five planes fly over, including some C-130 gunships to attack any movement they detected and to create a diversion.

The rear hatch of the C-130 was big enough so that all of us could go out together. We tried to stay in close order when we jumped, so we wouldn't get separated, but we didn't want to stay so close that our lines would get tangled up.

We free-fell down to 700 or 800 feet before we pulled our ripcords. By the time our chutes opened, we only had a hundred feet or so to go. A low-altitude jump at night is hard to detect. The higher the jump altitude, the easier it is for them to see you. The chute makes a silhouette against the sky, and you're up there longer. With a low jump, you're below the horizon, and by the time they look up, you're gone. It's especially hard to spot those green camouflage chutes if you go in against the face of a mountain that's covered with green vegetation.

The whole string landed within about sixty yards, but we'd been dropped off right in the goddamned trees, and two guys got hung up in some branches. They weren't hurt, so they just cut the lines and went for it. It was either climb down or fall.

By the time we got into our area of reconnaissance, the NVA had extended their patrols and strengthened them, and they had more patrols out. In fact, it seemed like every time you turned around there was a patrol. They didn't have many booby traps out because they didn't want their own men or the damned monkeys triggering them. Instead they just put out more manpower.

We took note of their weapons: a lot of AK-47s, a lot of automatic weapons, grenade launchers and bazookas, some SAMs and camouflaged antiaircraft guns. They had a hell of an ammo stockpile too. This had to be the main camp.

Getting close was like trying to break into the mint. They had guards out, some that would move around and others every thirty or fifty yards who were stationary. They were NVA regulars, well trained and very alert.

We were able to get inside their kill zone, but man, was it spooky! They had cleared out all the underbrush and a few of the trees for about sixty to eighty feet to make the zone, but they had left as many trees as they could, so they would still have foliage overhead to hide them from aircraft. They had put out concertina wire, too. Inside the fence of concertina wire was an area of about one city block.

They had set perimeters of punji sticks around some of their camp areas outside the wire. A lot of the troops, especially the sentries and patrols, slept outside the wire.

In the camp itself, little shacks had been built for the commanders. At night their fires smoldered under open-sided hutches with vented roofs that came way down low to conceal the glow from enemy patrols and low-flying helicopters.

We had brought along a camera with infrared film, and we used it to take pictures of the camp.

It took us two and a half hours to go fifty yards through the wire. Just for comparison, depending on the thickness of the brush, once you're experienced you might move through it two miles in an hour. That's a normal walking speed. They had put out stakes and tied the concertina wire down so it couldn't be dragged off or rolled back.

Lusk did the mapping. He stayed outside while Bob and I and Dasher and Magoun crawled in through the wire. We called in on our radios and told him our coordinates and everything we saw, and he wrote it all down. Then we came back out just as slowly as we went in.

We stayed in the area a while longer. We looked for weak points, tried to get an approximate head count, and tried to figure out how many sentries they would maintain through a twenty-four-hour period. We observed incoming and outgoing traffic. We timed patrols to see if they were keeping on a regular basis or if they were staggered. We watched where they went and what they did when they came back. There was a lot of activity around there during the daytime.

We found out the supplies were coming from the north, off the Ho Chi Minh Trail, and later we followed the traffic and found three or four bridges they were crossing as they came down. There were trucks and people on foot.

We didn't set any explosives or anything like that. We didn't try to hit the place, because we had more sense. We just went in, observed, and got back out. We gathered all the information and took it back to Intelligence, and they had to decide when to hit it and how.

Their most critical decision was how long to wait before they attacked. Should they wait until the buildup peaked and the NVA were about to launch their attack? That way they could destroy everything. Or should they hit them before they got all their strength built up? The problem was firepower. If they let the camp get too strong, it would take too many helicopters to get enough men in there, and they might have to move artillery into some firebases within range of the camp, thus tipping their hand.

In this particular case, they waited. They sent a company in to hit the decoy camps, to make Charlie think we were buying his trick. Then we moved in and hit the big one.

They sent us back in to blow the bridges, but they didn't want them blown until the main attack, so the communists would have no way to retreat. We booby-trapped the trails, and set explosives on the bridges and blew them up. Then we went back in toward the main camp and set booby traps and claymores so that when they came out, they'd run into them.

The results were very impressive. The enemy troops went this way and that, like a bunch of blackbirds scattered by a shotgun. They were dispersed all over the place, running and scared. Then it was just a matter of cleanup. We knew some of them would try to make it to the other camps, but the Marines had that escape cut off.

They probably got 180 kills on that operation.

Once the Marines had moved out, we went in and destroyed what was left. There wasn't much because they had bombed the hell out of it.

That was the last major NVA buildup in that area until after the goddamned peace talks.

A few days later we hit them again, to the west of that area, in Laos and in North Vietnam just above the DMZ. We went up by helicopter and were gone four days. We blew up some bridges and booby-trapped some waterways and streams. Charlie was coming down the rivers from the highlands on rafts and sampans, so we set explosives with their triggers just underneath the water. We also blew up a hell of a lot of swinging bridges and bamboo bridges.

The following week, as part of our familiarization with the area, we went into North Vietnam and blew the hell out of Highway 1 just about thirty-five miles out of Hanoi. We were just supposed to blow up the damned road and get back out. We set the charges, but we wanted to make a kill out of it, so we waited. The North Vietnamese were shipping some armament down that way, and we blew up four or five trucks out of a convoy of fifteen.

It was pretty country up there below Hanoi.

CHAPTER 6

Hill 484 is the highest peak on a steep and jungle-covered ridge that rises out of the coastal plains near Dong Ha, right up against the DMZ. It's an ideal observation post for artillery directed against the coastal plain. In 1966, the Marines went in there and kicked the North Vietnamese 324B Division off the ridge and back across the DMZ.

CINCPAC thought that as more and more American troops were withdrawn, the VC were moving back onto Hill 484 and getting ready to swoop down and take over as soon as we were gone. CINCPAC wanted a reconnaissance team to check and see whether Charlie was indeed reinfiltrating. They wanted to know if he had reoccupied bunkers left from before or was building new ones, and if he was moving back into huts in the ravines. We had been watching the area closely, but when the enemy made his move up north, we had to turn our attention toward keeping him as far back from the DMZ as we could. That's when Charlie decided to move back onto the hill.

We were flown in by helicopter and dropped off about three miles from the foot of the mountain. Hill 484 was nothing but pure hell, with lots of under-growth and an eighty-foot-high double canopy of brush and trees that made a murky darkness below. Movement would be slow and at times damned near impossible. It had rained for four or five days before we went in, and the slopes were still muddy despite the sunshine and heat during the days since then. In places where the sun got through it had dried out the leaves and made them treacherously noisy. Except for the battle in 1966, we couldn't have moved at all. When the Marines had come in, they had bombed the hill to clear out some of the undergrowth, and there were still patches less overgrown than the natural areas. They had used "daisy-cutters," which didn't make much of a crater. Other clearings were places where one side or the other had camped. The only trails were those the VC had made while moving in, and to follow them would have been a fatal mistake.

I was told the battle for Hill 484 was one hell of a battle. I may bullshit about the grunts, but they pay their dues, and in high numbers. They'd sure as hell paid for Hill 484. Now, as we pulled more and more troops out, the hill was being given back to Charlie.

This was a recon patrol, so we were to engage only when necessary. If needed, we were to call Cam Lo for artillery support or Da Nang for air strikes. We carried a pack radio to call for support, and each of us carried hand radios to use in the bush. We were also carrying our personal weapons, some claymores and C-3 and C-4 explosive, and five hand grenades apiece. We would set the claymores in a defensive perimeter if we laid up to sleep.

I had been lucky so far and hadn't screwed up, but this patrol would soon put doubts in my mind. There were twelve of us that went in: eleven from the Tacforce and one LDNN named Bac Vo. At the time, I didn't know only eight would return alive and unwounded.

Almost from the time we jumped out of the helicopter and left the LZ, I regretted bringing such a large force. It was tough enough to move through the bush without making noise, and twelve made more than twice the noise of six; I don't know why that is, but it always works that way. It was also tougher to keep them spread out enough and yet keep them moving as a group. In the lower terrain Bob and I took point positions, and we moved with a flanker on each side and a rear guard. On the steeper slopes they had a tendency to bunch up, and we ended up with more of a column.

We were all on Dexedrine. When we started up that hill it was like we were all eyeballs and ears and noses. It intensified every sensation.

We hadn't gone far when Tony found signs at the foot of the hill that Charlie had been there, and it hadn't been too long ago, either: maybe three or four days. There was some freshly cut brush, and the grass was trampled down. I couldn't tell how many there had been, but certainly more than one.

I told the guys to spread out and we would make short sweeps up the hill. I wasn't going to take any chances that Charlie was still nearby. I took the point, but couldn't go out very far because the bush was too thick and the visibility poor. I told everyone to watch the trees. If Charlie was in there, he'd have spotters out. I was also sure he would have booby traps out, and patrols. We had to be on our toes all the time.

I had a small funny feeling about it when we started up. At one point I said to myself, "Nope, I'm scrapping it. Let's get the hell out of here and go on back and just tell them we blew it. It wouldn't be the first time, and it's no real disgrace or anything." But they train you until you are totally mission oriented: the mission must be accomplished despite all. So I went on with it.

The sun was just barely up, but the humidity was already high and the temperature was rising. Little biting gnats were swarming everywhere. You could tell it was going to be a hot sticky day in the bush. We didn't want to make any unnecessary noise, so we didn't use our machetes. We moved by parting the undergrowth and slipping through, but that meant we moved more slowly than usual.

Thompson was carrying the pack radio, an AN/PRC-41. It was bulky, and it caught in the underbrush and made more noise than I was comfortable with. It also weighed forty pounds, and it was quite a burden to haul up a steep, muddy hill in the heat. Its range was line of sight, so it would be useless down in the ravines. We'd barely started up the hill before I decided to leave it behind. I convinced myself that if we saw anything, we could mark it on our map and report back to headquarters about it. They could hit a camp or an observation post by coordinates on a map without an observer spotting for them. We cached it and booby-trapped it and moved on.

The monkeys were plentiful on the hill. They chattered and screamed and barked when we frightened a bunch of them, and fled through the treetops. A few brave ones would stick around to scream at us and throw sticks and handfuls of shit. It worried me that they might give us away, but then I realized they could just as easily betray a VC patrol to us. Anyway, who was going to know if they were screaming at us or at each other?

We were about an hour onto the hill and about 150 or 200 feet up when we spotted the first patrol. There were seven of them, and they were moving fairly fast along a trail. They were carrying backpacks. We hid and let them go by, although we could easily have taken them out. Our mission was to find out what was on the hill, and if we took out the patrol, there was a certain element of risk that we would be discovered. If one man slipped up and let his man cry out or shoot, they'd know we were there. Or the bodies might be discovered by another patrol.

After they were well out of sight, we moved out around the mountain, following their back trail. I thought that by backtracking them we might be led to their camp or strong point. We had been following their back trail for a little less than two hours when Bob broke squelch on his little hand radio to get my attention and motioned for me to come over. When I got to him he said, almost casually, "Olfson just went down."

I immediately got a cold lump in my stomach, as if I'd swallowed an ice cube. I thought we were discovered already.

"Where was he?" I asked.

"About forty feet over that way," he said, and pointed to his left.

I signaled the others to hold their positions while Bob and I checked it out. There hadn't been any gunfire, so I thought he had been either shot with a crossbow or jumped. I hoped it was a crossbow. The VC that could take Olfson down as fast as he went down was someone I wouldn't want to meet in a dark alley—or jungle, either.

"You stay about twenty feet to my left," I told Bob. "You watch the trees and I'll watch the ground."

"You got it," Bob said as he moved out.

When a man goes down, you've got to figure whatever caused it has moved, so you don't go directly to that spot. You go a little ways ahead and a little ways behind where he went down and circle to try to cut their path. We did, and didn't find anything. So we went over to check on him.

Olfson had found a booby trap. A pit full of sharp bamboo stakes.

"Son of a bitch," I said, after I looked at him. There was blood foaming from one of his lungs where a stake had punched through his chest, and another one had gone through his neck and out his mouth. There was no sign of life.

"Damn," Bob said. "Why didn't he see it, Jay?"

I thought a damned monkey had probably distracted him.

It was suddenly clear what that patrol had been doing. They were going around the mountain checking their booby traps, to make sure they hadn't been sprung by some animal, and to see if they'd bagged any victims. That would be a regular patrol, and there might be more than one a day. Or the one that checked this pit going out might also check it coming back in. One way or the other, they would be back. If not today, then tomorrow. They would see the blood on the broken stakes and know they'd gotten somebody. Then they'd know there had been a patrol on the hill, and that it might still be there.

The backpacks indicated they planned to be out overnight, probably for several nights. It might be days before they were due back. Or this might have been their last day.

A couple of the guys started to climb down and get him out. I stopped them. I should have aborted the mission right then and let them carry him back out, but they drill it into you that the mission takes precedence over everything else. Aborting just didn't seem to me to be an option at that time. Still, I had an uneasy feeling about it. And I wasn't the only one. A couple of the guys had doubts. When you've got two guys that are feeling uneasy about a mission right off the bat, how are they going to perform?

I turned to them and said, "It's a hard decision to make. I don't know whether to go on or turn back. But I'd sure like to know what's up there."

Tony said, "Do you think we really should?"

And because Intelligence wanted to know if anything was going on in that area, and our mission was to find out, I said, "Hell, yes. Let's go for it!"

"But we've got to leave him," I told them.

"He deserves better than that, Jay," Tony said.

"Goddamnit, I know it!" I snapped at him. I'd never snapped at him like that before, or at any of the others. But my ass was in a bind between what I wanted to do, get the body out and take it back, and what I had to do, which was complete the mission. They weren't helping me make the hard decisions by appealing to my emotions. Didn't Tony know I felt the same way?

"Look," I went on, a little more rationally, "let's get that patrol. Catch 'em and get rid of 'em. Then we'll come back here and get him out, and I'll send three of you back with him. That'll leave me eight men; that's enough. It'll buy us some time. But we have to get that patrol first."

They left him reluctantly. I spread them out about thirty feet apart and paired them up, one man to watch the trees for spotters, and one to watch for booby traps. I took the point again and went out a little farther than before. I wanted to make sure I had enough time to get back to them and warn them if we ran into a patrol coming toward us. I picked up the pace a little. I thought we might have to overtake the gook patrol and pass it. If they were stopping to check their traps, we should be able to do it. Otherwise, we'd catch them when they made camp, or got back to their main camp if their route took them that way.

They had doubled back. I spotted them before we even got back to where we had seen them the first time. They weren't moving very fast, and they were walking in single file along a trail. I backed off from them until they were almost out of my sight, then turned and hurried back to the team and called them in.

"They're ahead of us, heading our way, in single file on that trail over there. There's twelve to fifteen feet between them. I'll take the seventh man, Bob'll take the sixth, Tony the fifth, and so on. Number off and get in position. The rest of you scatter out to the sides and cover us. Don't anybody make their move until you see me go first.''

They quickly numbered off and took their positions along the trail. The heavy underbrush was a definite asset now. We stayed eight to ten feet back from the trail so there was no danger of being seen.

When the gooks came by I could see they were NVA. They were in uniforms and wore boots and helmets. The seventh man had his chin strap fastened and pulled up tight. That would make it easier for me, but he had that damned knapsack on, and that would make it tough to get a grip on his shoulder. So I took out my knife and waited until he went by.

As soon as he was past I raised up to a low crouch and slipped over to the trail behind him. He heard nothing and just kept trudging along. I leaped forward, covering the few feet between us in a second or less. I stabbed him in the left shoulder and grabbed the front rim of his helmet with my left hand all in the same move. The knife buried in his shoulder gave me the grip I needed to hold my right forearm at the base of his neck while I pulled back hard on the rim of the helmet. His neck snapped without his ever having made a sound. I glanced past him as he went limp in my grasp and saw Bob in the act of leaping on his man.

We took them down one by one, from back to front, like dominoes.

I cut his throat and stabbed him in the heart to make sure he was dead, and dragged him off the trail into the bushes down the hill about twenty yards. I covered him with loose leaves and humus. The rest of the guys dragged their victims off the trail and did their best to cover them up. In a few hours they would start to smell anyway, and before long anyone that came that way would know they were there, but it might buy us a few hours.

There was some blood on the leaves around the trail, and scuff marks and bloodstains leading through the bush. We covered that up as best we could, and destroyed their weapons.

I should have stopped right there. I should have just counted the kills, aborted the mission, and got the rest of them the hell out of there. But we were so mission oriented. . . .

We went back and got Olfson's body out of the pit. I tolled off Quinn, Casburn, and Fitchew to cover the pit and take the body down. It was starting to smell already, because of the heat. Quinn had the strength to carry the body without any trouble. Fitchew and Casburn could spell him, and the two not carrying the body could watch the bush for the other one.

"You stop and get that radio on the way down," I told them, "so you can call in for a dustoff. Don't go to our LZ or to our pickup spot. Find another spot, and have them come to you. Then you stay around after they take the body out. We'll rendezvous about a mile from our LZ and get picked up together. Remember that ledge of rock that stuck up down by the bend in the river? We'll rendezvous there. We'll call you when we come off the hill."

It was mid-afternoon when the rest of us started back up the hill. We all stayed on the same side of the hill, because I figured the patrol we'd taken out was responsible for that sector. We followed off to one side of their trail. Soon we came to a long, gentle slope that went up the crest of one of the divides

between ravines. The trail followed the incline for
quite a distance. The trees formed an almost solid
canopy, and where there was an opening, the brush
grew up in a second canopy so the light came through
the leaves in little pencil-thin beams. When you were
in the darker parts, your eyes got accustomed to it
and you could see all right: it was like dusk. When
you came to one of the more open areas, though, the
light dazzled your eyes, and you couldn't see what
was lurking in the shadows. The monkeys gathered
near the open spots. You could generally tell you were
coming to a clearing from all the shrieking and chattering.

Magoun found a Malay sling. It was a sapling
mounted against a couple of trees and bent back so it
would whip across the trail just about waist high.
There were sharpened bamboo stakes lodged in it that
would be driven into the belly or groin of the person
that triggered it. We left it untouched.

Just before sundown we came upon a bunker right
at the top of a little knoll. We checked it out. It was
empty, and there were no signs that the enemy had
been there recently, so we moved on. Beyond the
knoll was a little clearing. It covered the crest of the
ridge. On either side of it the ridge fell off sharply
into ravines. The ravines were steep and heavily overgrown with bamboo and all kinds of brush, because the
trees were very patchy. The trail swung to the left and
through the brush at the head of one of the ravines. It
was an ideal site for an ambush or a booby trap, so we
avoided it. The choice was to cross the clearing or work
our way through the ravines.

We were all tired, and the idea of bucking the brush
some more didn't sound attractive, so I sent Vo and

Tony down for a closer look. They came back and said it was all clear, but the grass was short, so we'd best wait for dark before crossing. We spread out around the knoll and waited. Bob worked fifty yards back along our trail as an outpost in case we were being followed. Some of the guys took the opportunity to eat their C-rats or take a drink. I sat and studied my map and looked ahead at the terrain, as much as I could see of it. We were about a third of the way up, and the roughest country lay ahead of us.

It was dusk when we got ready to move out again. Bob and I were conferring before going out as points when he spotted two gooks moving out on the far side of the clearing.

I dug out the binoculars and watched them. There was no real need for a starlight scope.

"What are they doing?" Bob asked.

"I don't know, unless they just got tired of fighting the bush. Maybe they're looking for a place to bed down for the night. I do know one thing: they feel safe up here. And they're not in any hurry."

We held up until the dusk had deepened into dark. There was a full moon out. All the time, I was going over the possibilities in my head. If we tried to go through the brush at the head of the ravine, it would be a real bitch. The moonlight would help some, but we were going to make noise enough to make up for the extra cover we would have. If we cut through the clearing we might be spotted. And if we held up here until morning before working our way through the bush, Charlie would be moving too.

When we started to move out I told Bob, "We're not going through the clearing. Tell everybody to stay close. We'll go through the brush to the right of the clearing.'' It was more open and less steep than the other side.

"Fuckin' A," he agreed.

We worked our way through the bush just at the edge of the clearing. We were about halfway across when I heard voices. I had the others hold up, and then crept up closer. I could see at least two men, probably the ones I'd heard talking. With the starlight scope, I could see others in some of the bushes. They had an L-shaped ambush set up, but they weren't very serious about it. I could hear them muttering to each other every once in a while, and once one of them chuckled. If they'd kept their damned mouths shut, they could've had eight of Uncle Sam's best to brag about to Mama-san.

I backed away until I felt safe breaking squelch and called the team. I just mouthed the words into the mike in a very quiet whisper, but they heard it. Tony moved up near me, and we watched the ambush while Bob led the rest of the team into the edge of the clearing. They went one at a time, the rest crouching down to cover the moving man. They sounded like a herd of water buffalo to Bob, but I didn't hear them, and the Talking Ambush sure didn't.

After they were past, Tony and I followed them. We leapfrogged across the edge of the clearing, in the patchy brush as much as possible, one man moving while the other watched over him.

About 2100, in the thicker bush up the ridge, we laagered for the night. We lay in a rough circle, in pairs, each pair about fifteen feet apart. The guys in each pair were about three feet apart. One would sleep while the other kept watch. We were close enough to wake each other without much movement, and the pairs were far enough apart that Charlie couldn't get everyone at one swoop if he did hit us.

The monkeys and the birds had settled down, and except for the occasional call of a night bird, it was silent. At this season, at this altitude, there wasn't any noisy insect life or tree frogs. They'd come later. Every now and then you could hear a loud crack as the trees cooled and contracted. Green troops might have been panicked by it, but we were all used to it by now. It was a normal night sound in this area, due to the extreme temperature range.

Tony and I paired up. I had the first watch. I lay there and tried to concentrate on watching my zone of responsibility, but my mind kept going back through the events of the day. Had I made the right decision, splitting the team? As far as our own movement and security, I was sure I had. I could only hope the other three were making it all right. If they didn't make it, if they were spotted and ambushed, I knew I'd blame myself. On the other hand, it had seemed necessary for the morale of the group to let them carry the body out. No one wanted to think of his body being left behind to rot and become a part of Vietnam.

When we first stopped, my greens were wet with sweat, and I could smell the blood on them from the gook I'd killed earlier. Later, as the night cooled, the sweat sapped my body heat, and I got chilled. I started craving a smoke, but the smell would carry a long way at night and might give us away. There was nothing to do but lie there without moving, and look and think.

The moon was high and big and unobscured by clouds. That would give us an advantage if Charlie came by. I looked up at the moon and thought about that same moon shining over the hills back home in Arkansas, and I could almost hear the music of the coon dogs down along the Buffalo. I loved the moon back there. Not that I was a coon hunter, although I've been a few times. These moonlit nights were the best ones for a hot date and a watermelon roast down by the lake. Over here, the moon might be a help to you, or it might help Charlie. It seemed to change sides pretty often. I thought, "Whose side are you on tonight, moon? All I ask is: keep shining until daylight."

When I reached over to wake Tony for his watch, he woke up without jerking. I think he wasn't really asleep. I stretched out on my back and closed my eyes but never did go to sleep. I was aware every time somebody awakened for his watch. Time just seemed to drag on. I took my watch again, then Tony took the last. When he poked me the next time, it was getting light. It was time to move.

As we started up, we found a broad area that had been cleared by the bombing during the big battle. It was quite a bit easier to travel through, and we made up for time lost in the other areas. The monkeys were plentiful again, and we took that for a good sign that Charlie wasn't in the area in big numbers. Neither did we see any patrols until mid-afternoon, when we were nearing the top of the ridge. By then we'd gone three-quarters of the way around.

The patrol was larger than those we'd seen farther down: there were about a dozen men. I thought that might indicate we were close to the enemy's strong point, and when we saw a second patrol about the same size just a little way farther on, I was certain. I decided to hold up until dark. We searched the immediate area to make sure the two patrols had gone, and circled up to wait until sunset.

When we moved out, I put Bob out on the right flank and Tony on the left. I spread the group out just far enough so that we could still see hand signals. The bush was far more open than before, but we still had to take it easy or we'd make too much noise.

We had gone about half a mile when I spotted a patrol. I signaled the team to drop down and stand by. I didn't want to take them out.

They got closer and closer, and I got tenser and tenser. It looked as if they were going to walk right onto us. Actually, they did. They were spread out too, and for a moment they were all around and among us. Then they passed on. The rear guard passed within six feet of me. I thought, "You lucky slopehead asshole! If we were going down this hill instead of up it, I'd stick your ass!" They weren't carrying packs. That meant they weren't out for more than half a day, so we were getting close to their camp. They were probably a perimeter patrol, so there would be another not far behind them.

We didn't move until the last of them was out of sight. Tony gave the all-clear signal, and I motioned that we should move out. We were getting close now, and everyone knew they had to be more alert.

We hadn't moved much more than a hundred yards when I happened to look over to the left and saw Dasher relaying a signal from Tony—an indication that someone on the left had visual contact and wanted us to wheel in that direction.

We made a broad sweep, keeping our relative positions so that Bob ended up on the right flank, but we crossed our former line of movement at about right angles.

I could see a light ahead, thirty yards or so through the bush. The guys had automatically pulled in closer because the light was failing fast, and they were staying within sight of each other. I called them even closer so we could whisper and hear one another.

"Okay, listen up. Bob, you and Tony take the right and see what they have on that side," I told them. "Be damned sure to watch for booby traps." I still had Mike Olfson on my mind. "Dasher and me will take the left. Thompson, you and Vo cover the rear. You other guys hold your positions here. We'll meet back here in one hour."

Bob and Tony moved out to the right and Dasher and I went off to the left. We went about fifty yards before we turned toward the camp—a little area cleared of brush, with six huts in it. Four of them were new; the other two were run-down, seedy, as if they had been there for some time. They weren't much, just bamboo frames with some leaves to shed the rain. A gook was squatted down in front of one of the huts with his head resting back against it. The huts didn't have any doors, and I could see maybe ten people inside the one where the guy was leaning. There were about twenty more outside, standing or squatting around in little groups, bullshitting. Dasher counted four sentries around the perimeter, walking posts about a hundred feet apart within about twelve feet of the edge of the clearing, and he pointed out two more near the entrance to a bunker. They were standing there talking with their weapons slung, but their positioning suggested they were guarding something. In the middle of the clearing there was a small fire built underneath a bamboo frame with a roof to hide it from the air. The kill zone—the cleared area— on our side was cleared to about 200 feet from the huts. There were five sandbagged mortar pits. Everyone in the place seemed to be carrying AK-47s, and they were all uniformed NVA. I estimated there were probably fifty men in the camp, plus those out on patrol. We knew there was at least one patrol out, but I didn't know if the two we'd seen earlier had come back in.

We had watched them for about thirty minutes when Dasher pointed out one of the gooks talking on the radio. About five minutes later a patrol of eight entered the camp from off to our left. Three men from inside the hut came out and started talking to the leader. We couldn't hear them, but I could see the leader shaking his head from side to side. They talked for just a couple of minutes, then the leader went inside with the three that had come out to meet him, and the rest of the patrol dispersed.

I glanced at my watch. It was time to head back.

We rendezvoused back in the bush where Lusk and Magoun were holding their positions. The guys checking the back trail had already returned, and Bob and Tony had got back just ahead of us.

Thompson made his report. "We went about a hundred yards back and out fifty to each side, and seen nothing."

"There were five sentries over on our side, and the kill zone is about a hundred feet wide. The bush over there has been thinned down and it isn't as thick as it is over here," Bob said. "You can move around in it a lot easier, but there's still some patches of brush there for cover. It looks like it might be some kind of an escape route." Then he recounted essentially what Dasher and I had seen of the layout of the camp.

"Are there any huts in back of the main ones?" I asked him.

"There's one, a little one. Looks like a shithouse. I didn't get close enough to smell. And there's two sandbag bunkers. One of them has a machine gun in it, and a gook. The other I couldn't see very well."

"Do the sentries have a clear view of each other?"

"The ones right and left of them, yeah. And the ones on the end could see each other across the clearing if they looked. We could take out the middle three, and risk the other two missing them. They don't walk a regular post . . . sometimes they take longer on their route than they do other times."

I asked about booby traps.

"Didn't see ary a one."

"None," Tony agreed.

I told them what we'd seen, and about the patrol coming in. We sat there and thought over the situation for a while in silence.

Then Bob asked the Question: "Well, what are we gonna do?"

I made a show of studying the map while I thought. I lay down and covered my head with a shelter half and looked at the map with one eye by the light of my little penlight, but I knew what the map showed, anyway. We had covered the hill pretty well. Anything we had missed so far, we were likely to miss if we stayed another day on the hill. That really wasn't the question Bob was asking. What he was really saying was: "Okay, you stupid fucker, you left the pack radio at the foot of the hill. How do we call for artillery or an air strike?" I turned out the penlight and lay there under the shelter half while my eye readjusted to the dark.

I could see three options open to us.

One: We could leave, report the location of the camp as we had it on our map, and let them fire on it blind, or hit it with a blind air strike. More likely, they would send someone back in to observe and correct the artillery or the air strike. Probably they would send us, since we'd been there and knew the way in and what to expect. We'd have to climb the damned hill again. Or they might send the Marines in to clear Charlie off the hill. If they did that, some Marines would get killed. Maybe a lot of them.

Two: We could go down the hill, meet the other guys, and get the radio. Then we could come back up the hill and call in the air strike or the artillery. That would take at least three more days, and there was the risk of being seen by a patrol. As we got tired, we'd make mistakes, and the risk grew. That option was not as good as the first.

Three: We could hit the camp ourselves while we were up here. We had hit camps this size before with very few problems. Bob and I and a mixed bunch of Green Berets, 101st Airborne, and ARVN Rangers had hit a camp bigger than this, not once, but twice, and got away with it. When the claymores and the explosives went off, there was so much confusion that Charlie really couldn't organize an effective defense effort for several minutes. The idea was to hit hard and get out fast.

There were definite advantages if we hit the camp, even if they had to come in later with airpower or the Marines to finish the job. Psychologically, it was more damaging to their morale to be hit hard and hurt bad by a few men on the ground than to suffer the same destruction by air strikes or artillery. If they took twenty-five or thirty casualties from an air strike, they'd just think, "Look how much effort they had to put out to cause this many casualties—they used all those planes, and burned all that fuel, and dropped all those bombs, and it probably cost them ten thousand dollars to kill one Viet Cong!" But let six or eight men hit them and cause the same number of casualties, and they'll think, "Holy Buddha! What's going on here? They did all this with eight men? Let's hope they don't bring in a whole company when they come back!"

I pulled my head out from under the shelter half. Bob was sitting there looking at me. I started folding away the shelter.

"Well?" he said. "You see anything on that map you ain't seen before?" He knew I'd been thinking it over.

"Let's hit'em."

"Fuckin' A, man!" When he grinned his teeth made a white flash in the darkness.

We had a council of war there in the dark. We knew what lay ahead of us, so we could sit down and figure out what we were going to do: draw it out in the damned dirt. Put all of our heads together. It wasn't me telling the guys, "Well, we're going to do this or we're going to do that, and the hell with your opinion." A lot of times they made more sense than I did. I wasn't the type to want credit for whatever we all did right. None of us wanted individual credit for anything. We weren't glory-hungry sons of bitches like some soldiers I've seen.

We decided to hit the camp from one side to panic

them, so that when they tried to escape, they would run into trip-wired mines on the other side. We would wait until just before dawn, so that the patrols out for the night would be in, and the morning patrols would probably not have gone out. When we had worked it out, I repeated the plan to make sure we all had it right.

"Okay," I said, "Bob, you and Tony and Thompson set your claymores in that cleared area. Trip-wire them. Then move up and take out those middle three sentries and put delays in those two bunkers and the shithouse. Set your timers so they'll go off at 0535. Then work around to this near end so you can shoot into the camp, if necessary. Dasher and Vo and me, we'll take out the middle two sentries on our side, and set our charges on the bunker and the mortar pits for 0530. Lusk, Magoun, set a perimeter of claymores in the bush about fifty yards from this end of the village. Leave a clear path so we can get through. Then stay back here to secure our backs. We go in at 0500. Remember, the first charges will go off at 0530. Be back here by 0520, so we can get started down the hill. Is that clear enough to everybody?"

They all agreed it was.

"All right, it's 2218 now; we have a chance to get some sleep. We'll laager up here. We seem to be out of the path of any patrols. Two men will maintain a watch on the camp. Bob and I will go first. The rest of you count off: odd numbers take the first watch. Two-hour watches. Be ready to saddle up at 0400."

At about 2330, we were startled by a racket that turned out to be some men in the camp getting a little drunk and loud. Two of them got in a tiff over a bottle, and another man came out of one of the huts and chewed their asses out. We saw no patrols going out or coming in. Then, just before we pulled back and let Thompson and Magoun take over, there was some radio traffic that generated some excitement in the camp. One man left the commo hut—we could identify that by the antenna wires strung from it—and ran to one of the other huts. In a few seconds he scurried back with another man, probably the commander.

"Did you see what hut he came from?" I asked Bob.

"Yeah."

"Well, remember it. It could be their officers' quarters. Put your charge on that one instead of the shithouse."

We moved back and let the other two take over the watch. I took Magoun's spot in the circle, and Bob took Thompson's. When my turn to sleep came, I was too nervous to close my eyes. Mom had always joked that my brother and I weren't afraid of work, because we could lie down right beside it and go to sleep. That sure wasn't the case now. "Work" was fifty yards and three hours away, and I hadn't slept in seventy-two hours, and I still couldn't doze off. Maybe because the Dexedrine was still in my bloodstream. I don't know. All I know is I lay there and thought about everything that could go wrong.

At 0330, when Bob rousted me, I went around and double-checked on everybody, making them eat and drink, and empty their bladders and move their bowels, if they hadn't already. "When we start down this hill, we're going to be moving damned fast," I reminded them. "We won't be able to stop and wait while ya shake the dew off yer lily." I made sure they had their charges and claymores, and the detonators they'd need, and that their weapons were loaded and working properly. By the time I'd finished I hardly had time to check my own gear. It was time to move out.

I reminded everybody, unnecessarily, of the timing, and to make sure they got a clean kill on any sentries they took out. Then we saddled up. We left our packs behind and took only our weapons and explosives. I checked my rifle to make sure the banana clips were clear, and my knife to make sure it was free. Then I switched the rifle to full auto and popped some Dexedrine, and we moved out, me, Vo, and Dasher in one direction, Bob Brewster, Tony, and Thompson in the other, and Magoun and Lusk directly ahead toward the camp.

Only the sentries were moving around in the camp. A couple of drunks were still curled up on the ground by one of the huts, sleeping it off. It was a little too early for the sober ones to be up and moving around. They'd wake up at sunup—about the time our charges started going off. I was relieved to see there wasn't an early patrol going out.

At 0500 I signed to Vo to move in on his sentry. He was to delay five minutes before taking him out. That would give me time to get into position to get mine. We left our rifles with Dasher.

My sentry was holding his rifle in his right hand, by the pistol grip, but he didn't have his finger on the trigger. He'd laid the rifle back on his shoulder with the pistol grip forward, so that the barrel stuck almost straight up. He was short and wiry, as most of them were. He had his helmet on, but his chin strap wasn't fastened, so snapping his neck was out of the ques-

tion. He was walking too close to the bush, which
was to my advantage.

He was approaching me and about thirty feet away
when there was a disturbance in the bush. He stopped,
brought the rifle down into firing position, and edged
toward the commotion. My mind was racing: Was
Dasher doing something on his own? Had Vo mis-
understood his assignment? I got ready to run like
hell. Then the sentry bent down, picked up a rock,
and threw it off into the bush. At once there was
screaming and chattering as a monkey took off for
parts unknown, cursing back over his shoulder at the
sentry. The sentry relaxed and came on toward me,
mumbling.

He was probably cursing the monkeys. I know I
was.

When he passed, he had his rifle back on his shoulder and his finger off the trigger. Sometimes when
you grab a sentry and stick him, he'll pull the trigger
by reflex, so I was glad to see he didn't have his
finger on it. He'd put his left hand in his pocket,
probably because it was cold.

I glanced at my watch, and it was time to go.

I raised into a low crouch and stepped out of the
bush behind him. He was about eight feet ahead of
me and walking away, so it took me three quick steps
to catch up to him. I grabbed him under the chin with
my left hand and jerked his head to the left and back
so he couldn't cry out. He was so small I lifted him
right off the ground. He dropped the rifle and grabbed
for my left forearm. I placed the knife between his
shoulder blades, and it hit his spine and slipped off to
the right. For a second I thought I'd screwed up, but
I turned the blade to the left and forced it in, and it

went in front of his backbone into his lung and heart. He kicked a couple of times as I carried him into the bush. I left his rifle lying there. When I dropped him, I realized he was dead, but I cut his throat anyway, as a sort of double-check.

Over to the right, I saw Vo had taken his man out. I grabbed the demolitions and headed for the bunker in a low crouch.

It was that period of false dawn, when the sky lightens a little just before true sunrise. The moon was low in the western horizon, and together with the light in the eastern sky, lit the scene a little brighter than full moonlight would.

I had to pass one of the sandbagged mortar pits to get to the bunker. There was one guy posted there, but he was sitting on his ass, sound asleep. One of the guys posted by the bunker had gone over to the fire to warm his hands. The other one sat with his back and head leaning against the bunker. He wasn't asleep, though, because he would move his head a little and look around.

I was about thirty feet from the bunker when a man came out of the commo hut and walked right toward it. He was probably the radio operator on duty. I was in the open with nothing to hide behind. I pressed myself flat on the ground and became a bush. I concentrated on being a bush. I even dug my fingers into the ground like roots, and mashed my face into the ground and smelled the good rich soil and wished it would rain. There for a few seconds, I *was* a bush.

Either the guy wasn't alert or I sprouted leaves, because he went off to the other side of the bunker. I waited a few seconds and then went for it. He was taking a leak behind the bunker. I would have waited until he finished and left, but I was on a tight schedule. I set the timer and laid a charge by the front corner. Then I set another timer, laid a charge on the top, and went back to the rear. The gook was still there. It was sure taking him a long time. He may have been playing with himself. Anyway, he was making me run behind schedule. I needed to set a charge on the hut he'd come from, and I didn't want him coming back and interrupting me.

Cursing him silently, I drew my K-bar and stepped around the corner of the bunker. He heard something and turned to face me, his hands still on his penis. I grabbed him by the throat with my left hand, crushing his Adam's apple with my thumb, and rammed my knife into his solar plexus. He didn't even kick. He just stiffened up for a second and then went limp. I laid him down easy. I was tempted to cut off his penis—I'd seen what they did to our dead—but I didn't have time for such nonsense.

I glanced around the corner at the guy sitting by the front corner of the bunker. He had drawn his knees up and rested his forehead on them. He was breathing slowly and regularly. If he wasn't asleep, he was damned near it. His companion by the fire was standing with his backside to it, warming his buns, and watching one of the huts—probably keeping an eye out for signs of an officer or noncom stirring. If he looked back toward the bunker, he'd see me heading for the hut.

I worked my way around the other side of the bunker, crouched there, and checked my watch. I was about three minutes behind schedule. I was about ready to go for it when the jerk by the fire turned around.

I practically sprinted over to the hut. Not quite flat out, because every muscle was tense, and I was careful not to let my feet thud on the ground. I put the third delay on top of the hut. I wanted to put it inside the door, but with that asshole standing by the fire out front, it was out of the question.

After a quick look around, I worked my way back past the bunker to the mortar pit. The guy in there was still catching some Z's. He was propped against the back wall. I set the timer and lowered the charge over the sandbag wall until I felt the strap go slack. I let the strap go, praying the charge wasn't caught on something and that the gook had not wakened. I could imagine him calmly taking the charge out of my hand as I lowered it, then raising up over the wall and shooting me. Nothing like that happened, though, so I checked to make sure there was no one moving around, and slipped back to the edge of the clearing where Dasher was waiting.

Vo tapped his watch. "You late," he said disapprovingly. He was almost covered with blood from the sentry.

"I had to take another one out," I told them. "Let's get the fuck out of here."

CHAPTER 7

We rendezvoused in the clump of brush where we'd laagered during the night. Bob was cursing to himself as he slipped his pack on his shoulders. There were only seconds to ask him what was wrong, and while he muttered something about the detonator on the last charge, I was already thinking about calling in Lusk and Magoun, so whatever he said didn't register. I picked up my hand radio and called in the other two. I kept checking my watch as we waited, even though it only took a few minutes. We were still running late.

Then one of the damned claymores on the perimeter went off.

For about half a second we all stood there, frozen, looking at each other. Had a patrol moved into the perimeter? Had some gook slipped out of camp to go AWOL and triggered it?

I called Lusk and Magoun to see what was going on.

Lusk answered. "Stand by . . . Joe is checking it out."

Bob said, "I got the left flank!" and took off.

I pointed at Thompson and then to the right. The hill would soon be swarming with NVA, and we needed flankers out. Thompson was gone in a flash. The others spread out.

I called on the radio again. Magoun answered. "Alfa Blue One? Joe, what the hell?"

"It was a damned monkey, Jay."

"Get back here, fast." There wasn't any need to tell him they'd be all over the hill soon. "We'll move out north," I told them all over the radio. "They won't expect that. Joe, take the rear guard. Dasher, you drop back with him."

Magoun ran to catch up. There was no need to be quiet now. As soon as I saw him behind us, I signaled the group to move out. We moved away as fast as we could while still checking ahead. Any patrol still out would be coming back toward the camp, and we didn't want to run onto one without warning. I moved out front, taking Vo with me.

It wasn't the first time I'd had trouble with the damned monkeys. On my first tour, there'd been one place with so goddamned many monkeys we called it Monkey Hill. I guess a lot of outfits had their Monkey Hill, or Monkey Mountain. In our case, we were setting ambushes, and the monkeys got to messing around with our claymores. They didn't set any off, but they stole one from one of our team while his back was turned. We didn't get any Viet Cong that day, but we sure took care of the monkeys. Now it looked like the little bastards were getting back at us.

We'd gone about 150 yards when Vo reported contact on the left. There were two NVAs about fifty feet ahead of him, moving toward the camp. I turned the team downhill, to the right. It was probably a mistake.

The turn made me left flanker. I hadn't gone five yards before I ran into two gooks hurrying through the bush toward the camp. They looked at me, startled, and I shot them both from a range of ten feet. The rifle was still on full automatic, and it blew them backward into the bush. Then I heard firing behind me: Vo's M-16 and Bob's shotgun. They seemed to be coming from the left. I looked that way and there was another one. He saw me at the same time and fired. I could hear his bullets pop as they went by my head. The muzzle climbed on him as he shot. I fired from the hip and saw him go limp, then I ducked down into a very low crouch and looked around. As I did, the dirt in front of me flew up into my face. I couldn't see the shooter, but the angle of scatter told me he was to my right. I didn't study it. Things like that become instinctive or you don't last long. I blasted a nearby clump of brush and jumped behind a tree.

The first two time-delay charges went off, followed half a second later by a larger blast. There must have been ammunition in that bunker. Immediately, shooting started over by the camp. Either someone was blasting away at monkeys, or some small-arms ammunition was cooking off from a fire in the bunker. A flare shot up.

I figured we'd run into a patrol hurrying back to camp. They weren't sure what they'd run into. They probably thought we were the rear guard for a larger force attacking the camp. It sounded like the Fourth of July over there, with charges going off at irregular intervals and a lot of shooting. The patrol, if that's what it was, backed off a little to study the situation.

I took out the hand radio and told everybody to hold their positions and to listen and watch for movement. It was dawn now and getting brighter by the minute. I checked my rifle. The clip was empty. I reloaded and switched over to semiautomatic.

The radio crackled a bit as Bob reported, "Two moving in on my right, toward Vo." I started zigzagging toward Vo myself. I went about fifty feet before I saw them. They were approaching our position at an angle, leapfrogging—that is, one would move while the other crouched behind a bush and covered him. They were trying to work in between Bob and Vo. I raised my M-16 and took aim at the one squatting behind a bush, watching over the other. I had an angle on him because he was keeping the bush between him and Vo. I aimed at his left ear, and he went down when I fired as if he'd been kicked in the head by a mule. I crawled off to the left to get an angle on the other one, but he moved to his right to put a bush between us. A second later Bob's shotgun blasted him over the bush ass-end foremost.

Bob called in again. "I've got three working in on my left."

Magoun reported two moving toward the camp. There was a shot behind me, and Thompson reported he'd got a single. Tony reported that he'd gone fifty yards down the hill and it was clear. I sent Lusk and

Magoun twenty yards back toward the camp to watch for anyone coming from that direction. I told the others to head toward Tony.

It was as still as a tomb on that hillside. The noise from the camp had stopped almost as quickly as it had started. All the charges must have gone off. I could imagine them running around trying to get a defense organized without having the slightest idea what was happening. I broke squelch to tell the others not to shoot unless they had to. We tried to break contact with the patrol by slipping away downhill.

We hadn't gotten down quite as far as Tony when the claymores went off. There was screaming this time, and it wasn't any goddamned monkeys. I hoped we'd gotten a lot of the gooks. The monkeys sure screwed it up for us. If they hadn't set off that claymore, most of the NVA in the camp would have been in their huts, and we'd have taken care of a lot of them there. I figured most of them, by now, would have been mustered outside by their officers and noncoms. At any rate, they'd gotten into the claymores, and that, at least, would slow down their pursuit.

I glanced over to my right and saw Magoun moving down the hill. He stopped for a moment, then held up his hand and lowered it slowly. I couldn't see anything, so I dropped on down the hill a little. Sure enough, there they were. I didn't know if they were coming from the camp or were part of the patrol we thought we'd slipped away from, or if they were part of another patrol. They were trouble, anyway.

Magoun started to move. He was going with his knife after the gook he'd seen. A second one raised up and fired. Magoun went down and yelped, ''I've been hit!'' Vo and Bob were behind me. They opened up on the gooks as I hurried over to him.

He'd been hit in the side, but not real bad. The bullet had ricocheted off one of his ribs. It made a long, nasty-looking wound, and it bled a lot. The rib was probably broken.

"Son of a bitch, it burns," he said.

"Can you move all right?"

"Yeah, I can keep up."

Bob came sliding in like he was stealing third. "Don't give him any morphine!" he barked. He meant he didn't want the guy conking out on us.

"I didn't," I told him. "He ain't hurt bad. You stay close to him, though."

"Sure," Bob said.

"Sure as shit, Bob!" I snapped at him. His eyes widened a little. I never snapped at him that way. "Do it!" I told him.

"Okay, don't get your balls in an uproar."

I signaled for the group to move on. We went about a hundred yards downhill without seeing Charlie, and I called them in to regroup.

After I counted off to make sure we were all there, I laid out the situation for them, as if they didn't know it already. "All right, listen up! They know we're here, and they know which way we're moving. They also know we have to go downhill. I'm sure they'll try to get in position to ambush us on the way down. They'll expect us to drop straight downhill, though, because that's the fastest way out. So we'll go diagonally. That should throw them off a little. We'll veer to the left here about forty-five degrees.

"We ran a recon coming up this damned hill, and that's how we're going to go down it," I told them.

"Flankers out, two point men, and a rear guard. Magoun, you stay in the middle. Bob, take the point on the left; Tony, you take the left flank; I'll take the point on the right; Lusk, flanker behind me; Vo, Thompson, rear guard. Dasher, stay in the middle with Magoun. Keep an eye on him, he's been hit in the ribs. He's lost some blood, and he's still in some pain and could pass out on us.

"We don't have that much ammo with us and we can't be pissing it away, so set your weapons on semi-auto and make every shot count.

"We'll go to a Morse code system with the radios. No talking. Odd numbers on the left, number one being the point, number three the flanker, number five the rear guard. Even numbers on the right, starting with number two. You in the middle, seven and eight. Signal first that you've spotted movement by breaking squelch twice, then give your number in Morse code. Then signal how many you've seen. Three quick clicks will mean all clear. One click after your number means 'help.' They might run a decoy at us to draw our fire and get us to give our positions away, so make damned sure they're not decoys before you shoot. Let them go by if you can.

"It'll be early tomorrow morning before we can get down. If we get separated, keep going. Rendezvous with the other guys, but wait until tomorrow afternoon before you call in for pickup. If everyone isn't at the rendezvous by 1700, assume they're dead. Any questions?"

"Yeah." It was Bob.

"What is it, Bob?"

"Can we get the flock off this hill?"

"Move yer ass, then."

I glanced at my watch as we spread out and started down again. It was 0730.

It was mid-morning when we made contact again. I heard two clicks on my radio, followed by a short pause, three short clicks, and two long ones—Morse code for number 3. It was Bob. He sent four more clicks, meaning he'd seen four enemy. We all lay silent for nearly thirty minutes before he sent the all clear. We moved again, but hadn't gone ten yards before two more pops came: "five," the rear guard on the left. Two more pops told us he'd spotted two Charlies. Again we waited. This time it was almost an hour before we got the all clear. I had begun to worry that Charlie had gotten to him before he could shoot or signal.

This time we covered considerable ground before there was contact again. The left rear guard spotted a patrol of eleven Charlies. Then the left flanker signaled he'd seen two, and Bob, at the left point, spotted five. They may all have been part of the same group. I broke radio silence to tell everyone to hold their positions. They were moving fast and zigzagging back and forth across the slope, searching for us. They were moving too fast: their right flank almost stepped on our left flankers. But they went on past without incident, and moved ahead along our planned path.

I decided it was time to change direction and descend across the slope to the right. It was a steep slope and the brush was thick, but about a mile back that way was the little knoll with the clearing below it, and the long gentle slope down the crest of the ridge just beyond it. It was ground we were more familiar with, and we would come off the hill near where we'd started up on it. The chief problem with that route was that we would have to cross a ravine about 150 yards below us, a good place for an ambush.

We held our formation and swung around to the right about ninety degrees. That took us into the ravine to just below the narrowest part. Ledges of rock, dense patches of bamboo, and a thick carpet of dry leaves on the steep slope didn't make moving easier. The underbrush was heavy and tangled, and we had to yank it aside with our bare hands and rifle barrels, and twist our bodies through.

It was 1330 when we reached the bottom. The temperature was well over 100 degrees, and it was still and muggy. Even the monkeys and birds had called it quits and were lying in the shade. I popped a handful of salt pills, took one swig of water, then started up the other side.

About halfway up, Dasher called to say Magoun was getting run-down with the effort of working through the undergrowth. I was feeling pretty run-down myself. I hadn't slept in eighty hours, more or less. I called a break for his sake, and mine too. We found some thick brush and came in close together. We decided to stand one-hour watches, and two men awake at all times. I picked a number and wrote it in my notebook. The guys who guessed closest got the last watch. It was less effort than drawing straws or tossing coins. I would take the first watch. Bob volunteered to take it with me. We spread out about twenty feet apart and tied our pinkies together with string, all the way around the circle. If anyone passed between us while we were sleeping they'd trip on the string and wake us. And we could jerk the string and wake someone if we needed to. It was a system we used often on ambush.

I lay there during my watch and thought about Mike Olfson. He had a wife and three kids back in Minnesota. He'd told me that he and his wife had had to get married when they were both just seventeen. Her daddy wouldn't help them out at all, and Mike's parents couldn't, so they had to make it on their own. She had held down two jobs while carrying their first baby, and Mike did too, whenever he could. Mike was like that.

You could count on him. And he'd always known what had to be done before you told him.

We had taken some pictures three weeks before of him and me clowning around, and I still had them. If I made it back, I'd send them to his wife. It wouldn't be much, but at least he was smiling.

I heard something big moving through the brush and jerked around to look, expecting an elephant or at least a water buffalo. It was only Bob.

"It's 1630. Let's wake these guys and get some shut-eye ourselves."

I rousted Tony while Bob kicked Lusk in the ribs hard enough to wake him. I told Tony to wake me right before sundown. Then I checked on Magoun and saw that he was asleep. That was good. He needed it. Then I lay down on a cushion of leaves and crashed.

It was 1800 when Tony woke us up. I woke up feeling dehydrated and wishing I had a beer and a cigarette. Magoun was feeling a little better but was stiff from lying in one spot. The flies and other insects were swarming around his wound and worrying him.

We had some water and rations. I ate a chocolate bar and the last Vienna sausages I had.

It was 1820 when we saddled up and moved out. The small clearing was just around the ridge, and I wanted to make it before nightfall so we could take the clearing under observation for a while before crossing it. We still had a hundred feet of heavy brush to go before we got out of the ravine. We were moving downward. We really weren't climbing, but we were moving across the natural grain of the terrain, and the going was tough. And of course, when the going got tough, we tended to draw in together, as always.

Just when we reached the top, all hell broke loose. Charlie was waiting for us, and we were in a firefight again. Lusk was the first to return fire. Then Bob opened up on my left. I looked over toward Lusk and saw one moving my way. I raised my M-16 and fired twice, dropping him. That gave my position away and suddenly there was hot lead all around.

"Move back, damn it!" I hollered, and immediately followed my own advice. Firing from the hip at the bushes in front of me, I moved back toward the ravine. Only one or two Charlies would move at a time, but they were moving in. We kept firing and backing away, and it seemed like we were bunching up again. Probably Charlie was trying to work around our flanks, and the natural tendency is to back away from the fire, not straight back the way you came.

"Spread it out!" I yelled at them, and several of them repeated the order. We backed about seventy-five to a hundred feet before the firing slacked off. We had spread out more, and Charlie wasn't too eager to pursue us down into the heavy bush. An occasional shot still sang through the brush, but they were mostly nuisance shots thrown out to make us return fire and give away our position. I got on the radio and told the team to quit moving.

"Was anybody hit?"

Tony came on the radio. "Jay, Dasher's hit in the face."

"Is it bad?"

"It hit him in the mouth and came out his left jaw. He's lost some teeth and he's bleeding bad. But he can travel."

"You're fuckin' right he can. He'd better. Anybody else hit?"

There was no other response. I called Tony back and told him to get Dasher fixed up. He rolled up gauze and stuffed it into the wound where Dasher's teeth had been and then immobilized the jaw with a triangular bandage. That would have to do until we got back to medical facilities. After about five minutes Tony called back and said, "Okay, let's go."

Now I had to turn about and tell Magoun to keep an eye on Dasher and help him along.

I didn't really know what to do next. Our asses were in deep trouble. We were in danger of getting sandwiched between two enemy patrols, and I knew Charlie had a lot of firepower on that hill. It was time to make a decision, and I dreaded making decisions under pressure more than anything in the world. The problem is you're looking at these guys, and they're looking back at you, and their eyes are saying, "Okay, asshole, what do we do?" You've got to decide right now, and worry later if it was right or wrong. You don't find out until it's all over with, until you're back home or you're dead.

"Let's go for it," I thought. "We've got to go for it. Let's get out of this ravine and off the hill."

We moved down the ravine a hundred yards and tried again to come out. I think we'd barely flanked the enemy, because Thompson reported seeing two Charlies moving into the ravine behind him as we headed down the slope. We went at an angle again, trying to move fast but cautiously. We'd gone about a quarter of a mile when there was a *pow! pop!* off to my right and rear, and someone screamed.

"I've been hit! *Goddamn! I've been hit!*" I recognized the voice. It was Lusk.

I knew the louder sound was an AK-47 firing, and the *pop!* was an M-16 round—probably Lusk firing in reflex when he'd been hit.

I ran to where I could see him sitting up. I hollered and asked him how bad he was hit.

"I took a round in the belly," he said. "I think I can move, though." He got up and he went a little ways, then said, "Fuck it!" and just sat down.

Bob was hollering, "Get the fuck out of here! Let's go! Let's get the fuck out of here!"

Thompson came on the radio. "Sniper . . . one Charlie . . . I got him. Lusk is down."

"Hold your positions!" I told the team. "I'm going over."

He was grunting. I could hear him grunting before I ever got over there. When I got to him, he was lying on his back holding his stomach and pushing himself along the ground in agony. I dropped to my knees beside him and tried to pull his hands off the wound so I could see how bad it was, but as I would get one off and reach for the other, he would clamp the first hand over his belly again. At the same time he kept digging his heels into the dirt and pushing himself along so that I had to crawl along on my knees beside him. Finally I looked up to see Thompson backing toward us, watching the bush. There had been no more firing.

"Did you get the gook? Then get over here and give me a hand!"

He came over and sat on Lusk's knees and pulled the hands away for me. There was one hole, low down inside the right hipbone. The exit hole was in his left hip. Both were clean. The bullet hadn't tumbled, but he was bleeding badly.

"Ohshitohshitohshitshitshit!" he was muttering through clenched teeth. "It burns, it burns. My guts are on fire!"

"I'm going to put you out," I told him, reaching for my syringe of morphine.

"Oh, goddamn, hurry! I don't want to die looking at this shit!"

"You're not going to die," I told him as I grabbed his left arm and shot the morphine into him. I used mine, and then took his own and shot him again. It was only a minute before he relaxed.

"Is he dead?" Thompson asked.

"No, he ain't dead!" I snapped. "Get yer ass back out there and make sure there's none moving in on us."

I got on the radio and called Bob over.

"He's been gut-shot," I told him. "He's got a chance if we get him out. I want you to take the guys down. If you see you're getting your ass caught, bust a flare so I'll know where you are. Same with me. If I get caught, I'll pop a flare. If I'm not there by tomorrow afternoon, write me off and call the pickup."

"He's not going to make it, and you know it, Tyler. Leave him, and let's get out of here!"

"It's a clean wound," I argued. "He's got a chance. If we could call in a dustoff, he'd make it for sure. If I can get him down, he'll make it. You get the rest of them down!"

"Ah, you stupid asshole! Yer going to fuck around and git yourself killed! And he's going to die anyway."

I looked him in the eye—it was hard to do, because it was getting darker by the moment—and told him, "Bob, take over the goddamned patrol and get them down the hill in one piece. That's a fucking order! Do you understand?"

"Well, yes, fucking sir, Mister Petty Officer Tyler! Will do, can do, and all that do-do! But you'd better show up!" He turned and stomped off. I heard him snarl into the radio, "Awright, you simple bastards! Off yer asses! We're moving out!"

He'd gone before I remembered the starlight scope, so I took it out of my pack and gave it to Thompson as he went by.

"Take care, Tyler," he said.

I took what I could carry in my pockets and buried my pack and Lusk's. I looked around until I found his rifle, field-stripped it, and threw the parts as far as I could in different directions so the gooks couldn't use it. I used what gauze I had to stuff in the bullet holes and staunch the bleeding. I held the gauze in by wrapping our shirts tight around his belly. I took the ammunition that he had, and kept both our revolvers. Then I popped my last Dexedrine, set him up, and worked him up onto my shoulder. I used my M-16 for a brace to help me stand up with him.

I headed for the clearing and the long, gentle slope down the ridge crest.

I couldn't travel very fast. It was hard to keep my balance on the slope, and I had to stop and rest every ten minutes or so. I would shift him from shoulder to shoulder as my muscles on one side or the other would begin to ache. At first, I put him down while I rested, but each time it got harder to pick him up. Finally, I just leaned against a tree—I didn't dare put him down, or I would never have gotten him up again.

About 100 yards from the clearing I heard movement off to my left. I stopped to listen, but all I could hear was my own heavy breathing. I laid Lusk down in a clump of brush and covered him up. Then I slipped off about thirty feet and again listened.

I had about decided it had been my imagination when one of the shadows took the form of a man. The gook was moving very low to the ground with his rifle out in front of him. He moved very slowly and stopped frequently, looking off to both sides before moving on. He wore black, or a dark uniform, but no helmet. He moved like a hunter, and I figured he was hunting me. A chill passed up my spine as I watched him. Very few of them scared me, but he did.

I started to think then about Lusk and the morphine. I wasn't sure how long that stuff lasted. If it wore off, and he started making noises . . .

There were no other gooks with the stalker. After he moved off into the night I lay there for thirty minutes before I even thought of moving, then I made myself lie there another five minutes for good measure. I was stiff when I moved, so stiff I wondered if I could have handled the gook if he jumped me.

Lusk hadn't twitched a muscle since I hit him with the morphine, but he came around a little bit as I got back to him. He grunted a little bit, and said some words I couldn't understand. Then he passed out again.

I got him up on my shoulder again and headed for the clearing. It was 2048.

Time passed slowly. It seemed like I would never make it to the clearing, and when I got there my legs were as tired as if I'd been climbing stairs all the way. Yet only fifteen minutes had passed.

I put Lusk down in some brush about fifteen yards back from the edge of the clearing and covered him again. He still had a pulse, but his skin felt cold. I thought it was probably the night chill. I had nothing to wrap him in for warmth, since my shirt was tied around his belly. I could do nothing more for him but hope. At least he wasn't awake and begging me for water, or more morphine. I hoped what I had given him would last until I got him off the hill.

I went over to the clearing and observed it from a clump of brush. With a full moon you can look just over the tall grass, and if anyone is walking through it, you can see them. I saw nothing moving yet, but I thought about the Viet Cong manhunter I'd seen just a hundred yards back there and shuddered. He might be in the bush behind me right now. He might also be watching the clearing. I crouched there and kept an eye on the clearing until 2200. The moon was full and bright, and there wasn't a cloud in the sky. It hadn't rained in eight days, and everything was dry. The leaves crunched underfoot when you walked through the brush, and the bamboo rattled like dry gourds. "Monsoon, where are you when I need you?'' I thought. I looked at the moon, beaming happily down as if it were pointing at us and saying, "There they are, guys, go get them!" I thought, I know whose side you're on tonight, motherfucker!

I went back and checked Lusk's pulse. It was still there, but slow. The effect of the morphine, I figured. I covered him the best I could with long grass and sat down about thirty feet away where I could watch. I sure as hell wasn't going to sleep.

I wondered how the patrol was making out. I was sure Bob and Tony could get them down all right. They'd be slowed down by the two wounded, but not as much as I had been by Lusk. There had been no firing, so they must have succeeded in getting past the patrols. I wondered if they had come this way, or if they'd chosen another route. I thought about the two wounded guys and hoped they weren't in much pain. Magoun's wound wasn't that bad, unless the rib was broken. He would heal and come back. Dasher was going home. I wondered what the wound would do to his looks. He was a good-looking guy, in his way, and single. I didn't even know if he had a steady girl. I don't think so, because he talked like he had a girl in every port, and a dozen waiting to jump in bed with him when he got home. Well, the wound might put an end to that.

About 0100, I noticed some high, thin clouds covering the moon. Not enough to reduce the light much, but an indication that the weather might be changing. I looked back in the northwest, which was the only direction in which I could see very far, and thought I could make out some clouds beyond the mountains there. I slipped down to the clearing, but it was still well lighted. Too well lighted to cross.

About 0400, the moon was getting low in the west, and some broken clouds appeared around it. They just skirted its edge, though, and only covered it for a few minutes. Not enough time for me to cross.

By 0430, false dawn was beginning, and it was getting lighter. I went down to the edge of the clearing again and thought, "I'm moving out at 0500, clouds or no clouds."

The clouds were getting bigger and closer together, but they still weren't blocking out the moon for any substantial amount of time. It was almost as if they were purposely going around it.

When the time came, I rose and started back toward the bush where I'd left Lusk. As I turned my eyes away from the clearing something registered on the edge of my field of vision. Sometimes in dim light you can see objects better if you don't look directly at them. That's what happened in this case. Even as I turned back, I thought, "Bushes."

They weren't. Four men were walking across the clearing, line abreast. Even as I watched, two more appeared in the edge of the brush. They were sweeping across the clearing from my near left to the far right. They must have thought we were hiding in the grass. I wondered if they'd tracked me or followed me, or if the rest of our patrol had come this way before me. For whatever reason, they were ahead of me, and hunting.

I decided I could move around behind them, cutting through the left edge of the clearing just far enough into the brush to avoid being seen. They wouldn't expect me to be behind them where they'd just swept through.

There were fifteen or twenty in the line in the clearing when I moved back toward Lusk.

I heard a limb crack a little way ahead of me, back in the bush. That was a common sound in early evening but not in early morning. It wasn't the sap rising in the morning warmth, either. The only sap moving around that time of day had two legs. Was it an animal flushed out of the clearing by the patrol sweeping through it?

Off to the right there was a scuffle of leaves. I crouched as low as I could and pressed slo-o-wly back into the brush so as not to make a crackle.

Somewhere in front of me there was a faint *clunk* and a gurgle of water. A canteen bumping against something. Off to the right again, someone snuffled. Runny nose. I raised my M-16, but I wasn't sure if I wanted to shoot. I kept thinking of Lusk lying there wounded but alive in the brush, and what they'd do to him if they found him. If I fired a shot, those fifteen or twenty men in the clearing would be here inside of a minute. I might get away alone, but I'd have to leave Lusk. If I tried to use my knife, the sound of the scuffling would alert the others. There was only one course of action open to me: hide. I froze.

A gook stepped out from behind a bush not three feet from me. He moved very slowly, his rifle leveled and his finger on the trigger, but he was walking upright, like hunters do when they're not expecting to see game. He sniffed again, and wiped his nose with the back of his hand. Another appeared about five yards behind him. I could hear faint rustling behind me—a third one. So there was a line sweeping through the brush around the edge of the clearing too.

I crouched without breathing while two of them walked straight toward the brush where Lusk lay. When they found him still alive but wounded they'd know I was nearby. Even if they shot him to pieces they'd see he'd been bandaged. I decided I'd wait until they found him and clustered up. Then I'd shoot the shit out of them and run like hell down the hill behind me. I wished I had a grenade.

They stopped right beside the bush, and I thought I'd shit in my pants. My stomach knotted up as if I had eaten a pail full of green apples. My mind said, put your weapon on full auto and get ready. But my finger refused to move. They looked at each other, and then one made a gesture with his rifle barrel and they walked on, on either side of the bush.

When they were out of sight, I took a deep breath and let it out slowly. It caught a few times. I made myself wait five minutes. I broke out in a sweat and then got cold. When the five minutes were up, I was shivering. I went and picked up Lusk and got the hell out of there.

I went straight down the hill instead of around the clearing and along the ridge. I went fast at first, but slowed as I calmed down. I saw no more patrols.

I laid him down in the edge of the heavy brush at the foot of the hill and checked the more open terrain ahead. There were no gook patrols and no sign of any. It was almost noon. As I was picking him up again, it dawned on me that he felt cold. I checked his pulse and found none. His mouth was open and his tongue was dry. I listened for a heartbeat and put my cheek next to his nostrils to feel a breath. He was dead.

He wasn't stiff, though. He'd died sometime that morning.

At least he'd gotten his last request: he died unconscious, not "looking at this shit." I guess he meant the jungle. Vietnam.

I sat there for a while on the hillside. It was a long goddamned way to the LZ, and I was near exhaustion. I was out of water and out of rations. I could have justified leaving him there and going back for the body later. I was alone, and carrying a burden like that made it tough to watch for enemy patrols.

I'd carried Billy's body out the same way. I had made a mistake and got Billy killed, and now my mistake had got Lusk killed too. I owed him the same last favor. So we went the rest of the way together.

I called ahead to let them know I was coming in. I ran into Fitchew and Quinn, who were outposted, as I approached. They were tired and ragged, but they looked great compared to the rest of the guys, who were all sitting around in a little sheltered area, looking worn out and beaten down. Their uniforms were rags, and every one of them was covered with welts and cuts from the underbrush. Come to think of it, I guess I looked like that too. I counted heads as I walked in. They were all there. Olfson's body was lying on the ground in a little clearing. They hadn't called a dustoff for him.

Tony helped me lay the body down beside Olfson's. He just looked at it, and said, "Shit," and walked back to Dasher and sat down beside him. Dasher had Tony's blood-soaked shirt pressed against the side of his face. They were all staring at me. It was like I'd just cursed aloud in church. I knew what they were thinking: "He fucked up. If he hadn't left that goddamned pack radio at the foot of the hill, we wouldn't be shot up like this.'' I could see it in their eyes. I'd fucked up, and they were wondering if they could trust me anymore.

Bob was staring at me too. I knew he was thinking of something to say—like, ''I told you so.''

''Don't say a fucking word, Bob,'' I told him. ''Not a fucking word.''

He didn't say anything for a while. They had some water there, and I got a drink and sat down. After a time, he said, ''There's the radio. Call the pickup.''

''I know where the damned radio's at!''

I looked at the men, and they were looking at the ground. All except Bob Dasher, who was staring at me. It pissed me off, him sitting there staring at me that way. ''Why don't you just turn yer fucking head? Goddamn!''

I went over to the radio and jerked up the handset and called for extraction. I gave them our coordinates and told them to come get us there instead of at the LZ. Then I sat down and folded my arms on my knees and rested my head on them.

Bob came over and squatted down beside me. I thought he was going to put his hand on my shoulder.

''Just keep yer hands off me, damn it!''

Finally, he said, ''Yer right about this patrol leader job. I wouldn't want it.''

It was a quiet trip back.

CHAPTER 8

All the way to Quang Tri I psyched myself up to meet the criticism I expected from the officers and the team. Not that I wasn't being critical of myself. I'd screwed up bad, leaving that pack radio at the foot of the hill. A man died because of it, and two more were shot up. Mike Olfson—well, he might have died in that punji pit anyway. Or hell, he might not; he might have missed that booby trap if he'd been carrying the radio. You could play a lot of "if" games.

I kept remembering what Captain Gartley had said: "If you get in a firefight you've probably screwed up and failed your mission anyway." We had accomplished our mission, but I'd damn sure screwed up.

At the debriefing, Bob said he'd tried to count explosions, and he thought one of his hadn't gone off.

He said he thought the timer on the detonator was screwed up somehow. It was the one that was to take out the officers' hut. If it had gone off with the officers in the hut, the gooks might have been too disorganized to pursue us.

I figured that when the monkey yanked on that claymore trip-wire he woke up everybody in the camp, and they all ran outside. Only a few of them could have been hurt even if all the charges went off.

Captain Gartley took the casualties hard, but he didn't seem especially perturbed about the mission. We gave him our estimate of NVA strength and the number of casualties we caused, the location of their camp and all the booby-trapped areas we saw, and he took it all to the ARVN brass. They screwed around for weeks. When we left Quang Tri, they still hadn't done a damned thing with it.

After I'd screwed up on Hill 484, I thought the guys would want a new patrol leader. After all, we had lost three men up there. Two killed and one wounded that was sent home to recuperate. All of them SEALs. We didn't often lose that many SEALs on a job. We sure lost a lot of the other guys that worked with us, but being a SEAL usually meant survivability. It was a matter of training. And, I guess, aptitude. Some absorbed more of the training than others did.

SEALs and Marine Recons were about the most highly trained of the outfits the U.S. had over there, along with the older Green Berets. The Army expanded the Green Berets too fast, and turned out too many men only partially ready. Still, they were better off than your run-of-the-mill soldier, who got only a few weeks of the most rudimentary training before being tossed into the meat grinder. The average Marine was better trained than the average soldier, but after a few of them died in a training accident and there was a scandal, they let up on the trainees. They only killed more by doing that—not in accidents, but out in the bush of Vietnam. It didn't help quality when they started drafting kids into the Marines either. There were some other good units over there: the 101st Airborne, the 82nd Airborne, the Army Rangers: they got good training too, but maybe not enough. The brown-water sailors weren't trained enough when they were sent over there. They were hardly trained at all for fighting on land, but they did one hell of a lot of it. They'd go out with us when we needed more strength for a mission and couldn't get any other SEALs or other special forces. We sure got a lot of them killed off, too.

If they survived the first few firefights, though, guys usually did pretty well. They learned battlefield survival. Sailors, soldiers, any of 'em. There were individuals who did well no matter how much training they'd had. Fighting and surviving seemed to come natural to them.

After the debriefing I crashed for two days. When I finally came around, I felt considerably better, except for being so hungry I was nauseous, and completely dehydrated. The mess hall took care of the hunger, and hoisting a few with Bob and the guys took care of the thirst.

The barracks seemed mighty empty without Lusk, Dasher, and Olfson. Magoun left the hospital on the third day. His rib wasn't broken, but he was on the invalid list for the next couple of weeks.

One afternoon, I got the team together. "Look," I told them, "we've been on a major operation now. We had two men killed and one wounded and sent home. If you want another patrol leader, I'll understand."

They all sat there and looked at me without saying a word. I had the idea they all really wanted to pick somebody else, but nobody wanted to be the first to say it. So I looked over at Bob, who was studying me with his head tilted over to one side, and an unhappy frown on his face.

"What about you, Bob? You want it?"

He looked at me for a while without saying anything. I thought he was thinking it over. Finally, he said, "Naw. I told ya out there when ya come in with that body I wouldn't want the job. They ain't nobody else could do no better than you, anyway. You keep it, Tyler."

I looked over at Magoun, then. He had been wounded, and he had more experience than the others; if anybody was to say anything he surely would be the one. He was grinning like a possum in a persimmon tree. "Is it gettin' to be too much for you?" he asked.

"Well, no," I admitted, "not really. But I thought some of you might have a few doubts about whether I can handle it."

"I've done the job before," he said. "I'll take over if you get hit, but I don't want it till then. There's too much responsibility for me."

"What's happened so far, hell, you weren't to blame for it," Tony chipped in. "Up on Hill 484, we all had a part in those decisions. I didn't want to carry that fuckin' radio up the fuckin' hill any more than you did. And as for going on when Olfson got into that punji pit, you didn't get any argument, did you? If it hadn't been for the damned monkeys, we might have gotten off the hill without anybody more than Olfson being hurt."

"Well, here's somethin' to think about: they had me

once. They captured me, and I sure as hell don't intend for it to happen again. There ain't no bastard going to get me down and tie me up and kick my ass like they did," I told them. "I might get you killed tryin' to avoid it."

"I don't intend for 'em to get me alive, anyway," Bob said.

"All you got to do, Bob, is fart: they'd all run off," Tony told him.

"He couldn't do that," Casburn replied. "Gas warfare is against the Geneva conventions."

"You bastards is just jealous."

I never could get them back to the idea of picking another squad leader.

When they mustered us in for the next briefing, we went down to the Marine headquarters at the base. There was a tight security area where we had to show our identification to get in, and we had a little card to insert into the door lock to open it. Just like James Bond.

When we went in for briefings, we usually knew all the officers there: Captain Gartley, Admiral Jameson of COMPHIBPAC, some general's aide, or a Navy Intelligence captain. Every now and then there was a CIA man.

This time was different. Gartley was there, and so was a man in civilian clothes. They were sitting behind a long table with some maps laid out on it. Captain Gartley looked up and nodded when we came in, then introduced us to the man with him. "Gentlemen, this is Mr. Smith," he said. "Mr. Smith is with a federal intelligence agency."

He was a tall, ruddy-faced blond man, about my height, but somewhat overweight, and sweaty-looking. He had a big mustache and bushy eyebrows several

shades darker than his hair, which was starting to recede a little. There was something busy-looking about
him, but he didn't talk much.

A black steward brought in a tray of mugs and a pot
of coffee. Captain Gartley and "Mr. Smith" helped
themselves and Captain Gartley waved casually at the
mugs, indicating we were to take some for ourselves.
We did, then sat down in some chairs they had there
on our side of the table.

After the steward left the room, Captain Gartley
started the briefing.

"When Mr. Tyler first reported to me, I told him
the missions he would be assigned were of the kind
that, if there was any shooting, he'd probably already
failed to accomplish the mission," he said. He paused
for a moment, looking from one of us to the other.

"I lied.

"The missions you've had so far, including this last
one up Hill 484, were the usual type of recon mission.
You were to engage the enemy at your own discretion.

"You will have no such discretion on this mission.

"What we want you to do is guide a team of agents
into Hanoi." He paused to let that sink in for a while.

Bob repeated "Hanoi" very softly, as though it was
something he wanted to commit to memory. No one
else said anything. I glanced around at the team, and
they were all looking attentively at the captain. With
considerable interest, I thought.

"Mr. 'Smith' here has a team of five men he wants
inserted into Hanoi," the captain went on. "We want
you to guide them to the city, and back out again when
their mission is accomplished. You are to lead them
through the countryside, keep them clear of booby
traps, help them avoid patrols, and cover them.

"You must avoid contact with the enemy. If you encounter an enemy that must be taken out, absolutely must be, do so as silently as possible. Your presence must remain undetected on the way in. On the way out, use your discretion. Remember, if you get pinned down exchanging fire with an enemy patrol, you are a long way from home, and a long way from help. It would be better to avoid contact altogether, but if you have to shoot your way out of a situation, do it. If you get into that kind of a situation on the way in, you'll have to abort the mission and call for us to get you out. *Do not* continue on to Hanoi."

That made a lot of sense, considering how far into North Vietnam we were going to be, and it really was no different from the way we operated on recon patrols. If we got into trouble going in, we'd normally abort the mission: the enemy was tipped off that we were there, and it wasn't likely that we would be able to slip in and observe them without being spotted ourselves. That had been one of my mistakes on Hill 484, and I wasn't going to repeat it.

"Mr. Smith" then took over. "This is a sterile mission," he said. "You will be provided with 'neutral' uniforms—that is, uniforms made outside the United States and not designed for any specific country, available over the counter to anyone. You will be provided with Soviet-made weapons, and you will carry no identification linking you to the United States. No personal matter, no letters, no pictures of sweethearts. Your Saint Christopher's medal or lucky rabbit's foot is okay, so long as it says 'Made in Japan.'

"If you are caught or killed the United States will deny any knowledge of this operation, *and* your citizenship. That's right: we will deny that you are Americans. You will become men without a country, and I assure you that you will be treated as international criminals by the People's Republic of Vietnam. If they should offer to return your remains for burial, the offer will be refused. Your family and friends will be told you are Missing in Action.

"If it looks as if an agent will be taken alive, or if one has been taken, you are to eliminate him if possible.

"They are not combat veterans. They can handle themselves well in hazardous situations that may arise during the normal course of their mission, but if they are caught in a combat, they may not recognize that they cannot escape until too late. You must protect them as much as possible and get them out alive if you can, but if in your opinion one of them, or all of them, are about to be captured, you must eliminate them. Consider them as valuable assets to be kept out of the hands of the enemy at all costs, and not to be destroyed unless absolutely necessary.

"The nature of their mission is not your concern. You will observe one man working with maps and air photographs, and another man carrying photographic equipment. Outside the obvious function of ground-checking aerial mapping and photographing enemy installations and bomb damage, you have no need to know other details. They are professionals, as adept at their jobs as you are at yours.

"Do you have any questions at this point?"

I glanced over at Bob and saw him looking at me. I wondered what he was thinking. Was he wondering about the possibility of having to kill an American? I used to think of Bob as absolutely cold-blooded, somebody who could cut an American's throat just as quickly as he could cut a Viet's. I knew better now.

The others were sort of looking around from face to face too.

"Mr. Smith" waited a few moments, and when we didn't ask him any questions, he turned the briefing back to Captain Gartley.

The captain, pointing to one of the maps spread out on the table between us, showed us the insertion point, and our route into the city.

"What size force are we going to have?" I asked the captain.

"We want to keep this thing as small as possible to minimize the risk of detection," he replied. I couldn't have said it better. "Since there are five agents, I think we should keep it to the six of you in this room. Eleven all together."

"That ain't many shooters, if the shit starts to fly," I told him.

"That far from help, you might as well write yourselves off anyway," he pointed out.

"No way," Bob said. "I ain't writin' myself off of nothin'. I'll get my ass out of there if there's any way. Just be sure you do your part and send help if we need it."

"You say we're supposed to bring the agents back out again after they've completed their mission?" I asked. Both the captain and "Mr. Smith" nodded. "And the mission isn't really a success unless we get them back alive?" Again they nodded. "Don't worry about it, Bob. They'll send help if we need it or they'll have to write the mission off too."

"How long will it take you to cover this distance?" the captain asked. "The route is about forty-four miles as the bird flies."

"It depends on the terrain, and how many people

are moving around on the route,'' I told him. "Maybe four days. Maybe eight."

"That's too long!" the Agency man snapped. "Four days at the outside. If you can, get this thing off the ground inside of sixteen hours!"

That told me what I wanted to know: timing was critical to the mission. Something was coming down in about four and a half days, and he wanted his men there when it happened. I just stared at him awhile. Those spooks made me uncomfortable. They'd ''write you off'' in a minute—eliminate you, in other words, if they thought it was the thing to do, without a second thought. So let him be the uncomfortable one.

"Ya shoulda come to us yesterday," Bob told him.

"That's fairly open ground up there," Quinn reminded us. "It's not dense shit like we just came out of. We ought to be able to make it in four days, easy."

"Yeah, we can," Bob said, "but what about them damned agents? Can they keep up? Or do we have to carry their asses?"

"They can keep up!" "Smith" snapped. "They're in excellent physical condition."

"They better be," Bob told him. "If they're a bunch of pussies, we'll leave 'em along the way. We're goin' to be humping to cover that kind of ground in four days."

Actually, I thought we could make it in less, probably in three days, but I didn't want to reassure the Agency man.

"Well," I told Captain Gartley, "we'll need to study the air photos and the maps, and discuss it some more between us. We'll let you know later just how quick we think we can make it. Right now, we need to get some other things clear. We need to know details about the weapons we're going to carry and the uniforms we're going to wear. We need to figure out what kind of radios to bring, and how many, and what the radio procedures and codes will be. How much ammunition we need to carry, what kind of rations and how many.''

The captain seemed kind of relieved to get back to his ''script.'' ''Well,'' he said, ''we've got AK-47s for all of you, and four thirty-round magazines. You'll be issued Makarov nine-millimeter automatics to replace your thirty-eight revolvers. You'll carry Japanese-made knives. We considered Russian or Japanese radios, but our opinions favor American made.''

He went on from there, and after he'd covered all the details, we started picking at them. We wanted more ammunition, and ended up with six magazines for each AK-47. We wanted revolvers, too, but there weren't any foreign makes to compare to ours except the British Webley and a Chinese copy of it that shot nine-millimeter automatic ammunition from half-moon clips. We gave up on that and accepted the Makarov pistols. I don't believe that any of us had ever had an opportunity to use our .38s anyway. We were loaded up with Russian grenades, too.

We carried U.S.-made radios, one large set with the range to reach a communications plane if we needed help or wanted to be picked up, and individual sets to communicate with each other. The larger set was a PRC-77, chosen because it was only slightly more than half the weight of the standard AN/PRC-41 used by ground troops. The small sets were AN/PRR-9 receivers and AN/PRT-4 transmitters. The receivers were normally mounted on a helmet, but had been modified so they could be worn over a bush hat or with no hat at all. The transmitter was limited to line of sight, and the antenna had to be angled about forty-five degrees toward the receiver for best transmission, but they only weighed about two pounds apiece. Everyone, including the agents, wore one of the receiver headsets and carried a transmitter. You could talk over them or send signals by breaking squelch with the transmit button.

To get ready for the operation, the first thing we did was strip. We got rid of our socks, our underwear, our handkerchiefs, everything. We took off our dogtags. That part wasn't unusual: we didn't wear our dogtags on missions anyway. We left everything personal behind, anything that might identify us or that might suggest we were Americans: our watches, our pocketknives, you name it. Like the man said, "Made in Japan" was all right, but "Made in Schenectady" was definitely out.

They furnished everything we might conceivably need, from the skin out. Then we laid out everything we were going to take with us, *everything*, and Captain Gartley and "Mr. Smith" checked over our stuff to make sure there was nothing that would give us away.

Possibly the worst part was wearing new boots, and having to break them in on the mission. There weren't enough hours between the time they were issued and the time we had to mount up and leave to break them in before we left. Fortunately they fit well. Casburn had to swap the first pair he was issued for a second, but then anybody that wears those pointy-toed shit-kicker boots all the time has funny feet anyway. I wore mine from the minute I got them to break them in as much as possible before we got out into the bush, which was a hell of a place to get blisters.

I checked over my AK-47 to make sure the action worked smoothly and the cartridges fed through the clip without hanging up. I worked three clips of ammunition through the action before everything worked to suit me. The AK-47 assault rifle, made by Kalashnikov, was introduced into the Russian army right after World War II, and its design was based on lessons the Russians learned fighting the Germans, who had a similar weapon. Along with the folding-stock version, known as the AKS, it became the most widely used of all small arms produced since the war. It's gas-operated and air-cooled, and allows the shooter to select fully automatic or semiautomatic fire. It uses an intermediate-size cartridge that's lighter and less powerful than the 7.65-millimeter round used in our M-60 machine gun or M-14 rifle, but faster in operation. The round is more powerful and has greater range and accuracy than the .45 ACP or 9-millimeter rounds used in submachine guns. It has a cyclic rate of fully automatic fire at 600 rounds per minute, but its practical rate of fire is about 100 rounds per minute. It uses a 30-round magazine, and changing magazines slows the rate of fire a little, but the main reason for the slower practical rate is that it is prone to overheating, making the weapon hard to handle and sometimes causing rounds to "cook off" accidentally.

The "AK" is simple, rugged, and reliable. That's why guerrillas and other forces that have a supply problem or poorly trained personnel like to use them. They can even be manufactured by machine shops and gunsmiths in less-developed countries. About the only real mechanical weakness of the weapon is the exposed gas tube, which can be dented easily. Dents in the tube lead to malfunctions due to uneven gas pressures.

One combat weakness of the weapon is the maximum effective range of the cartridge—on automatic, only about 200 yards; on semiauto, about 300. The lower muzzle velocity allows the action to work faster, but it also gives the bullet a very high trajectory. The short distance between the sight blades makes drawing a fine bead difficult, and the bullet loses accuracy very quickly anyway. Of course, there weren't many firefights in Vietnam where lack of range was any problem.

Where we were going, the "AK" would have two advantages over the M-16 or any other American weapon: we could replenish our ammunition supply off almost any NVA we killed, and they wouldn't be able to distinguish us from their own patrols by the different sound our weapons made when fired.

We dressed in the new uniforms and packed our new packs and laid out our new weapons and ammunition. Then we checked each other's pockets to make double damned sure there was nothing incriminating or identifying. Mail call had come while we were getting ready. Most of the guys had looked at their mail and then stuffed it in their seabags to reread when they got back from the mission. Casburn had stuffed a letter into his shirt pocket, and I had to chew his ass about it. The letter was from his girl in Texas, and if found on him, it would have been enough to identify him as an American. How that would have affected the U.S. or the course of the war I don't know, but I was responsible for the team, and my butt would have been in trouble.

Seeing his letter reminded me that I hadn't gotten one from my wife in about a month. That wasn't so long that I was going to get upset about it, but I had to wonder why I hadn't heard from her. Before we went up Hill 484 I thought, "It's probably just delayed in the mail." Well, maybe it had been lost. Maybe she had written, and her letter had been lost, and now she was wondering why I wasn't writing her. I'd have to write her as soon as I got back from this mission.

When we were all set to go, I did some Dexedrine. Then we shouldered the packs and picked up the weapons and rode out to the helipad.

To that point, I hadn't had much time to think about anything except getting ready and making sure the guys weren't taking anything they shouldn't. On the ride out, I went back over everything in my mind, just to make sure I wasn't forgetting or overlooking something. We saw some guys we'd been drinking beer with a few days before, and they waved and hollered. We waved back, and yelled insults at them, and the thought sneaked into my mind: "I wonder if I'll ever see them again?" It's a common thing to think when you're going out on a mission. Usually you don't dwell on it. Your mind is on the details of the mission, checking and double-checking, or should be. So you acknowledge the thought, and answer yourself with a little personal philosophy, like, "What the Hell, you can't live forever." Then you go back to your mental checklist.

This time, though, I had a premonition. Nothing strong, just a disquieting feeling that something was wrong or was going to go wrong, as if my subconscious mind was trying to tell me I'd overlooked some detail.

I'd had that sort of a premonition before, and the damned NVA sappers had placed a mine underwater that goddamned near finished me off.

Then we were rolling up to the helipad, and there was no more time for premonitions.

CHAPTER 9

"Mr. Smith" was at the helipad, with five other guys. They were dressed just like we were, but their packs were even larger. Part of their load was gear, because the cartographer had to carry his alidade and altimeter, and the photographer had to carry his cameras and lenses and film. And they all carried the same weapons that we carried. Another part of their load was civilian clothing they had to have to go into Hanoi.

We dropped our gear beside theirs and started introducing ourselves. There were two white Americans and two Vietnamese. The fifth man was an Oriental of some kind. They were friendly enough and shook our hands, but they only gave us one name each, and I suspected those weren't their real names. The mapmaker called himself "Kilroy" and the photographer was "John." The two Viets were "Duc" and "Dinh," and the other Oriental said his name was "Cesar." He spoke really good English with a trace of an accent I couldn't quite place. Duc and Dinh spoke very little English. They may have understood more than they spoke. They would chatter in Vietnamese between themselves, and sometimes Cesar would join in.

I sidled up to Kilroy and asked, "Where y'all from?"

He just kind of smiled and scratched his ear and said, "Saigon." I got the message.

"John" was in charge of the other four agents. "Mr. Smith" stressed that "John" was responsible for their actions in Hanoi and for the successful completion of the mission.

"Let's get it straight before we leave. I'm in charge when you're with this team, going in or coming back out," I told him. "I won't stand for any arguin' or questioning my orders. You got that?"

He nodded.

"See that ya remember it," I added.

I wouldn't have been surprised if our transportation had been a Russian-made helicopter, or at least a French model. It turned out to be a Jolly Green Giant. They were about the only helicopters with the range to get us that far into North Vietnam. The Air Rescue and Recovery Service used them to rescue pilots out of North Vietnam when their planes went down. But this wasn't a rescue helicopter. I think it was from an Air Commando unit. It was painted in an odd camouflage pattern, very dark green and very dark brown, so it looked almost black. There were two others with it, but we only loaded onto the one. The other two were decoys.

When we threw our gear on board and climbed in, the crew seemed to know the intelligence agents. The door gunner greeted them like they were old buddies, and Kilroy stuck his head in the cockpit and said something to the pilot. Cesar and the door gunner started rattling to each other in Spanish. That really took me back. I looked at Cesar again and began to wonder if he really was Oriental.

The first part of the flight was over the China Sea. We took off and headed east and a little north until we were well off the coast, out near Yankee Station. When we got near the fleet there, we dropped down to just above the water and headed north for a while before we turned northwest. We made several course corrections a few minutes before we reached the coast, turns of forty-five degrees or more, first to the north, then south, then north again. I wondered at first what the hell they were doing, but then I realized they had to coordinate their landfall with jamming and a diversionary aerial attack. They were tacking back and forth to kill time.

The noise level inside the chopper was enough to discourage talk, even if everyone hadn't been busy with his own private thoughts. I started my mental checklist again, even though it was too late to get anything I might have forgotten, but I was scared going behind the lines like that, really behind the lines, right up to the enemy capital, and going over my checklist kept my mind off my emotions.

Landfall was at the mouth of a river. We came in low, flying between the trees for several miles upriver. The night was dark, with scattered clouds that got thicker as we went farther north. The surface of the river was only a little less dark than the black mass that was the jungle on either bank. I wondered how the pilots could see well enough to fly that low at that speed. When we reached a place with low hills on either side, we pulled up a little, just enough so that we could fly a more or less straight course above the trees instead of swinging back and forth to follow the bends of the river. After a few more miles, we swung westward between some low hills, and fifteen minutes later the pilot signalled that we were approaching the LZ.

We passed low over a small clearing, visible through the open door as a patch of gray in the hummocky blackness of the jungle canopy. I saw one of the other helicopters dropping into it. I knew he would hover just above the grass and simulate an insertion.

I was really getting uptight now, breathing shallow quick breaths through my nose with my jaws clenched and my lips pressed together. There were too many hot LZs in my recent past.

I noticed Tony was staring, unblinking, at the other door. His eyes were focused far beyond any possible view from the door, probably on his memory of one of those LZs. Quinn was rubbing the sweat from his palms onto his pantlegs. Magoun was sort of grinning, but without mirth. Only Bob seemed his natural self, absentmindedly scratching his crotch, totally unconcerned. On the surface, anyway.

Two or three other small clearings slipped by underneath us, and then I felt the helicopter rear back as it started down. I picked up my pack and swung it up on my shoulders and yelled "Lock and load!" to the others. I locked and loaded my own AK-47. The helicopter dropped quickly into the clearing and hovered just above the grass. It didn't touch down, because they didn't want to leave a skid mark. We jumped out and gouged deep footprints in the muddy soil where we landed. As soon as we hit we humped for the treeline, bending way low to duck under the rotor. The agents were the last out; the last of them gave the thumbs-up signal to the door gunner, and the helicopter tilted forward as it lifted upward maybe fifty feet, then spun around and headed south.

A minute or two later, the third helicopter came over, also heading south like a scalded dog. By then we had laagered up in the treeline, AKs bristling outward like spines on a porcupine.

Everything got quiet.

Well, not too quiet. When you take those uppers, you can hear the crickets sigh and the cats walk, and you're ready to shoot the sons of bitches. You're not just alert, you're wound up tight, and you jump at the slightest sound. For me, with poor hearing in one ear, they were a definite help. I didn't even notice being partly deaf, and when I did, it was because a sound was coming from the left side, and I couldn't tell whether it was from in front or in back or straight off to the side. I would have to turn my head and listen for it, and hope it came again.

We formed up in the treeline on the northwest side of the clearing, and moved out right away. Bob and I took twin point positions, Fitchew and Magoun were the right and left flankers, and Tony and Quinn were twin rear points. The five agents made up the central group, and Casburn was with them. They were protected all the way around. We moved out to the southwest, going up toward the ridge line but away from

Hanoi as a little bit of misdirection. When we got to the ridge line we held up for thirty minutes to see if the North Vietnamese were going to react to our insertion. Then we moved north.

We had illuminated compasses for traveling at night, but you can't keep stopping every few minutes and looking at your compass. Even that faint light will degrade your night vision. We'd take a bearing and look for some natural object that was just about in line with the bearing. Then we'd go toward it.

If you knew where you were on the map, you could use the slope for a guide. You could go along the side of the hill or directly up or down, and you could tell when the angle of the slope or its direction changed. This night it was cloudy and misting rain. It wasn't pitch black, but it nearly was. The ridge top was wide and nearly flat, so the slope wasn't a good guide. We had to use our compasses pretty often, and when the slope seemed to steepen we'd turn away from it, back uphill.

Bob and I carried spray cans to mark the path for the agents, and to mark any booby traps we might come across. The spray was a powder, like a dry spray deodorant. It would fluoresce in ultraviolet light. We used a lot of it to mark safe paths and booby traps when we were on recon patrols. We might be marking a safe path out for ourselves, in case we had to get out fast, or we might be marking a safe path in for a search-and-destroy patrol or attack group following us in. We didn't use much on this patrol, because we weren't going into an area that was likely to be booby-trapped, but we had it handy. Of course, it would wash off in the rain.

I didn't expect that we would see many patrols unless we had been spotted landing. Still, we were cautious. We didn't just stroll along single file, and we stayed away from clearings. We moved fast when we moved, and then we'd stop and look and listen for a few seconds, and move again. We covered a lot of ground that night, considering how dark it was.

About 0200 we came to a peak. It wasn't much of a peak, just the highest part of the ridge. We could see enough to tell it was broad and rolling, with some scrub bushes around it, and some rocks sticking up. We went on across a clearing there.

I led them over the clear ground and into the brush on the other ridge, the one that led off to the northwest. We held up there, waiting for it to get lighter. We'd come about seven klicks, or four and a half miles. I figured we were a safe distance from the LZ, and anyway, I had been whipped in the face by branches and had stumbled over rocks and logs in the darkness until I was tired of it. The agents were grateful for the rest.

We laagered up in pairs, lying in a circle facing outward. One man in each pair was supposed to be awake and watching while the other slept. Naturally I couldn't sleep, with all that Dexedrine in me, and I didn't want to anyway. I was too worried about being so goddamned many miles from "home" in South Vietnam. It was a long walk back. If anything went wrong, if, for some reason, we missed our pickup . . .

I put that out of my mind. Nothing was going to go wrong. I was just getting uptight. I made myself think about something else, like home. Like my wife. I hadn't thought much about her since I'd been back in-country. I wondered: did I really care about her, or had I married her just to cover up some of the other problems I was having? Maybe she was just a kind of anchor for me, to keep me from losing contact with the States completely. It was hard to know. I'd been concentrating on surviving and hadn't had much time to think about her. I pictured her the way I'd first seen her, through the haze of smoke in a bar in Coronado. I pictured her face. Then I tried to picture her naked body. It didn't work. I couldn't see it. I remembered swimming with her down on Silver Strand Beach, and I thought of her body in the swimming suit, and tried to remove the suit mentally. It still didn't work. I tried to remember cuddling with her, kissing her, anything, but all that came to mind was that cocksucking GI insurance.

Then I realized I was losing my alertness, and I made myself concentrate on the shadows that were trees and rocks in the darkness, and listen for the slightest sound, or a change in the natural sounds.

We laid up there, on the ridge just beyond the peak, until it began to lighten up. On a clear day, that might have been as early as 0400, but as cloudy as this day was, it was about 0530 before it was really light enough to see the trees and bushes before you walked into them. We moved out then, down the ridge and toward the northwest.

It was about four miles to the Phu Ly road. We made it by 0730, and while it was considerably lighter by then, the clouds that were down in the valleys when we started our walk had risen to the level of the ridge, and we were moving through a fog with visibility at about a hundred yards. We were right on top of the ridge, where the road crossed the pass. It was a good place to cross the road because any trucks approaching would have to climb several switchbacks on the way up, giving us plenty of warning. The only drawback was the lack of dense brush on either side of the road for cover. We had to move from clump to clump to conceal ourselves.

I sent Fitchew and Magoun out about a hundred yards in either direction along the road to watch for traffic. When they gave us the all clear, I crossed, then Bob. We took up concealed positions to cover the others. Casburn sent the agents across one at a time. Tony and Quinn followed, and Fitchew and Magoun moved last.

I wanted to move away from the road right away, but we had to delay a few minutes while Kilroy checked his altimeter.

"I thought those things had to be corrected for barometric pressure," Tony said.

"They do," Kilroy told him, "but I'll record the date and time and the location, and when I get back, they'll have records of the daily pressure changes."

"How do they get records from way up here?" Bob asked.

"We've got weather stations scattered all over this country. Some of them are automatic, dropped by aircraft. Others are run by special units. They radio out their information, and it's combined with satellite data down in Saigon."

About two miles from the road we came across a clearing right on the crest of the ridge. We studied the maps and air photos and decided it was the extraction LZ. Kilroy couldn't get a sun shot with his sextant to confirm it, but he agreed it seemed to be in the right place. We avoided it, as we did all the other clearings, by working our way around the edge. I looked around at the terrain and tried to memorize what it looked like, so I'd know it on the way back.

I kept them moving until we got about two miles beyond the clearing. The ridge turned slightly east there. We could either move on down the ridge, where the going was probably easier, or descend into the valley and follow the stream. That route would be rougher, but safer.

It was 1000, and the fog had lifted. It was now overcast and drizzling. While it wasn't likely that we would encounter an enemy patrol in this area, I didn't feel comfortable moving around in the scattered brush on top of the ridge in the daylight. The NVA might even have patrol planes out. Just down the side of the ridge was a thick patch of timber and brush. It looked like the next best place to hole up during the day. The best place would have been the brush along the stream in the bottom of the valley.

I moved them down the hillside and we laagered up in the brush. We stayed there until about 1800. It rained off and on all day, and the temperature got up to 85 or 90 degrees. The rain didn't seem to keep the insects away, either. The agents and a couple of the SEALs managed to nap a little, despite all, but I still had too much Dexedrine in me.

Cesar was paired with me. I had the first watch, and he napped. He woke up by himself at the right time.

"My watch," he said. "You'd better get some sleep."

"I won't sleep," I told him.

"You got to sleep sometime."

"No."

He was quiet for a while after that.

"How long can you go without getting some sleep, man?" he finally asked.

"The whole fucking mission, if I have to. Knock off the damned talking."

I lay there for a long time, until finally it was my watch again. I told Cesar to get some more sleep if he could. He shrugged and laid his head down on his arm.

"Where you from, anyway?" I asked him.

"You know I'm not supposed to tell you anything."

"How many languages you speak?"

"Three, counting English."

"Jesus! I have 'nough trouble with one. Ya go to school to learn to do that?" All this was spoken in a whisper, of course.

"I learned Vietnamese in a service school."

I didn't ask him any more right then, but I was still curious. He looked a little bit Oriental, but if you saw him on the street in Tijuana, you would have had a tough time telling him from a Mexican.

We moved out just before dusk. We worked our way slowly down the hillside to the valley floor, where the treetops formed a solid canopy above us. The going was somewhat easier there because the undergrowth wasn't quite as thick, but it was darker. We stayed near the stream, where the noise of the water would drown out the sounds we made moving through the brush.

The agents weren't as quiet as my men were, and they weren't as fast. They hadn't been taught to move the vines and branches aside and slip between them. They tried to bulldoze their way through. After a while, it wore them out. I told Casburn to teach them how to do it properly as we went.

We kept going as far into the night as we could. I wanted to reach the river before we stopped, so that we wouldn't have to make up time the next day. It was still cloudy and drizzling, and that made it pitch black down on the valley floor. Even with our night vision fully developed, all we could see was black shadows on a background only slightly less black. We changed to single file, each man touching with one hand the shoulder or pack of the man in front of him to maintain contact. The point man had to feel his way along, moving very slowly, with one hand out in front of him so he wouldn't run into a damned tree. Since I didn't trust anyone else in that position, I took the point. As we groped forward I kept imagining that the next thing I touched would be a cobra or a python, and every time I put my hand out and touched a damned vine, I *knew* I'd found one. Finally I gave up and called a halt. We crept in close together, took a head count to make sure we were all there, and stopped for the night.

I sat in the blackness and cursed myself for not starting earlier in the afternoon. Was this going to be another mistake that would endanger the mission and the men?

Of course, the uneasiness came back, stronger than ever.

We sat there in that absolute blackness and strained our eyes into the darkness. There was nothing to see. The rain dripping off the canopy of leaves overhead made a constant soft patter that was just audible. Every once in a while there would be a louder sound, perhaps a splash as some large leaf got overloaded

and dumped an accumulation of water. That always
brought you instantly alert, because it could easily be
a splash from someone stepping in a puddle.

The night passed uneventfully, however. Finally—
I won't say "soon," because it wasn't—it was light
enough to begin to make out the dark trunks of the
trees, and we moved out. It was late, nearly 0700,
and we would have to make up for the lost time by
moving earlier in the afternoon and traveling later in
the morning. I also tried to move them a bit faster.

We soon broke out of the really densely canopied
area and began to travel faster. We made far too much
noise, but we only had limited time left to get the
agents into Hanoi. I thought the risk was justified.
We were just hitting our stride and moving along at
a pretty good clip when we spotted a patrol.

Bob saw them first. He gave a couple of warning
clicks on the radio and we froze. Then he came back
with his position number and the number of gooks in
the patrol, all signaled by the number of times he
broke squelch with the radio. Obviously they were
close enough that he didn't want to talk.

I crouched behind a big plant that looked like it
ought to be potted and growing in a dentist's office,
and prayed they weren't coming our way.

Finally, Bob signaled "all clear."

I broke silence and called him on the radio. It was
taking a chance, but I wanted to know more about
them.

"What'd ya see?"

"Patrol. Twelve of 'em at least, going from our
left to right, about sixty or seventy-five degrees to our
course. They were following a trail, but with points
and flankers out. Allowing for the flankers I couldn't

see, there were probably fifteen or eighteen. We were overtakin 'em.''

"They gone now?"

"Out of sight."

I thought awhile. If they were following a trail it was a good bet they were on a routine patrol instead of searching for someone. It was unlikely they would zigzag or change their direction of movement much. Somewhere up ahead was a river we had to cross, so it seemed smart to work to the other direction, to our left. Upstream, according to my map.

"We'll bear left forty-five degrees," I told them. "Bearing three-one-five. Stay with it until we hit the river. And stay quiet."

Pivoting left would mean the right point and right flanker would have farther to go than the rest of us, so I moved very slowly at first. We came to the river much sooner than I had anticipated, and sooner than I liked. I wanted the gook patrol to be farther away.

It really wasn't such a bad river to cross, this far upstream. The current wasn't fast, and the tree canopy almost touched over midstream. There were also several fallen logs and tangles of debris in the channel to provide cover. We found a shallow spot and waded. The water came to our chests at one point.

On the other side, we were in broken bush. We had veered to the west of the course we'd planned to take, so we followed a bearing of 360 degrees until a spot I estimated to be five miles north of the river. Kilroy took a shot on the sun and said I wasn't far off. We turned east from there. It was only a short way until we got into rice paddies and a populated area, so we stopped there until dusk.

I dreaded crossing the damned cultivated area.

There wasn't enough cover out there for me to be comfortable. The VC did all right, hiding in such areas, but the villagers helped by hiding them.

It was the morning of the second day.

We started off again just before dusk and had gone only a little way before we saw another patrol. I saw this one first. They were crossing a little open area, moving from our right toward our left. There were only eight. The careless way they carried their rifles and the way they strolled unconcernedly across the clearing told me two things: they weren't expecting to encounter anything they couldn't handle, and there were no mines or booby traps to worry about, at least not nearby.

After they were out of sight we moved on.

Crossing the cultivated area was not soothing to the nerves. There were places where we could find no cover to follow, and had to just cut right across the paddies or risk getting too close to the villages we were passing between. Not only were there more people moving around near the villages, but every one of them had a pack of damned dogs that did what dogs all over the world do best: bark. They were constantly barking. If it wasn't us they were barking at, it was the local peasants or the soldiers or some animal, so it wasn't anything unusual to hear. I had a nightmare sometimes that we were slipping into a village or a camp to grab somebody, and a damned dog got wind of us and went apeshit. In the nightmare he would stand about three or four feet away, barking and growling and making a dive for me every once in a while, like they do when they have an old boar coon backed into a corner. I would stand there, unable to hit the son of a bitch with my rifle, and not wanting to shoot him, because that would wake the whole camp. That's why I steered the patrol as far away from the villages as I could. Later, I found there weren't that many dogs in most of North Vietnam. Maybe the Vietnamese had eaten most of them.

We had come a little farther north than we'd planned, and we had to swing back to the south to skirt a little lake. Then, according to our map, we had to go due east to cross a small river below its junction with a canal. If we crossed north of the junction, we'd then have to cross either the canal or a second river before we got to Highway 1. Of course, in the dark it was easy to misjudge, and it turned out that the lake we detoured around wasn't the one we expected but a smaller one west of it. We soon came to the shore of the second, larger lake, which drove us still farther south. On the southern tip was a little village, about six or eight fishermen's huts and at least that many barking dogs. We lay in the bush and cursed the dogs and prayed until an old man came out and started throwing rocks at the dogs to either shut them up or drive them away. He cursed them just like we were doing, only he did it at the top of his lungs. After several of the rocks hit, the dogs scattered and we bugged out. Only one of the dogs followed us into the bush, barking like we'd just stolen the mint. Bob wanted to cut its throat, and it was tempting to let him, but that would just tip them off that we were around.

When we came to the river, it was only twenty or twenty-five yards across, but the channel was full from bank to bank, and it took us forty minutes. The water came up to my neck, and the two Vietnamese had to ferry their packs and guns across on a raft of limbs. Fortunately, the current was slow.

About three miles beyond the river we crossed the next highway. There was more traffic than we expected on a spur road, and Kilroy made a note that something was going on, probably down where the road ended.

We crossed without incident and headed east through the rice paddies. There was one more river to cross, and it proved to be very much like the last one, except wider. This time we all made rafts of branches for our packs. I found a bar about halfway across, and from there on the water only came to my waist, but it had been at least neck deep in that first stretch.

In that more open terrain, on such a cloudy night, we could travel all night if we needed to, and so we did. Bob and I were both reluctant to try to find a place to lay up during the daylight hours out in that paddy country. There would be too many people moving around during the day, too much chance we might be discovered. I conferred with him, and also got opinions from the rest of them, but the decision had to be mine. We were all tired, the agents more than the SEALs, even though they had slept and at least some of the SEALs had not. I tried to judge how tired I was, and if I was to the point of making stupid mistakes. I looked at the map to see how far we had to go. Then I popped some more Dexedrine and signaled them to move out.

We came to Highway 1 about 0130, and while there was construction activity and traffic on the highway, the only delay in getting across was waiting for Kilroy to take his notes and take a star shot when the clouds opened for a few minutes. He marked the construction on his map. He had a penlight for reading and posting notes. He covered his head with a dark cloth so the light wouldn't show. I assumed they were repairing bomb craters, but he said they were widening and resurfacing, probably getting ready for the increased traffic when they moved their heavy combat forces south, after we pulled out of South Vietnam.

Sometimes he'd just make a mental note and jot things down when we stopped to rest, but he said this was too important.

We went only about a mile east of the road before we turned north. That was halfway between Highway 1 and the Red River. At that point we were only seven and a half miles south of Hanoi, and I knew it would start getting more populous as we got closer. I didn't want to blunder into a village or an AA gun emplacement in the darkness, so I signaled the group to hold up, and we rested until 0400.

We could hear truck traffic on the road as we rested. It had begun to rain lightly just after we stopped, and the moist air carried the sound well. There was a lot of air traffic, too, and once there was an air strike to the south of us. Flares lit up the night, and we could plainly hear the *crump!* of bombs. The jet jockeys had probably spotted some trucks moving. I was glad we weren't down that way trying to cross the road.

We moved out again at 0400. We moved much more slowly, for we frequently spotted AA gun emplacements and missile launching sites. We didn't see foot patrols, but there was truck traffic and there were people on the roads. We had to take it very carefully and stay hidden much of the time. We finally got there in late afternoon, just before sunset. Just outside the edge of the city we came up onto a low ridge. We stopped there and waited until dark before we went in closer. The agents got their civilian clothes out of their packs and got ready to go into town.

I squatted down by Cesar while he dressed.

"Something puzzles me about you," I told him. "You look kind of Oriental, and you speak Vietnamese, but you said you learned that in a school, and you chattered Spanish to that door gunner. Just what the hell are you, anyway, a Mexican?"

"Would you believe black?"

"Hell, no!"

He laughed. "I'm Japanese, man. Grew up in L.A. speaking Spanish and English. I didn't learn much of my native tongue, although hearing an Oriental language spoken at home probably helped me learn Vietnamese."

"Well, you sure sounded like a Viet to me when you were talking to Duc and Dinh. And you sounded like a Mex talking to that door gunner."

He finished changing clothes and started sorting out the gear he was going to take into Hanoi. He packed a couple of cameras and some lenses into a canvas bag along with a lot of film. He kept glancing toward the city. I could tell he was nervous.

"Now that I risked my ass getting you here, why don't you tell me what the hell you guys are going to do in there?"

"I'm going to take pictures, can't you tell?" he said with a nervous little smile.

"Yeah, but what the heck of? I mean, they've got all these damned recon planes that can take a picture from thirty or forty thousand feet so you can read the date on a nickel lying on the street."

He exhaled with a short sigh, as if he were getting tired of my questions, and looked at me out of the corner of his eyes. He looked like he was trying to judge the risk of telling me. Finally, he said, "Prisoners. I'm going to photograph some POWs."

"POWs?" I said it too loud, and got an angry look from him. "How are you going to get close enough to take pictures of 'em?"

He didn't answer. He just took one of the lenses out of the bag and let me get a look at it. It was a telephoto.

"What about John? Is he going to be doing the same thing?"

He just shook his head.

We were right on the outskirts of town, as close as we could get without losing most of our cover, and you could see the lights of houses and the street lamps. It surprised me at first, because I just assumed they'd be blacked out, but I then realized that with radar and infrared bombsights, it wouldn't do any good. The city wasn't lit up much, anyway, at least this far out.

John, Kilroy, Cesar, Duc, and Dinh left us there and all went in together toward the edge of town. I didn't have any idea if we would ever see them again. They told us nothing except that they would be met at the edge of town and guided in. And that they would see us in two, maybe three days. If they didn't show up in seventy-two hours, we were to assume they had been discovered and start back without them. As they walked off into the darkness, I began to feel uneasy again.

CHAPTER 10

We sent a prearranged signal that we were moving back to the ridge. That was so that if they had to come back out suddenly, they'd know about where to find us. From the ridge, we watched the outskirts of town through binoculars and checked with the agents as long as we dared send and they dared receive. When they made it to their safe house, they signed out.

Now we were on our own, so to speak. We had no specific assignment except to wait for the agents to come back out of the city, but we had to do something to occupy our time. There's nothing worse than sitting and waiting in enemy territory. If one of those guys was caught and talked, half the North Vietnamese Army would be out scouring the countryside for us. We'd have about as much chance of getting away as a one-legged blind man crossing an L.A. freeway.

We split up into two groups of three. Three didn't have much firepower, but if we were spotted up here, firepower wouldn't make a whole hell of a lot of difference anyway. One group was to patrol around the rendezvous site to make sure the enemy didn't surprise the seventh man, who was left there in case the agents came back out, and to monitor the radio in case they called. The other group of three—it happened to be Bob and Tony and me—was to patrol westward, recording the locations of AA batteries and SAM sites, foot traffic and vehicles on the streets, noting how many military trucks and tanks we saw, how well the area was patrolled, and how heavy the air traffic was. The airport was over that way. All of us carried our radios, and never took our headsets off. The guy with the big radio could monitor for a signal from the agents while keeping in touch with the two patrols.

Three men can move a lot quieter than six or ten, hide in a smaller area, and see just as much—and the loss of three men wouldn't be as significant to the successful completion of the mission as the loss of a bigger group would be.

We went as far as we dared, avoiding NVA foot patrols and sentries around AA gun emplacements and missile launchers. There were radar vans and trailers around: they'd move them a quarter mile or so away from the guns and hide them under trees or camouflage netting, and of course they'd set sentries out around them. We noted their locations, and locations where we saw trucks or soldiers moving around on foot. There were plenty of foot patrols in this area. We knew they had been patrolling for some time, because the trails were worn out where they'd walked. Whether they were on training exercises to keep the men on their toes, or they were expecting some sabotage, I don't know. I suspect some officer was keeping the troops busy. They were very lax.

We could see quite a way into the city, even though the ridge was only about eighty feet high. There was one building in there we decided was a whorehouse. Big staff cars would often pull up to the door and some older man would get out. Usually he was dressed as an officer: anything from a colonel to a general. He would usually stay several hours, but sometimes all night. There might be four or five of these guys in the building at one time. Bob swore he could recognize the cars when they came back for a second time. "That's the Mercedes," he'd say, or "That's that Citroën again. Second time today. The old boy must really be horny." They all looked the same to me. I never was good at identifying those foreign makes. Some of the officers were recognizable, though, the second time they came.

The second day, we headed on toward the airport. This time we got to a little low hill overlooking the end of the runway. It was very sandy, with some trees growing right on the top of it. It was probably a sand dune that had been there a long time. The trees provided the cover we needed so the planes wouldn't see us as they were landing, and the height was just enough so that we could see the whole airport with binoculars. I was a little let down that I didn't spot any MiGs, just cargo planes. Some of the guys I'd talked to said they'd seen MiGs up here around Hanoi, but it must have been at some other base.

There were some big Russian cargo planes out

there, and planes from several other countries, including some of our NATO allies. I wished I had Cesar's camera and that telescopic lens to record some of it. Even my own little 35 millimeter. We watched about a hundred big muscular guys in civvies unload from an Aeroflot airliner. They were dressed in slacks and sport shirts, but they fell into ranks to wait for their duffel bags, and marched off the field in single file. "Tour group," Bob growled. "Ya can always tell the damned tourists by the way they're dressed."

We had to leave our observation post too soon to suit me. Going back to the ridge, we traveled a lot faster. We knew where the gun and missile emplacements were, and the radar vans, and we didn't have to stop and record them. We could avoid them easily and not worry about suddenly coming upon a sentry.

When we mustered at the rendezvous site, Fitchew wanted to go out and scout around. He had done his turn holding the ridge position while the rest of us got out and looked around the town. I had to pull rank and keep him there. There was too much chance that the agents would come back out in a hurry, like chicken thieves out of the henhouse with dogs on their heels. I wanted him around in case we had to move out quickly.

They didn't signal that evening, though, and the hours started to drag. Even though I knew very well they might be gone for the full three days, I started thinking about all the things that could have gone wrong. We had seen no excitement on the streets that might indicate they had been discovered, but still we grew more nervous as the hours passed.

Then an NVA patrol came by. That didn't help my state of mind at all. They crashed through the brush like a herd of water buffalo, and called to each other in loud

voices, a sure sign they weren't looking for anyone, but
I still got apprehensive. Suppose the agents returned and
were discovered by that bunch, or one like them?

As soon as it was safe I pulled the guys together
and told them four would stay on the ridge while three
went down to the edge of town to wait for the agents.
I picked Quinn and Magoun to go with me. If we
didn't return before dusk the next day, the others were
to get the hell out of Dodge.

We waited there by the road at the outskirts of Hanoi
until early dawn the next day before we got the signal,
and let me tell you, I was getting nervous. So nervous
I got a bad case of the shits. The more time passed
without them calling, the more uneasy I got that something had gone wrong. Even after we got their signal, I
was uneasy.

It started getting light, and they hadn't shown up
yet. Fortunately, it was foggy. I really got uptight
when they were late. I was ready to pull back to the
ridge without them because it was getting so light
when the radio broke squelch, and from the strength
of the signal I could tell they were close. I signaled
back ''all clear'' and soon saw this figure appear
through the fog. It was just a vague shape at first, and
I tensed up until I was sure it wasn't carrying a rifle.
It was joined by two others, moving confidently along
the road, then by two more, and finally another single
figure. They walked along as if they were heading for
the next village and wanted to be there by breakfast.
If they were our agents, they would walk along the
road until hidden from prying eyes by brush or fog,
and then take to the underbrush. So far, so good.

Except, where five went in, six were coming out.

My heart started pounding, and my stomach felt

like it had been quick-frozen. Who was the sixth figure? Was he holding a gun on one of them, forcing them to lead him to us? Whoever it was, we had to be ready to take care of him and get out of there fast.

I glanced around at the guys and signaled them "alert." They looked at me like I was crazy. I held up six fingers to let them know the reason I was suspicious, even though I had to lay my rifle down for a moment to do it. Then I assigned them their targets, using hand signals.

When I looked back at the oncoming figures, it was over my rifle sights, and they were much closer. Even in the fog and morning light, I could see the leading figure well enough to identify it. It was John. After him came Kilroy and Dinh.

What the hell was going on? Who was number six?

I signaled Magoun and Quinn to hold their fire.

When the next pair came into sight, I could see it was Duc and another Oriental. Not Cesar. This man was dressed in a raincoat and a fedora. His hands were in the pockets of his coat. I settled the butt of the rifle firmly against my shoulder and pressed my cheek to the stock. What was he carrying in there? Was he holding a gun on Duc? I took a fine bead on his left temple. Where was Cesar? I began to squeeze the trigger. The sixth figure took form and emerged from the fog; it was Cesar. He was carrying his camera bag and a briefcase. I eased off the trigger and tilted the barrel upward over the fedora.

I signaled Quinn, who made a bird-whistle sound. John glanced casually at the bushes where we sat, and kept walking for twenty steps or so. Then he casually turned and walked over to the side of the road as if he was going to take a leak, and just walked on out into the bushes. The others followed him after a few seconds.

We joined up with them about a hundred yards from the road before heading back to the ridge. The sixth man held back as if he was shy.

"Who the fuck is he?" I asked John.

John didn't want to say.

"Enough of this secrecy shit," I told him. "We almost blew your butts away when we saw six where we were expecting five. Now you talk fast and tell me who the hell he is, or we'll slit his throat and bury him here and now."

"He's a defector," John admitted grudgingly.

"Not good enough," I told him. "Did you jist happen to meet him on the street? Who checked the bastard out, anyway?"

"I am not accustomed to having my actions questioned by an enlisted man."

"Get used to it. Your responsibility for the mission just ended, and mine started."

He stood there and glared at me. I kept the rifle pointed at the midsection of the "defector," and my finger on the trigger, but I was glaring at John. We stood like that for a few seconds before John shrugged and half turned away.

"It was part of the mission to pick him up and bring him out. I decided that the less any of you knew, the less you could divulge if you were captured. So I didn't tell you. I meant to call ahead to you when we got out into the bush and I could get the radio out without risking being seen. I thought I'd tell you then that there would be six of us. I didn't think you would wait down by the road."

"Quinn, search him."

"Mr. Quinn, don't do that. It would be an insult to him. We want to keep him well disposed toward us so we can get as much information as possible from him when we get back."

Quinn stopped and looked at me. I was watching the "defector" but talking to John. The man was looking from John to me to Quinn and back again, and there was something in the look that made me suspect he understood what we were saying. His face was as expressionless as a wooden mask, but his pupils had contracted even in the dim morning light.

"I think he would understand. I think he'd have you or me searched if the shoe was on the other foot."

"Mr. Tyler, I have to protest. In my opinion, and I think I'm more experienced in this intelligence game than you are, to search him could do irreparable harm to his value to us as an intelligence asset."

"Not searching him might do irreparable harm to this mission and the men on it. We don't move until he's searched." It wouldn't make sense to take him up onto the ridge and let him see the full strength of the force before we checked him out. Not that he could do much damage with any weapon he could have concealed on him. It was a radio transmitter I was worried about. Not necessarily a voice transmitter, either. Just a repeated beeping signal could lead the enemy right to us.

Of course, I really wanted to get the heck away from that road, too, but I wasn't going to give in. We stood there in a kind of Mexican standoff until John finally sighed and said, "Go ahead."

Quinn searched him thoroughly. I told him to look for a small radio beeper, especially in the guy's hat and coat, and I'll swear the man's pupils contracted even further. Quinn didn't find anything, of course, and John got to say, "I told you so."

When Quinn finished the search, I said, "All right, he can come with us, but he'd better be able to keep up. If he slows us down, we'll have to kill him. Now, let's get out of here." And I signaled to Quinn in deaf-mute signs, "Stay close and keep your gun on his back."

When we were about five minutes out, we called ahead and told Bob we were coming in with an extra man.

The agents wasted no time. In fact, they seemed to be in a real hurry, but then, I guess that would be normal. I was eager to get the hell out of there myself. They dug up the gear they'd cached, changed out of their civilian clothes, and picked up their weapons. The "defector" took off his raincoat, and someone gave him a jacket. He kept his fedora, though, and it sure looked stupid over that camo jacket. They buried the civvies and tried to conceal the evidence of the burial by scattering the dirt and raking loose topsoil over the disturbed area. Then they shouldered their packs and we formed up.

I started up to my point position. Cesar grinned as I walked past, and said, "Home, James!"

I was still pissed at John. I just looked at him like I was thinking, "Grow up, you dumb shit," and walked on past.

We covered ground a lot faster coming back out than we did going in, because we knew the terrain. It stayed foggy until early afternoon, so we were able to travel almost all day. We reached the crossing of Highway 1 before the fog broke and lifted, and held up there until dusk. That gave us all night to cross the cultivated area and get back into the bush-covered hills before we stopped again, and we made good use of the time. The weather cooperated too, giving us a moonlit night with scattered clouds. Coming back out, we knew the best places to cross the rivers, so we gained some time there, and since we had already recorded the activity on that secondary road we crossed, I wouldn't stop for Kilroy to make more notes. I told him to take mental notes and fill in his notebook when we laagered up the next morning. We skirted way south of the lake and avoided the fishing village with the pack of dogs. The "defector," if that's what he was, kept up pretty well.

We crossed the last river and climbed up into the hills just as the morning was getting light. We could have pushed on another two hours or so without running too much risk of seeing a patrol, but we hadn't stopped but four hours in almost twenty-four, and everyone was tired. I was happy with the ground we'd covered, so Bob picked a brushy spot where we could take cover and keep a good watch all around us, and we rested until late afternoon.

Cesar was busy with some of the crap in his pack. I went over and squatted down beside him. He was sorting through a bunch of photographs.

"I'm splitting them up, just in case," he explained.

"Just in case what?"

"In case I don't make it back and my gear can't be recovered."

"Hell, you got it knocked now. Getting in and out of that damned gook city without getting caught had to be the worst part."

"That was easy. We just walked in like we belonged there. They never once stopped us."

"All of you went in? I figured Kilroy and John stayed in the safe house."

"No, why should they?"

"Well, it's real obvious they're Caucasian. They're so damned much bigger than the Viets, they got to stand out like a sore thumb even if they wear some kind of makeup to make 'em look Oriental."

"Hell, there's all kinds of Caucasians in there. Besides the Russians, there are French, Italian, and Australian reporters, not to mention the usual diplomatic staffs. I don't even stand out: there are Chinese and North Koreans in there, and they're big too."

"I seen some of them damned Russians," I admitted. "I sure wished you was along, with your camera, while we was watching the airport. There was lots of airplanes out there from countries that are supposed to be our friends and allies."

"They see them all the time on air photos, you know. Not only can they tell what airline, they can read the numbers and identify individual planes. You ought to see the ships in the harbor at Haiphong. . . ." He suddenly realized he was saying too much, and stopped. He finished sorting the photos and started packaging them up in waterproof envelopes, and then put them all in a heavy waterproof bag. "I want you or someone else to carry these," he said. "They're duplicates or near duplicates of the ones I'll carry."

"What do you mean, 'near duplicates'?"

He showed me. He took a photo out of each group. They were two slightly different views of the same building. Then he showed another pair, telephoto shots of a Caucasian man's face taken from different angles and with different shadowing, showing the man had moved.

"If I don't make it, you get your set back out," he said. "It could be important." He put the two photos back in their respective bags.

"How'd ya develop these damned things anyway? These ain't Polaroid pictures. Was there a darkroom in your safe house?"

"Keep them in the plastic wrapper so they don't get ruined when we cross the rivers."

I could see he wasn't going to answer any questions, so I rewrapped the bundle and put it in my pack on the very top. "After all," I thought, "if there's all them damned reporters for the communist newspapers in there, there has to be plenty of darkroom supplies."

Things had gone very well up to this point, and I had lost most of the uneasy feeling that had been bothering me. Then, at about 1430, a patrol came by.

We saw them coming, so we laid low. I kept a sharp eye on the agents to make sure they didn't panic and shoot or anything, but they stayed calm. I guess the ability to stay calm and controlled when the enemy is around is a definite asset to a spy.

The patrol was well out of sight when I got the guys ready to move at 1600, but I cautioned Bob and the two flankers to keep a sharp eye out, in case the gooks changed directions and crossed our path. I planned to take the same route back we'd come in by, the densely canopied valley. It would be dark in there at midday, and virtually impossible to move through on a cloudy night, so I wanted to go as far as we could while there was plenty of light. It was my goal to gain the ridge top before we stopped during the darker hours, and move on to the LZ in the early morning.

We made good time at first, but as it got darker the going became slower and slower. I could see we weren't going to make it to the ridge by the time I'd hoped. Finally, I called the points and flankers in and told them to stay tight. It was getting so dark we might get separated, and we had to go back to moving single file. When we formed up, I led off, feeling ahead of me with one hand and moving only a foot or so per step. But when I took my compass bearing, I led them away from the stream, toward the south.

When you can't see anything at all beyond arm's length, and only shadows at less than that, you don't realize at first when the slope of the ground changes. The most marked difference as we got away from the stream was that the rushing noise in the background diminished until we began to hear our own movements again. Finally it became so faint a rustle that even the soft night sounds could drown it out. About then, I noticed that there was a slight slope to the ground, but it seemed a long time later that the tree canopy began to open up, as we got to the thinner soil on the steep slopes. The darkness around us gradually faded from pitch black to dark gray, and we could begin to make out tree trunks and clumps of brush again. Then, when clouds parted and let the moon shine through, a beam of moonlight pierced the canopy ahead like a spotlight. A few yards beyond that, dense clumps of vegetation gave way to small clearings of grassy slope.

I spread the men out into our usual patrol formation again, and we headed up the ridge.

Near the top, I thought I heard movement and broke squelch to signal a halt. I waited for what seemed like five hours—but was really about five minutes—to hear the sound again, then, when it didn't come, cautiously moved a few feet. Off to my left there was a sudden rustle in the brush. I reacted: turning, crouching, almost firing before I realized it was some little critter scurrying away. Maybe it was one of those little deer they have over there. So I relaxed and was just turning back to start up the ridge again when I saw movement in a nearby clearing.

I crouched down in the shadow of the bush next to me and waited. After a few moments I saw a second movement, and this time I saw it was a man, where none of our group was supposed to be. He was moving slowly, in a crouch, with his weapon ready. He moved out of sight behind some bushes, toward my left. Still I waited and watched, finally spotting one more higher up on the ridge. He was also moving to my left. They were going parallel to the ridge crest, and we were moving up it at an acute angle. They were moving toward our left flanker. I signaled my position and how many I'd seen and waited for several minutes. If Magoun had not gone too far up the ridge before I stopped him, he'd be safe.

There was no scuffle in the brush, and no shots were fired. Finally, Magoun signaled that he saw them, and there were four, not three. When he gave us the *all clear*, we moved out carefully. I took everybody up to the top of the ridge, and we laagered up for the remainder of the morning.

"That last patrol worried me," I told Bob. "They were looking for somebody. They moved different from the others we've seen. They weren't as casual."

"Maybe they're combat vets."

"What are they doing way up here?"

"Could be a unit that's rebuilding. One that got their asses kicked and had to pull back."

"But why are they patrolling up here at night?"

"Training the new guys."

Well, that sounded like a good explanation, but I wasn't totally satisfied. My uneasiness had come back. We'd seen two patrols in a stretch of less than three miles. The Lord only knew how many we might have passed in the dark down under the trees. I shuddered as I imagined feeling my way along and putting my hand on somebody's face. A firefight, blind and at that range, would have been devastating to both sides.

By this time we were not in the best of shape. We had been out seven days already. Our uniforms were torn by the brush and had mildewed on our bodies from the constant moisture. We'd developed rashes of several kinds, and some of us had infections where the brush had scratched us. Our shoulders were chafed raw from carrying our packs over wet clothing. I slept while we were outside Hanoi, so I had recovered somewhat from being alert twenty-four hours a day on the walk in, but I hadn't slept since we started back out, and neither had the other SEALs. The agents had. We were getting low on food and were stretching the rations by eating less, so we were more tired than we would have been on full rations. We were all looking forward to a hot bath and a beer, some clean clothes, and getting the rashes and infections taken care of.

The "defector" was tired, but he was in better condition than the rest of us at that point, because he'd started out rested, dry, and clean. I noticed he'd lost his hat.

There were sighs and groans when we saddled up to move out for the last stretch, and the first few yards, moving with stiff and sore muscles and weary minds, we were noisier than we should have been. Fortunately, we were back in the groove before we went very far, because after we'd gone about a quarter of a mile we hit another patrol.

There were at least ten of them, coming down the ridge toward us, and they were moving slowly and cautiously, as if they expected to find something. That gave us time to pull our group back and down off the ridge toward the east, so that they passed on while we hid ourselves in a dense grove.

I turned to Bob and said, "What the fuck is going on?"

He shook his head. "Don't know. Looks to me like they're hunting. Do you suppose they found our trail?"

"Nah, it rained too much after we passed this way. Do you think they might have caught on to these guys when they were in Hanoi?"

"Yeah, I've been wondering about that. When you get tied up with these spooks you can never tell what's going to happen. They may have been discovered. Or they may have been double-crossed. And I don't trust that son of a bitch they brought back with them, either. I thought he might have a little radio beacon on him, but Quinn searched him and didn't find anything. Then again, any one of them may be a double agent."

"Well, what do ya suggest, damn it? Search 'em all?"

"Shoot 'em all, and get our asses out of here."

"Let's just get our asses out of here and back to the LZ."

When you're very tired or very cold your brain just doesn't work right. You don't think clearly. I was very tired, and I made another mistake. I led them on along the ridge.

We were about three miles out from the LZ, by my estimation, when I started getting uneasy. Something wasn't right. Something was missing: animal sounds. When we'd hold up for a few minutes to listen or take a look around, we didn't hear the sounds we'd heard on the way up—no birds or monkeys hollering, and even the insect sounds were subdued. When I got to thinking about it, I realized we hadn't spooked a monkey or deer all morning. I called a halt, and we all gathered up to talk about it and rest for a little while.

I told them what I'd noticed, and Bob said he'd noticed the same thing. ''Maybe a patrol has come through here,'' he said.

''More than one, I'll bet,'' Magoun added. ''It takes quite a bit of activity to move the animals out of an area.''

''Let's not follow the ridge all the way,'' Tony suggested. ''Let's take a different route.'' We all agreed that was a good idea.

I pulled out my map, and Bob and I both looked at it. I pointed to where I thought we were on the ridge. ''Let's go down this side about half a mile, and then head toward the LZ.''

''We can't get too far down the slope. We might walk right into this damned village here, this Duck Key place,'' Bob pointed out.

''We'll be all right if we don't get more than half a mile from the ridge crest. We'll follow the route we planned to take, just half a mile to the east of it. It won't be easy walking, because we'll be 'side-hilling' all the way, but it'll be better than walking into an ambush.''

''Lead on.''

The others agreed, so we deviated from our route a little.

CHAPTER 11

We moved down the slope to the east of the ridge until we thought we'd gone half a mile, and then turned back to the south. The bird sounds and animal noises had returned to normal, and I felt less uneasy. The going was rough, though. We had to fight thicker brush on the slope, and we had to cross ravines and hollows. We were slowed down by the brush, the terrain, and our own exhaustion.

When we judged we were about a mile from the LZ, we started working our way diagonally up the hill. The LZ was right on the crest of the ridge, in a little saddle. As we got closer, I started getting uneasy again. I had the agents hold up, and Bob, Tony, Magoun, and I went on ahead to check it out.

We were still about a half mile out when Bob spotted

someone in the bush to our right. I moved up beside him and we used the binoculars to see what they were up to. At first we only saw a couple of heads, but as we scanned the area, we started picking out more of them. They would move a little, or shift their positions, or scratch, or flick a bug off and give themselves away. We counted eight, wearing NVA uniforms, in a quarter-arc so that they faced along the slope as well as down-hill. They were waiting where they would have the best killing zone against anyone moving up the slope, but we'd approached unseen by moving through the thicker brush and avoiding the trail.

We crawled backwards away from our observation spot, keeping very low, and then worked back to where Tony and Magoun were waiting.

"What do ya think?" I whispered to Bob.

"Looks like they're expecting us," he whispered back. "I don't think they'd ambush this slope just as a routine."

"They weren't watching uphill too well. We might be able to work past them on the uphill side."

"They might be easy about that side because there's another bunch up there," he pointed out.

"Maybe that patrol that passed us was supposed to cover the ridge," I suggested.

"They were too far out," Magoun objected. "They were probably just a perimeter patrol."

"Well, the four of us can check it out, anyway. We can do it a lot quieter than if we brought the whole bunch up."

"Bet there's an ambush right at the top," Bob said.

There was. We spotted one guy's silhouette before any of them saw us. We pulled back to the main group.

"Well, Charlie's up there," I told them. "He's

waiting on us. He's got between us and the LZ and set ambushes on this side. Can anybody tell me what the fuck is going on?''

Cesar said, "Oh, my God!" I accepted the remark as a normal reaction to the news, but something about the way he said it made it stick in my mind, and I kept recalling it as we discussed what to do.

Just then, I was mainly interested in how we were going to get around those bastards and get to the LZ.

We studied the map and the hillside and tried to remember the details of the ground around the LZ, but no one had any good ideas.

Finally, I suggested that we try to circle around and below the ambush site and come into the LZ from the southeast.

Bob and Magoun and Tony and I went off again. We'd gone about eighty yards when we saw movement. An NVA patrol was coming our way. It would have passed behind us, and in front of the rest. We backed up out of their sight, then hurried to warn the group.

There was just enough time to find some good hiding places before they came upon us. Fortunately, the bush was thick—that's why we'd chosen that spot in the first place. We lay there while they passed by. They never did come within sight of us, but they did come within hearing distance. You could hear them going through the brush, the leaves and branches brushing against their clothes and their boots. They moved like deer that've been spooked, in short rushes with short stops in between to listen.

When the noise got fainter, we moved out. All of us. I didn't dare leave the group behind while we scouted ahead. We cut in behind the gook patrol and went on south along the ridge. Every now and then we'd try to turn back uphill toward the LZ, but we'd spot a patrol or an ambush. We stayed almost three-quarters of a mile east of our original route, and every time we tried to cut back in toward it we saw gooks.

We went well past the LZ, and still we saw gooks. We went on past the highway, and they were still up on the ridge. They had us cut off. That meant we'd have to be extracted from one of the alternate LZs. LZ Charlie was almost due east of us, but none of us had ever seen it. We would be at a definite disadvantage trying to approach it without knowing the terrain. LZ Alfa, the drop zone, was also an alternate. I couldn't say that we really knew the area well, but at least we had been on the ground there, even if it was pitch-dark night at the time. Of course, if the NVA had spotted us coming in, or tracked us, they'd be there waiting for us to come back. If we pressed on to LZ Alfa, and they were there, we'd have to turn around and come back north to LZ Charlie. I doubted I could convince this tired bunch to turn around and walk back north. On the other hand, if we went east to LZ Charlie and the gooks were waiting there, I was damned sure I couldn't convince them to turn around and climb the ridge again.

And if they were at both the alternate LZs . . .

Goddamn! I thought, this ain't gonna cut it! I can't just call in for a pickup if they've got us cut off. I'll have to pick a spot I can locate on the map and give them coordinates. And the damned gooks may be listening in! They couldn't just fly over and spot us: we'd have to be out in the open and pop smoke or a flare, and I didn't want to risk it. The NVA had captured some American radios—hell, maybe they'd bought a bunch of them somewhere, too—and they used them to listen in on our transmissions. A lot of them could understand English pretty well, and if we didn't use code they'd know what we were sending.

I had to make a choice. I led them down to LZ Alfa, the clearing where we'd come in, and sure enough, those suckers were there, too. Waiting for us.

I was thinking, I am not going to go through it again. I am not going to be captured again. They're not going to get their goddamned hands on me! But it was looking mighty grim.

We pulled back down the side of the ridge and found a little clearing where the slope flattened a little bit. We looked at it and decided it was big enough to get a helicopter into, barely, and level enough to land on. And it was far enough from the first LZ so that the chopper could get in and out before the gooks could get there to stop it. We were pretty desperate by then, of course, and it probably *wasn't* big enough, or flat enough either.

We broke out the radio and started calling.

We got an answer on about the fourth try. From the call sign, Royal One Four, we figured it was someone offshore. We gave them our coordinates, as we figured them from the map, and asked for a helicopter pickup. The radio operator on the other end repeated the coordinates to make sure he had them right.

"Hold five," he told us.

Then in a few minutes he came back: "You are non-recognized."

"What's this 'non-recognized' shit?" I came back. "I don't expect ya to know me—just send a helicopter and get us the hell out of here! The gooks are onto us! They're all around, and we can't avoid 'em very long! Just get us the hell out of here, for God's sake!"

"I'm sorry, but you're non-recognized."

"What do you mean, non-recognized? This is Hotel India Two Niner Sierra, requesting a slick. We've had to change LZs. You have the new coordinates. Over."

No answer.

After a few minutes we tried again. We got the same fucker. We identified ourselves, made our request, and gave our coordinates. He was off the air for about two minutes this time.

"Hotel India Two Niner Sierra, you are non-recognized," he said when he came back on the air. "Royal One Four, clear."

Bob started cussing a blue streak.

"Try a different frequency," Tony suggested.

We changed the frequency and called again, hoping to get someone else. The same guy answered again. Royal One Four.

"Try him again," Tony urged. "Maybe they'll know who we are on this frequency."

But the reply was "non-recognized." He didn't even go off the air to check with anybody this time, just came right back with it.

"Check with the goddamned NISO in Quang Tri, you bastard!" I told him.

No answer.

"What was that other frequency? Weren't there three?" I asked.

"Sixty-five, I think. Try sixty-five," Tony urged.

I set the radio to 65 mhz and tried again.

The same bastard answered.

"Jesus!" Bob said. "The bastard's on all the channels!"

I repeated everything to him again, hoping we'd be recognized on this frequency.

He came back "non-recognized" almost before I could say, "Over."

I said, "You *fucker*! Forget the goddamned formal bullshit! Take your non-recognized crap and stuff it up your chickenshit ass! Check with Captain Gartley with NISO, and then get us a fucking helicopter up here!"

"Tell him who Babe Ruth is!" Dinh suggested. I glanced at him. He was pale and his eyes were big. He was scared.

Whoever Royal One Four was, he wouldn't reply to any more transmissions.

"Gartley told us it would be hard to get air support once we got away from the LZ," Magoun said bitterly. "He didn't say it would be impossible."

Bob said, "Somebody fucked up. That Royal bastard on the radio doesn't know who we are. Somebody didn't pass the word."

I had a different idea: maybe we weren't being recognized because we weren't where we were supposed to be. But what could we do about it? We couldn't get back to the LZ where we were supposed to be picked up. We might call in and give those coordinates, and then try to get the helicopter to divert to the new site after he was already in the area, but he might figure it was an ambush and just abort. More than likely. We had to get them to send the chopper even though we were at a different location.

Casburn was outposted to watch for patrols while we made the call. He called in now, on his little radio, and said there was one coming toward us, like they were coming to check out the clearing. We moved away at right angles to their path, down into a little valley. We held up again in the valley, and I put Casburn, Quinn, and Fitchew out as outposts again.

I called the others together again and told them, "Okay, you know where we are: we're back to where we came in. We're way past the alternate LZ. There's gook patrols and ambushes all along the ridge. We've got to get the hell out of here or we're going to wind up getting our asses kicked. We can't hide from these guys forever.

"We've called in for a pickup, and they keep telling us we're not recognized. In other words, they don't believe we're really Americans on a legitimate mission. Maybe somebody forgot to pass the word. More than likely, they've got instructions not to send the chopper anywhere but the prearranged LZ.

"Now, as I see it, we've got two choices: we can go on and try to get closer to the coast before we call in for a pickup, or we can try to go back to the alternate LZ. If we go on, they might not recognize us at the new location, either. If we go back to the other LZ, we may find Charlie all around it, too. If you've got any opinions, let's hear 'em.''

John said, "What the hell is going on? Why are they all around like this?"

I looked at him, and at Cesar kneeling beside him, and remembered Cesar saying, "Oh, my God!" when I told them about the ambush at the LZ. Something about the way he said that was still bugging me. The "defector" from Hanoi squatted a little ways behind John, his eyes shifting nervously from me to Bob to Tony to Magoun and back again. I was sure the bastard understood English and knew exactly what was going on.

"I hoped you could tell me," I said to John.

"What the hell do you mean by that?"

"I don't think they found our trail, and I don't think they saw us coming in. I think something happened in Hanoi. Somebody was spotted, or somebody talked." John's mouth opened and he rose slightly as if he were going to stand up and say something. I pointed toward the "defector." "Or that son of a bitch is an agent, a plant, carrying a little radio beeper to signal our location."

John glanced over his shoulder as if to make sure the guy was back there being quiet and not flashing signals with a mirror or something. Then he started shaking his head. "No. No, he's clean," he said. "He's been thoroughly checked out. We're absolutely sure of who he is. He wouldn't have anything to gain by betraying us to the North Vietnamese. You can be sure of that."

"We've only got your say-so for that. And you could be a double agent, for all we know."

"I wouldn't be fool enough to come along if I'd betrayed the route or the LZ to them. After all, I'm just as likely to get shot by you as by the Vietnamese if it looks like we're going to be captured. And the same goes for the others."

"If you were expecting it, you might be able to get away," I pointed out.

"How far would a white man get, running away from a firefight? A Viet might have a chance, but not me. And not Kilroy, and probably not even Cesar. He's too big. Anyway, even a Viet would have trouble getting away in these uniforms. They'd shoot him down with the rest of us."

"So maybe you were seen in Hanoi," Bob insisted.

"Maybe you guys were seen outside Hanoi," John countered.

Quinn called in. The patrol was moving slowly along our trail toward us. The guys started looking at me expectantly.

"I want to search this son of a bitch again," I told him, nodding at the "defector." Somebody behind me shifted nervously, itching to go.

"Goddamn it, you've searched him once. Aren't you satisfied?" It was a stupid question. Obviously I wasn't. "You're going to insult him. He's given his word that he's not carrying any kind of transmitter. If you insult his honor, he won't talk when we get him back to Quang Tri."

It was interesting that he'd given his word about it, since none of us had asked. Either John had asked because he didn't really trust the guy, or he was lying.

"If we don't search him, he ain't goin' back to Quang Tri," Bob told him. "I'll cut his throat and leave him right here."

"He's my responsibility. I'll make the decisions that concern him," John insisted. "I won't have him searched again, and I can't let you kill him. If you do, I'll see you're charged and court-martialed when we get back."

"For God's sake," Cesar spoke up, "they're getting closer while you argue. Let's move on, and you can search him later."

I just shook my head. "We search him before we move, or we leave him here. No use moving just to have them follow a radio signal right to us."

"What's up, Tyler?" Quinn called in. "Those gooks are getting awfully close."

"Just hold tight a minute," I told him.

"John, they mean business," Cesar said, trying to reason with him instead of me. "You're going to blow this mission, insisting they take your word Vuyen is clean. Let 'em search him. The rest of the mission is important, too."

That was the first time the "defector" had been called by name.

Vuyen now leaned forward and said some words to Duc in Vietnamese. Duc chattered back for a few moments and then said, "He wants to know what is happening."

I *knew* he understood English! He knew very well the NVA patrol was getting nearer, and that his life was hanging by a thread. He was trying to conceal that he understood by asking what was going on. Maybe he was trying to give Duc the chance to tell him we wanted to search him, figuring that if he offered to let us do a search, we'd think he was clean, and we wouldn't bother.

Sure enough, he said something else in Vietnamese to Duc, who replied briefly, and then Vuyen stood up, his arms spread, offering himself to me. John looked daggers at me as I stepped past him to frisk the Viet. I did it as quickly as I dared, but carefully, pinching the seams and pockets to make sure there wasn't a little beeper sewn in there. He'd lost his hat, or I would have checked that, too. He was clean as a whistle.

John had the last laugh after all. He sat there smirking at me.

Of course, I checked Vuyen's pack. I emptied it and even turned it inside out. Nothing.

Tony called Quinn and asked about the patrol.

"They're about twenty yards from me," Quinn told

him. "They're moving very slowly. They've almost been stopped for the last two or three minutes."

"How many?" Tony asked.

"I can see four."

"Why are they moving so slow?" Bob wondered.

"Maybe they know we're here and they're being cautious," Cesar suggested.

"They know we're here, somewhere," Tony told him. "They're following our trail. But they're being awfully slow about it. It's almost like they don't want to catch up yet. It could be that there's only four or five, and they know there are more of us."

"They'd have sent somebody for help," Bob pointed out. "They're hanging back until some more gooks get here. Then they'll move fast enough."

"We'd better get out of here before their help arrives," Kilroy suggested.

I grinned and pointed at Vuyen's boots. He took them off. They smelled, but there wasn't any radio transmitter in the toe or built into the heel.

"Are you satisfied, for God's sake?" John snapped, when I handed Vuyen the second boot.

"No," I told him. "He could have slipped a transmitter into someone else's gear. Let's get a look at your stuff now."

"GOD ALMIGHTY JESUS CHRIST!" John exploded, jumping to his feet.

"Sh-h-h-h!" I hissed at him. "They'll hear you."

He balled his fist like he was going to hit me, but he knew better than to try it. He just waved it around for a minute while he got red in the face and cussed to himself. "It's absolutely . . . you have no authorization . . . I never heard of such . . . no need to know . . . that material . . . damned nonsense . . .

not for your eyes . . . you can't . . ." he spluttered around for a minute. Finally he regained his temper and his dignity and shook his head. "No," he said. "You cannot search our packs. The contents of our packs are Agency materials, classified documents, and you can't go through them. It's outside your authority as patrol leader."

"I don't want to go through any documents," I pointed out to him. "I just want to search for a radio beeper."

It was Bob's argument that convinced him. Bob pointed his AK-47 at John's middle and loudly snapped the safety off.

"Our orders was to eliminate you fellows if it looked like you was goin' to be captured," Bob reminded him. "Now, it looks to me like they're about to catch up to us. We can search yer junk now, or we can search it after. It don't make no difference in the end."

We didn't find anything.

Quinn called in again while we were still searching. This time he was whispering.

"For Christ's sake, what's going on back there? They're only ten yards away! I'm moving back!"

We broke squelch twice to acknowledge that we heard and understood. Then we finished the search.

Nothing.

"All right, load it up," I told them. "Let's move on out before they get here."

Now I had to make a decision, fast, and I decided we'd go back to LZ Charlie. If we failed there, we could try for the coast. It would only add a few miles.

John was giving me dark looks when we moved out. I told Bob it gave me a funny feeling to have John behind me with a loaded rifle, he hated my guts so right then. He just grunted and scratched his ass and moved on over toward his point position.

Fortunately, LZ Charlie was south of the road, so we didn't have to cross it again, but I was worried that there might be troops around.

There were.

When we were close, we left the agents laagered up and went on ahead to scout the approach. We'd long since outdistanced the gook patrol behind us. We'd waded almost a mile up the little stream that ran down the middle of the valley, although it finally got so small we were walking single file. I had no doubt that the gooks knew we were here now, but with any luck we'd thrown them off our trail long enough to get a helicopter in before they found the trail again and caught up with us.

We went up and located the clearing and checked out the perimeter. Three-quarters of the way around it was all clear, but then we saw six or eight NVA working their way through the thick bush right at the edge of the clearing. We pulled back so they wouldn't get between us and the rest of the group and had a council on what to do. We agreed to break radio silence again and see if we could get the helicopter. If they dispatched it, we could go right through six or eight gooks with no problem. If they didn't, we'd have to head for the coast anyway.

I tried not to think about that. It was a long walk, and if they wouldn't pick us up here, they wouldn't come get us there, either. We'd have to steal a sampan and try to make it south on our own. That would mean dodging American air and sea patrols as well as the gooks.

I should've written that letter to my wife. It looked

like it was going to be a long time before she got one from me. She might never get one.

We pulled back to where the others were waiting and told them there were some gooks at the clearing and we'd have to take them out, but we didn't think there'd be a problem. Then we broke out the radio. I think everybody there was praying, or had their fingers crossed, or something, when we started signaling.

Royal One Four answered on the third call. My heart sank when I heard the call sign, but it helped when Bob pointed out, "The other bastard's gone off watch." He was right. The voice was different.

We gave them our call sign, and told them we needed a pickup at Lima Zulu Charlie, location November Quebec Romeo Niner Three Four Zero Two One.

"Hold five," the fellow on the other end told us while he checked it out. It seemed like it took forever. We sat there and looked around at one another and worried, and watched the damned bush around us. The tension was so thick you couldn't have stirred it with a stick. I should have been worried about how the others would take it if they came back and said we were non-recognized again, but I was only thinking about my ass, and whether, if they didn't send the chopper, I could keep it away from the Charlies long enough to get it to the coast to steal a boat and make it south on our own.

Then the radio crackled again, and the operator came back. It was probably only two minutes later, but it seemed like hours.

"Two Niner Sierra, Royal One Four. I need an identity confirm. Over."

"Roger, One Four. This is Two Niner Sierra Actual. Fire away. Over." An identity check was standard practice on one of these "over the fence" missions. We'd all filled out a little card that had things like our favorite color, our mother's maiden name, our favorite sport, and so on. "Actual" just meant they were talking to the unit leader.

"Actual, what is your favorite color? Over."

"Green, until I came to 'Nam. Over."

"Wait five, Two Niner." He was relaying this to someone else who had the information. Probably Captain Gartley at NISO.

"Two Niner Actual, Royal One Four: What is your middle name? Over."

What the fuck? That wasn't one of the questions on the little card. It wasn't even proper procedure. I hesitated, wondering what was going on. But I wanted that chopper so bad I would have told them my life history and details of my sex life if they wanted it.

"One Four, it's Ellis. What the fuck? Over?"

"Hang tight, Actual."

I was squeezing the damned mike until my knuckles were white and wishing it was the balls of whoever had fucked us up. Royal One Four came back again.

"That's a confirm, Hotel India Two Niner Sierra."

Man, did we ever feel like cheering! I thought for a moment some of the men might. Big grins spread across their faces, and you could almost feel them relax. Cesar looked as if he were going to faint and fall over in relief. Even the Viets were grinning.

So what if there were six or eight NVA between us and the clearing? We'd worry about them when the time came! The helicopter was on its way, and for the moment, that was all that was important.

Then came the bad news.

"What's the Echo Tango Alfa on that Hotel X-

Ray?'' we asked. How long do we have to wait for the whirlybird to come and take us away from here?

Again, he replied, "Wait five," while he checked, then came back in a couple of minutes. "Ahhh, Hotel India Two Niner Sierra, that Echo Tango Alfa is a deuce and a half."

Two and half hours!

Well, I could have figured it out. We were in the air just over two hours from the time we left Quang Tri until we inserted. They'd have to have time to get the crew into the helicopter and warm it up, even if they were standing by. I didn't know where it was based, either. They just picked us up in Quang Tri, and I hadn't seen any of those big black jobs around there. In two hours we could be in a peck of trouble. We'd best have some help available in case we needed it.

"Royal One Four, there is heavy November Victor Alfa patrol activity this area. The Lima Zulu may be hot. Can you arrange some muscle to help us out? Over."

"Roger, Two Niner, zoomies will be standing by. Anything else I can do for you? Over."

"One more thing, Royal One-Four: Have the helo give us a call when he's three zero minutes out."

"Roger, Two Niner. Big Bird will ring you at Echo Tango Alfa minus three zero."

"Hotel India Two Niner Sierra, clear."

CHAPTER 12

We laid up for the next hour and a half, waiting for the helicopter, in the densest thicket we could find, about half a mile from LZ Charlie. I sent Tony, Casburn, Fitchew, and Quinn to outpost, and Bob and I outposted in the direction of the LZ. Magoun stayed with the agents. They laid up in a circle, watching in all directions. Magoun stayed in the middle of them watching out, but also watching Vuyen.

When you're very, very tired, as we were, to sit and wait and watch for an hour or more may give you some needed rest, but it's damned hard to stay awake and alert unless the enemy is right there and the danger is apparent enough to make your heart pound and the adrenaline flow. The afternoon heat made us draggy and lethargic anyway, and to sit silent for that long meant we had to fight dozing off the whole time. Then, when you do have to move again, your muscles are stiff and sore, and your body protests having to stand, to walk, and to fight the brush again.

Those are times when you get to craving a cigarette, but you can't smoke, because that odor can carry a long way in the still air under a jungle canopy. The smell of a cigarette could give you away to a patrol. Smoking dulls your own sense of smell, too, and if you light one up, five or six hours later you might fail to smell a gook's B.O. or the *nuoc-mam* sauce on his breath as he slips in to knife you.

Of course, I'd like a beer to go with the cigarette, so cold the sweat on the can freezes into little slivers of ice. The water in our canteens, scooped from little streams in the hills, was hot and tasted of halazone and plastic. I could almost hear the pop as I opened the can and felt the cold brew trickling down my throat. . . .

After a while, I got very drowsy. I tried to fight it off, but my mind would start to wander, and I would go into a sort of trance. I was in that state when I started having a nightmare that I'd been captured by the NVA and was trying to escape again. They beat me and kicked me until my muscles wouldn't work, then they left me with my hands and feet untied, as if they were daring me to try to get away. I tried and tried, but my arms and legs wouldn't move. Then, somehow, I got into the water, but instead of swimming away, I was drowning.

I finally woke up, sweating and exhausted.

Nothing happened. Although I was expecting the bunch that had been following us earlier to find our trail again and track us to the thicket, we didn't even see a patrol.

When the hour and a half was up, I called the outposts in and we got ready to approach the LZ. Bob and I took the point positions again as we advanced on the clearing, and I left two men back to guard the rear.

The NVA were still there, waiting in ambush at the perimeter of the LZ. They looked as if they were expecting us to show up. That was good—for us. We knew where they were, and they didn't know where we were. It would have been different if they had been patrolling around.

Bob and I pulled back and conferred with Tony and Magoun. It seemed the best thing to do would be to hit them while they were between us and the LZ. That way, we would either scatter them, or drive them back to the LZ and have them in the open.

Then I faced another dilemma. I wanted to spread the Tacforce out in a line, so we could completely flank the enemy patrol. But what would I do with the agents? Did I leave them with one SEAL, who would have orders to kill them if anything went wrong? Bob was the best man for that job, but I wanted him up front. In the end, I decided to have them right up front on the line with us, to strengthen the middle and beef up our firepower. I would put Bob on their left. I would be on their right. Tony would take the far left flank, and Magoun the far right. Cesar carried the radio, and I would keep him close to me. When we got the half-hour warning call from the helicopter, we would spread out and advance on the enemy in a line. That would give us time to move into contact with the enemy and finish him. I passed the word, and we crept into position in a thicket about two hundred yards from the LZ to wait.

It was hot and still in the thicket, the air so thick

with humidity it pressed down on you like a wet blanket. Even when one of the scattered clouds drifted between us and the sun for a few minutes, you couldn't detect a change in the temperature. We were shaded by the brush and trees anyway. They kept the sun off our backs, but they also trapped the air and kept off any breeze there might have been. You felt as if you were breathing the same used air over and over again, as though the thicket were a closed coffin. The locusts were making a racket, as if they were trying to warn us of something. There was no other sound except the occasional buzz of a big fly. Once we heard the rumble of jets somewhere in the distance, and I got my hopes up that some air support was on its way, but the rumble never got any closer, and slowly faded away.

It was 1626 when we first picked up the transmission from Big Bird.

"Two Niner Sierra, Two Niner Sierra, this is Big Bird. Two Niner Sierra, come in. Over."

I had the sound turned down so that someone five feet away couldn't have heard it, but I was sitting with my back to Cesar, my head against his pack, and I heard it clear enough. I had the mike in my hand all ready to reply.

"Two Niner Sierra. I read you, Big Bird. Over."

"Two Niner, I need an identity check. Over."

"Big Bird, this is Hotel India Two Niner Sierra, Actual. Go ahead. Over."

"Actual, do you have a dog? Over."

"No . . . where would I keep a fuckin' dog? Over."

Wrong answer. Too late, I realized they wanted a name. They didn't give a flying fuck if it was a dog or a cat or my brother-in-law. There was silence for a long moment. I got a cold, heavy feeling in my belly, like I'd just drunk a gallon of ice water, even though all the water I'd had for days was tepid. If there was a fuck-up this time, I'd just made it.

"Big Bird, this is Two Niner Sierra, Actual. The name you're wanting is Chester. Over." Chester was a damned gimp-legged old boar that used to chase me around the farm when I was a kid. It was the only name I could think of when I came to the question about childhood pets.

"Ah, roger, Actual. You called it. Touchdown minus thirty, Lima Zulu Charlie. At November Quebec Romeo Niner Three Four Zero Two One. Over."

"That's a roger, Big Bird. We are moving toward the end zone now. There are unfriendlies in the way. Do you have some help, just in case? Over."

"Roger, Two Niner. We have fast friends on the way. We'll rendezvous at the site. Over."

"See you later, Big Bird. Two Niner Sierra, out."

That was our signal to move. I thumbed the mike button on my little transmitter twice, then twice more. I couldn't see more than five yards in the dense brush, but I knew that out there the guys were locking and loading, patting their grenades to make sure they were handy, and wiping the sweat off their foreheads. Then they would rise to a low crouch, look around carefully, part the brush, move, stop and look ahead and back, and move again.

I knew they were doing it, because I was.

I patted Cesar on the shoulder as I slipped past him, and motioned for him to move ahead and to his left. Then I slipped over toward the right—not far, just far enough so that they couldn't get us both with one burst. Quinn was out to my right, but I only caught an occasional glimpse of him through the brush. Fitchew was posted back behind us about thirty yards. He had the "defector," Vuyen, with him, so he could keep an eye on the one person I was most suspicious of.

We broke out of the dense thicket and into a more open area after about twenty yards. It was still brushy, but there were plenty of open spaces. The treeswere mostly large ones, mahoganies with trunks two or three feet thick, and their shade choked out a lot of the smaller growth. Just over halfway to the LZ we had to pass through a strip about forty yards wide where there were not many trees at all, only dense brush and clumps of reedy grass about five feet high. There was water about ankle deep in there, and underneath that was a tangle of roots slippery with mud. The devil must have designed the place himself. As for Charlie, he was moving.

We were out in the middle of the mudhole when Bob spotted them moving out of a line of trees ahead of us. "Four coming your way, Jay," he whispered into his mike. "Fifteen yards in front of me. Looks like they got tired of waiting for us."

"How far down the line from you?"

"Twenty, thirty yards."

That would put them nearly in front of me.

"Tyler, it's Cesar: I've got two in sight."

It was one of those times when in seconds you have to make a decision that may cost you your life or those of some of your friends.

If there were four patrolling in front of us, there were two to four others somewhere else. Maybe they were still at the ambush site. Maybe not. They might be around on the other side of the LZ.

It looked to me as though they had made a mistake

and divided their forces. Even though we couldn't hit them all at once, we could probably wipe out these four, and then the other four wouldn't be much of a force to reckon with.

"Push on ahead. When you see 'em, shoot 'em. Flankers, try to close 'em off." I had to point the antenna first at the guys on my left, then at those on my right, and repeat the message. Then I checked to make sure my AK was off safety, and I'd hardly done that before the first shot was fired.

I think Cesar fired it. It was awfully close to me, just over to my left. I jumped like I'd been shot myself. After all, it was an AK-47, and I was used to being on the wrong end of those weapons. I suddenly needed very much to pee.

That's all there was for the moment: just one shot, followed by a splash, and then I heard somebody cursing softly in Spanish. I thought, "Oh, my God! He slipped or tripped and squeezed off a round, and now they know we're here!"

Then I heard somebody splashing toward me—not loud, as if they were running, but softer, making swishing sounds to move fast but quietly. An NVA stepped from behind a clump of reeds about five yards from me. I saw his feet first, then he took another two steps and stopped where I could see all of him clearly. He was looking toward the source of the shot. His face was screwed up into a snarl and flushed red. I knew . . . I knew, with an enlisted man's instincts, he was a non-com, probably a sergeant, and he was going to give somebody a hell of an ass chewing for being so damned careless as to give their position away.

He saw me just an instant after I saw him. His AK-47 was lining up with my midsection when I squeezed off a short burst into his chest. The first round hit him and knocked him backward before he could shoot. He splashed into the shallow muck without making a sound.

Before I could move again, somebody fired a short burst in my direction, walking their shots right up to me. The line of splashes started about ten yards away and came at me faster than I could react and stagger backward away from them. The last round splashed water up between my feet and soaked my crotch just as I tripped on a root or something and fell on my ass onto a mud bank. I rolled away and got to my feet, wondering if I could be so lucky again.

I saw one of the little fuckers about twenty yards away, through a narrow space where some chance had parted the brush. I caught just a glimpse of him running toward the right as he tripped and fell on his face in the mud. I pointed my rifle that way, but he was gone before I could draw a bead. I was looking around for others when a movement in that direction caught my attention again. It was the same fellow, this time high-steppin' off toward the left like a chicken thief with a load of buckshot in his britches. I could tell it was him because he was coated with mud from head to toe. I pointed the AK-47 at him again, but he slipped and fell on his ass in a shower of slime just as I was cranking down on him. I sent a short burst his way, but I think all it did was hurry him on his way a little.

The volume of fire had really grown. It seemed that I could hear firing all down the line, but I couldn't be sure, because all the weapons sounded alike. That must have confused them a little, too. They seemed to be spraying shots all over the place, firing high for the most part, on fully automatic. Then they'd slack off for a while and start up again, really pouring it on. I could tell when they were shooting, even though the weapons all made the same sounds. I could tell by the goddamned bullets whipping by my ass. There'd be the *crack-ak-ak-ak!* of full automatic fire, and the thud and splat of bullets hitting the mud and barking the trees, and two or three ricochets. The bullets made sort of a popping or snapping noise when they went past your head.

I wanted to move forward, out of that mudhole and into the thicker brush beside the clearing, but there seemed to be a lot of lead in my way. I pulled back out of the water and started trying to raise people on the radio.

Bob was the first to answer. "What the fuck do you want now?"

"What's it like over there?"

"Did ya ever get into a hornet nest?"

Tony said he was getting pretty heavy fire, and Magoun thought there must be more than six or eight. I agreed.

"Break off. Pull back to the treeline," I told them. "Cesar! Get over here with that goddamned radio. I'm going to call for some air support."

He came crawling over, cursing quietly in Spanish. Or praying, maybe.

"Big Bird, Big Bird, can you read me?" I called. No answer. I begged, I pleaded, I cursed, I threatened. "Big Bird, *come in, for God's sake!*"

"Two Niner Sierra, this is Red Horse Leader. Big Bird is below your radio horizon. Can I relay a message? Over."

"Send us some help, Red Horse. Anybody. Anything. The shit has hit the windshield down here."

"Two Niner, we are on station at fifteen grand. We have eight five-hundred-pound retards and sixty-seven mike-mike rockets. Also twenty mike-mike. Mark your target. Over."

So they were up there somewhere. Shit, I hadn't even heard them over the gunfire.

I checked with the guys to make sure they were all back in the treeline. All of them rogered back that they were, and that they were unwounded. "I'm going to pop smoke for the flyboys," I told them. I pulled out one of the wooden-handled Russky smoke grenades they'd given us, yanked the pin, and threw it as far as I could toward the clearing. It landed in the middle of the mudhole area and started spewing black smoke.

"Red Horse, I've marked the target with smoke. They are in the trees between the smoke and the clearing. Do you see my smoke? Over."

"Roger, Two Niner, I see black smoke. Gooks in the treeline. We're on the way."

"Put 'em on the money, Red Horse. We're in pretty close to them. Over."

"We always do, fellow." He sounded a little pissed.

There wasn't any warning. The gooks were shooting at us and we were shooting back, and the smoke was drifting around out in the thirty or forty yards between us. If the zoomies were making a run I couldn't hear it over the gunfire. Then suddenly there was a series of sharp cracks followed immediately by explosions. Mud and black earth were thrown up in front of us in geysers, and shrapnel started flying around thudding into the trees, bringing down limbs and leaves onto our heads. The explosions started somewhere to my right and moved from there toward the left in a sort of roll that lasted four or five seconds. Each was about as big as a mortar round would make. Rockets. Rocks and chunks of earth started raining down around us. I had been crouching by the radio looking toward the LZ. When the rockets started hitting, I doubled over to the ground and covered my head with my arms. About the time my mind registered that the shriek I'd just heard was a jet passing over instead of someone getting hit, I heard a strange, fluttering hum. Then the ground dropped away from beneath me and came back up to knock me sprawling over Cesar and the radio. Mud and a fine spray cascaded around us.

I grabbed the radio mike and thumbed the button. "Goddamn, Red Horse, too close! The other side of the smoke. *The other side!*"

It was too late. The second Phantom was making its pass, and the rockets were starting to hit in the edge of our treeline. Seconds later he dumped his load of bombs. They tore up the ground just in front of us.

"Goddamn! *Stop!*" I yelled into the mike. The third jet pulled up and went whistling over without dropping anything or firing rockets.

". . . how was that? Over," Red Horse Leader was saying when the ringing in my ears subsided enough for me to hear again.

"Hit the other treeline, goddamn you! We're in this one!"

"Mark the target better, Two Niner. We went after the smoke. Over."

"Wait five," I told him. Then I called up the guys on our little personal radios. They were all okay, but they sounded dazed. I told Magoun and Tony to pop smoke with me on the count of eight, and to throw the damned grenades as far as they could throw them.

Then everybody was to pull back. I gave them the signal to start the count, then grabbed my own grenade, stood up, and threw it, taking a running throw despite my wobbly knees. I couldn't tell if this one went much farther than the first one had, but if praying could make it fly, it did. As soon as I had turned it loose, Cesar and I pulled back twenty yards.

Then I got back to Red Horse Leader.

"We've popped smoke, Red Horse Leader. We marked both ends of our line and the middle. Hit the trees on the *other* side, by the LZ. Over."

"Red Horse Leader to Red Horse Three, do you copy that?"

"Roger, Red Horse Leader. Hit the treeline by the clearing, east of the smoke. Going in."

This time I heard the whine of the jet engine as Red Horse Three started his run.

"Take cover . . . here they come!" I told the men.

It was just like before. By the time he'd completed his run, I was begging them to hit closer to the clearing. Number Four interrupted me by dumping his load almost on our heads.

Again, when my ears stopped ringing, I called the guys. They were all okay. A few of them had nicks and cuts, but nothing serious.

"Two Niner, Red Horse Leader. We still have twenty mike-mike. We can make about two more passes each. Over."

"Hold off, Leader. Let us check the situation out," I told him. To the men, I said, "Let's move up. Charlie can't do as much to us as the damned Air Force. Let's take that goddamned clearing."

We moved out again and got to within thirty yards or so of the treeline before they opened up on us. The mudhole was now a mess of water-filled craters and tangled exposed roots. There were small craters from the rockets and big ones from the bombs. It was bad footing, but the piles of dirt and debris and the craters gave some cover. I thought I was about where I'd been when I shot the NVA noncom, but instead of a crumpled body in the mud there was just a large double crater where two bombs had hit almost together. I could see the treeline had been hit, but not as hard as the middle ground. The gooks were still in there, and they opened up full auto again when we got close.

Bullets started snapping around my head and clipping splinters off a nearby overturned bush. When I ducked, I stepped into the edge of the muddy crater and went sliding down feet first, hoping the water at the bottom wasn't over neck deep. I heard someone cry out nearby about the time I splashed down. Cesar came sliding into the hole after me, so I thought he'd lost his balance and slipped in like I did. It didn't sound like someone wounded.

I glanced at my watch. It was 1650. We had to make it to the LZ soon and get the NVAs out of that damned treeline. We couldn't bring the helicopter in with all that shooting going on, and we didn't want them orbiting around forever. With the fighting and the air strikes down here, there were probably several hundred gooks on the way down the ridge already.

I tried moving forward, but the slick walls of the crater slowed me down, and I was stepping out three feet and sliding back two and a half by the time I got to the top, a slow-moving target for Charlie, who opened up on me right away. I stopped trying to run, crouched below the dirt rim of the crater, and slowly slid right back to the bottom.

Bob called in: "You okay, Tyler? I heard somebody yell like he was hit."

"Yeah, I'm okay, but I can't see what's going on from this fucking hole. Have we made it to the treeline yet?"

"Not over here. I'm in a damned hole myself. Anybody made it yet?"

No one replied in the affirmative, but several of them came on and said they'd gone as far as they could, that the firing was too intense to go on. Tony guessed there was an entire company of NVA up there. Quinn said he was next to the treeline, but the bombs had made such a tangle of limbs and vines he could barely worm through, and some fucker was sniping at him every time he moved.

"The zoomies have got to do it for us," I decided. "Every fucking thing we've tried has gone sour for us. If they would just hit Charlie, instead of us, he'd be blown out of there, and we could mop up." But Charlie appeared to be just as strong as before the air strikes started. It was almost as if the air support was for *his* benefit.

"Wait a fucking minute," I said.

Cesar said, "Huh?"

I'd just put two and two together and come up with an answer other than three. First, the NVA seemed to know where our LZs were. Second, when we called in for a pickup at an LZ where there weren't any gooks, we were "non-recognized." Third, we'd been told that we were supposed to kill the agents rather than let them get captured. Fourth, the air strikes seemed to be aimed at us, instead of the gooks. It all seemed to add up to one thing: someone wanted to make sure the agents didn't get out alive.

That someone had to be in a position to order the pilots to hit us instead of the enemy. It had to be someone in our own camp. Either the CIA or the NISO. Maybe MACV headquarters, but that was an outside chance.

I got real pissed off. The agents were to be eliminated, and to hell with the rest of us. That's the kind of people we were working for. Even if we'd killed the agents for them, and then got ourselves out, they probably would have gotten rid of us anyway just to keep our mouths shut. Sent us on a suicide mission or something.

I called Bob and told him what I thought.

He didn't answer. He was either pissed off or still thinking it over.

I turned to Cesar. "What do you think?"

He looked trapped. He looked at me, then hurriedly glanced away toward the edge of the crater. Maybe he was just checking to make sure no gook was slipping up on us, but it looked like he was trying to think of some lie to avoid answering me straight.

"I . . . I don't know what to think."

"Back there, when I told you the gooks were waiting for us at the LZ, you said, 'Oh, my God.' What did you mean by that?"

"I don't remember saying anything."

"Well, you did. And you said it like you knew they might be there."

"Well, I guess I meant 'Oh, my God, what do we do now?' I didn't . . . I hadn't worried about it. I hadn't thought about it," he said.

He would just go on denying that he knew anything. That was how they were trained. It wasn't even worth asking if Vuyen was the cause of the problem. If Cesar knew, he wouldn't say.

Of course, if the jets were under orders to get rid of us, what about the helicopter? Who would have a better opportunity than the door gunner? As we came running up, one long burst would get us all. But then, why send the helicopter at all? In case we avoided the enemy and didn't call in the air strikes. The helicopter was the last chance to get at us.

Well, if we were expecting it, we could handle it. We'd stay scattered out and approach the helicopter from several different directions, a few at a time. Some of us would have the door gunners covered at all times. If they started to shoot, we'd have the gunner first, and the helicopter would be in flames before it could get away.

I was determined now. I would get back, and get to the bottom of this.

In the meantime, how were we going to get through the gooks to the LZ? They were still there, shooting, although the volume of fire had fallen off to random sniping. They must have had lots of ammo, or else they knew help was close.

Well, if the jets were here to hit us, why not let them? Or let them think they were. We'd just mark the gook positions and call them our own.

"Tony, Magoun, get ready to pop smoke!"

"Again? Wasn't it bad enough for you the last time?"

"Throw your grenades into the treeline by the LZ. Then get back twenty or thirty yards, fast! I won't call in the zoomies until we've all had time to get back. The rest of you start now. Check in and let me know when you're ready."

I got my own smoke grenade ready as they checked in, each of them saying his name over the radio.

"Quinn."

"Casburn."

"John."

"Kilroy."

"Dinh."

"Bob."

"All right. Tony, Magoun, you ready?" I waved at Cesar to start back, and he scampered up the wall of the crater, making two long gashes where his feet slipped in the mud.

"That ain't all of 'em." Bob's voice.

"Who else, then?" I asked him. "Cesar's with me, Fitchew and Vuyen are already back there."

"Let's see. . . ." I could picture Bob counting them off on his fingers, trying to remember who had called in. I did my own quick count: six called in, Cesar's gone back, there's three on the line and two outposting the rear. That's twelve. That's it.

"Duc," Bob said. If he hadn't said it so matter-of-factly I would've ducked. I almost did anyway. Not that I was getting nervous, or anything, with both sides after my ass. Then I realized he was right. Duc hadn't called in. With Vuyen along, our original twelve had grown to thirteen.

No wonder everything had gone sour for us.

"Has anybody seen Duc?"

"He was in position when we moved out last time. He may have been the one that yelled," Bob said. "I'll look for him."

"Don't get your ass shot," I told him, and tried calling Duc on the radio a couple of times. There was no answer. I waited in the bottom of the crater for a few minutes, thinking if he was wounded he'd answer the call, and if he was dead there was no use delaying things by looking for him. Of course, if he was only unconscious, calling in the jets might finish the job. It occurred to me that he might have been a double agent and gone over to the enemy as soon as he thought he could get away from us. He could have done it while we were moving through the heavy brush. But I'd heard the yell too. It hadn't been a scream so much as a yelp, and I'd assumed it was Cesar losing his balance and falling into the crater. It wasn't the type of sound that signaled anything worse than a flesh wound.

When Bob didn't call back, I called him.

"No luck yet," he replied.

Well, I was the patrol leader. I had the responsibility of deciding whether to look for him some more or call in the jets. I knew if I was out there wounded, maybe with my transmitter shot up, listening to all this, I'd want them out looking for me.

"Bob, don't shoot my ass. I'm coming out."

I scrambled out the back of the crater the way Cesar had gone and then cut over to my right. A few shots kicked up mud and clipped twigs around, but nothing close.

It wasn't hard to figure why it was taking so long for Bob to find him. The going was extremely bad. With every step your feet slipped and slithered and tripped on roots. Spotting a crumpled body in that mess wasn't going to be easy. Add to that the fact that I didn't know exactly where he was and it got to be nearly hopeless. I spent precious minutes looking anyway.

"Tyler, Tyler," Cesar's voice interrupted my looking. "Big Bird is on the horn. Wants to talk to you."

As soon as he said it, my mind registered the distinctive whopping sound of a helicopter rotor just audible between shots.

"Tell him to hold off, to orbit until I get back to him."

I went another ten yards, looking around quickly as I dodged from bush to bush, trying to stay out of the snipers' sights. Then Bob called up to say he'd found him.

"I got 'im," he said. "Pop your smoke."

"Is he hit?"

"Yeah . . . he's dead. I'll get him back. Go ahead with your smoke."

I checked with Tony and Magoun to make sure they were ready, and then we threw the smoke and ran back as fast as we could. I tripped once and slipped down while I was staggering to regain my balance, and then slipped down again after I'd gotten up, bruising my thigh on a root. When I got back to Cesar, I was breathing so hard I could hardly talk into the mike.

"Red Horse Leader, you still there? Over."

"Roger, Two Niner. Not much longer, though. We're getting close to Bingo fuel. Over."

"We've marked our position with smoke. Do you see the smoke?"

"Roger, I see white smoke, three places, like before, Two Niner."

"The smoke is us, Red Horse. Make a run on the ground you chewed up before, where all the craters are."

"Say again, Two Niner? The smoke is on your position, and we make a run on the same area we hit before?"

"That's affirmative, Red Horse. Two Niner clear."
To Cesar, I said, "What frequency is Big Bird on?"

"The same one."

Red Horse was obviously using a different frequency to chat among themselves, because we weren't picking them up. I thumbed the mike and called Big Bird, who came back just as Red Horse Leader was making his approach.

"Big Bird here," they replied to my call. "Hear you're having some trouble with the natives."

"They're definitely unfriendly," I told them.

Big Bird came back, but it was drowned out by the roar of Phantom 20-millimeter cannon. I looked up, but couldn't see the rounds impact. I could see the tracers, though, and it looked like they were going right into the smoke. Both Red Horse Leader and his number two plane were making the pass at the same time. Numbers three and four were already entering their approaches.

In the brief respite between passes, I heard Big Bird talking to someone, but couldn't make out if they were calling us or Red Horse.

After the last two planes streaked overhead, Red Horse Leader got on the horn to us. I didn't answer.

"Aren't you going to answer him?" Cesar asked.

"No," I said. "Let him think he did his job." I held on to the mike, but pushed the transmit button on my hand-held radio. "All right, let's go get that LZ," I told the Tacforce.

We moved out into the blasted mudhole again, slipping and tripping and cursing.

Red Horse Leader finally gave up and called Big Bird.

"Big Bird, Two Niner does not answer. We have Bingo fuel. We'll have to Romeo Tango Bravo and leave you to finish up here." Romeo Tango Bravo was RTB: Return to Base.

"Okay, Red Horse Leader. We will orbit as long as we can, or until things get too hot, and try to raise them."

Red Horse Leader signed off and the jets rumbled off into the distance. The helicopter kept circling at what seemed about a mile or so out.

There was some half-hearted sniping from the treeline, but we returned the fire in volume and the sniping died out. The strafing appeared to have done a good job.

We halted at the edge of the treeline, looking out across the clearing. Bob dropped Duc's body, then he and Quinn swept toward Magoun to make sure there was no one hiding out on that flank to sneak in and snipe at us when we were feeling secure. Casburn and Kilroy cleared the left flank as far as Tony's position. There were still some gooks out that direction, but they weren't too enthusiastic for the fight anymore.

Duc had been shot in the neck; his carotid artery was severed.

Big Bird was on the horn to us. The jets were long gone, so I responded.

"Where have you been, Two Niner? We've been trying to raise you for ten minutes now. There are boocoo truckloads of NVAs on the road about a mile north of you. They're unloading already, and they'll be on top of you in ten minutes."

"We've been securing the LZ, Big Bird. There are still a few snipers, but they can be suppressed. We're ready for that ride home."

"Roger, Two Niner. We're on our way."

"Two Niner, this is Chickenhawk. I have a mini-twenty and lots to say. Where are these snipers?"

"Negative, Chickenhawk. They're all mixed in with our people, and we all look alike from up there. Hold off until we're airborne."

"Are your people over by the road?"

"Negative, Chickenhawk. We are all at the LZ."

"I'll go discourage those Charlies a little, then."

I was suspicious, to say the least, that he'd be strafing the treeline on his first pass, but when I heard the hum of the minigun, it was from the north, toward the road.

"Stay about five yards apart in the bush," I told the men. "When he lands, go out two at a time. Stay as far apart as possible. And *get in* the chopper when you get there. Bob, Tony, Quinn, you guys keep an eye on the door gunner. If he starts shooting at us, waste him."

Fitchew called in from his outpost position. "Tyler, there's a gook patrol moving in. Ten or twelve in a big hurry. We're pulling back."

"Get your ass on up here," I told him. "The chopper's coming in."

Big Bird popped up over the treeline on the far side of the LZ and reared back as it slowed down less than a hundred feet from our side of the clearing to hover just above the ground. The pilot wanted to be airborne to get a faster start when he lifted off. He turned the big ship parallel to the treeline so the door gunner would have a clear arc of fire. I hesitated for a few seconds to see if the gun would open up on us, then ordered the men out. John and Cesar went. They ran low but straight toward the door. They were just ducking under the rotor when the shooting started.

CHAPTER 13

The shots came from somewhere on the left. It was a short burst, just three or four rounds. Both John and Cesar went down but scrambled up again almost at once and ran for the chopper door. The door gunner swiveled his machine gun and opened fire—at the treeline, much to my relief. There was a sudden flurry of shots from that direction as Tony and Casburn found themselves having some trouble breaking off from the gooks. Just before he reached the helicopter door, John arched his back and fell heavily against the machine. Even without the blood splashed on the helicopter's airframe, I knew he was hit. Cesar was already inside. Bob and Quinn ran up, picked John up by the arms, and passed him to a crewman and Cesar, who pulled him on board.

Dinh and Kilroy were running for the helicopter, and

Magoun was backing toward it, watching the treeline. On the left, Tony and Casburn were moving in short sprints, leapfrogging one another, firing back at the treeline when they paused. Fitchew and Vuyen came tearing through the bushes and raced for safety as if the whole North Vietnamese Army was hot on their heels.

"Zigzag! Zigzag!" I yelled at them, and Fitchew immediately started cutting back and forth. Vuyen either didn't understand or didn't care. He could sure cover the ground fast for a short fucker.

It dawned on me then that everyone else was on his way to the chopper and I was still standing there like a spectator. I said to myself, "You're a part of this three-ring circus; you'd better get your ass in gear or you'll be the main attraction in Hanoi." So I picked up Duc's body and started for the helicopter. He must have bled nearly dry, because he hardly weighed anything at all. It was like picking up a kid. I zigzagged a couple of times just in case someone was trying to draw a bead on me, and got to the door about the same time as Magoun and Tony. A crewman took the body from me and laid it on the floor, and somebody gave me a hand up. Once inside, I emptied my last clip into the treeline while the gunner started yelling, "Go! Go!" into his intercom and the pilot hit the throttle. Casburn was lifted in by Tony and Bob, his feet scrabbling in the air as the chopper lifted off. We were forty feet up by the time he was inside.

Looking out the door past the gunner, I could see a second helicopter raking the treeline with his miniguns. A dozen or so NVA had spilled out of the brush into the edge of the clearing and were firing up at us until he scattered them with a strafing run.

We'd obviously gotten out with no more to spare than a squeak and a hair.

For some reason, I noticed the shadows of the trees extended halfway across the clearing. In an hour or two it would be dark. It had been a *long* fucking day. I lay down on the floor of the helicopter and put my palms over my eyes and pressed until I saw funny-colored swirls on my eyelids, and kept them that way until we were somewhere over the Gulf of Tonkin near Yankee Station.

When you've just come in from a long, nasty mission and you go into debriefing, all you can think is: let's get this shit over with and hit the shower and the sack. You've been four or five days without sleep, hiking and climbing and running through the goddamned jungle, and you're exhausted. You've had nothing to drink but warm, foul water for days, and nothing to eat but C-rats, and you have diarrhea so bad you walk bent over from the cramps and your ass is raw as hamburger. And you're uptight. Charlie's been trying to kill you out there. Bullets have been flying around you, and your people have been getting killed. Your nerves are shot. Then people start asking you the same questions over and over again, in two or three different ways, and you get pissed, and you snap and bark at the dumb fuckers.

So I screwed up in debriefing. I realized it later, and then lay there in my bunk thinking about it.

When we got off the Big Bird at Quang Tri, we were loaded on a bus and taken right to Special Forces headquarters. A guy in civvies took our AK-47s and our pistols and grenades, and two others took Vuyen away. An Army Special Forces sergeant led us into the debriefing room and closed the door behind us. Captain Gartley was in there, and "Mr. Smith." Kilroy, Cesar, and Dinh joined us for this session, but I knew they'd have their own debriefing later on what they did and what they saw in Hanoi.

"Get comfortable, men, and let's get this over with," Gartley said.

There was a coffee urn in the corner. I went over and helped myself. It wasn't beer, and it had all the endearing qualities of Mekong River water—it was full of sediment and it was fishy-tasting—but at least it was wet. I killed half a mug while standing by the urn looking at Gartley and Smith over the rim, and thinking about the gooks around the LZs, and the air strikes that hit our positions, and the "non-recognition" response we got. I refilled the mug before the spigot had stopped dripping and sat down on the edge of a table. Some of the others were getting coffee, and Gartley was waiting until they settled down to start the debriefing. I watched the two of them over the rim of my mug until I couldn't keep quiet any longer.

"Just what the fuck is going on?" A lot of hostility was loud and clear in my voice.

Smith was chewing gum a mile a minute. He stopped chewing abruptly and looked at me, but his pudgy pig's face never changed expression. His eyes did, though. They seemed to lose luster, as though a plastic curtain had dropped in front of them. Gartley looked startled for a second, then assumed a look of innocence, like a kid caught with his hand in the cookie jar. Then his innocent look quickly turned into anger as he reacted to my insubordination in a way any officer typically would.

"I'm not sure I know what you mean, Mr. Tyler," he

said, his voice practically crackling with ice. My coffee instantly got ten degrees cooler. "This is our usual debriefing."

I really hadn't known how to start, but he gave me the opening I needed.

"Yeah . . . but it wasn't our usual mission, was it? I mean, it was a one-way mission, and that ain't our usual type."

"I don't know what you're talking about. You were to see to it the agents got in and back out alive," Gartley protested.

"And kill them if they were about to be taken alive. And we were going to have all this air support if we got in trouble. But when the gooks got onto us somehow, and we called for a helicopter to pick us up, they kept telling us we were non-recognized. They didn't ask for an identity check, they just said we were non-recognized."

Gartley opened his mouth to say something, but I cut him off.

"*Then*, when we finally got hold of a different radio operator, he sent a helicopter up for us, and air support, but the damned flyboys kept dropping their bombs and rockets right on top of us. They kept hitting *us*, not the enemy. We finally marked the enemy's positions with smoke and told them they were ours, and they came in and knocked 'em out for us. *They were trying to get us!*"

"Now, calm down, Tyler. You just caught some friendly fire, that's all. An accident," Gartley tried to tell me, but I wasn't having any of that bullshit, and told him so.

"I've had air support before, and I've called in artillery from firebases and a cavalry division, and even a damned ARVN outfit, and they didn't screw up. They put their shells and their bombs right where we told them to, or right where we marked them. They didn't screw up. Why would the U.S. Air Force screw up, not once, but over and over? It wasn't no accident. They did it on purpose, and they did it because they were ordered to. Somebody was trying to get rid of us, damn it.''

"Stop and think, Tyler. That doesn't make any sense. Successful completion of the mission involved getting agents to Hanoi *and* getting them back alive. And getting the defector out too, I might add.'' Gartley was doing all the talking, I noticed. Smith was just standing there watching me. Every once in a while he'd glance at Gartley or one of the others, but he kept turning his gaze back to study me.

"Then maybe what I'm saying, Cap'n, is that somebody wanted this mission to fail.'' I thought it was time to mollify him a little by going back to military courtesy. I lit a Marlboro and took a long draw on it to give myself a moment to think. I'd been chain-smoking since the helicopter reached Yankee Station.

Gartley looked at Smith and then around the room at the others. Out of the corner of my eye I noticed Bob's head nod imperceptibly.

"It sure looked that way to me, too, Captain,'' Tony spoke up.

Smith looked at somebody with narrowed eyes. There was only one thing that look could mean: don't dare say a fucking word. I glanced over my shoulder to see who he was looking at. Cesar, Kilroy, and Dinh were sitting in a tight little knot, and he was looking in their direction. He could have been looking at any one of them, or at all of them.

"Somebody tipped off those gooks,'' I went on.

"Either somebody told them we were in there and how we were getting out, or we were seen going in, and these guys were seen in Hanoi, and they put two and two together. I think somebody told them where to look for us."

The captain still wasn't ready to accept that. "It would have to be somebody in the Agency or NISO or MACV," he pointed out.

"Sounds like a lot of people knew where to find us," Bob observed.

"Not that many." Gartley was immediately defensive again. "Only a limited number of people in any of those staffs have access to classified operations plans."

"Well, that narrows it down. You don't have so many to check out." I think it was Quinn who said that. It looked like they were all behind me on this.

"We don't need to check out anybody," Smith spoke up. "The NVA obviously spotted you after you left Hanoi and moved men into the area to intercept you. Then you called in air support, and they dropped a little close to you, and you panicked. This is all a product of your overactive imaginations. Get a little rest and sleep and you'll see there's really nothing to it."

"Bullshit!" I couldn't handle that kind of crap right then, especially from a bastard that made his living double-dealing. "Those troops weren't 'moved into the area.' They were moved right to the goddamned LZs, all three of them, Alfa, Bravo, and Charlie, and they weren't at any of the other goddamned clearings in there. And that's another thing: when we found a clearing without troops around it, we were 'non-recognized,' but when we went to LZ Charlie, with the fucking troops there waiting for us, *then* they recognized us."

Smith and Gartley both started to speak at once, and

both hesitated, waiting for the other. Smith deferred to the captain.

"That's standard operating procedure on that type of mission," Gartley pointed out. "We only recognize pickup calls for the designated LZs. There's too much risk of the North Vietnamese capturing a team and radio and calling the helicopter into an ambush. The teams carry no identification, but it's hard to deny that helicopter is one of ours. People all have the same kinds of features, but helicopters, especially long-range ones like we use, are distinctive, even without markings."

"That's why you use identity checks," I pointed out.

"The North Vietnamese monitor our radio traffic. They know the procedure, and the questions to ask a team member. They might be able to respond to an identity check correctly."

"If they can find that out, they can find out where the LZ is," Bob pointed out.

"I hope you people realize how stupid this argument is," Smith interrupted. "The fact that the helicopter went out and picked you up proves there's nothing to your theory that someone was trying to terminate your mission. Otherwise, the helicopter would never have gone." That was just like him, that cold-blooded phrase "terminate your mission." Why couldn't he just say "kill you"?

"It don't prove nothing at all," I told him. "If the helicopter hadn't come, there wouldn't have been any need for the damned jets to try to kill us off before they got there. If Captain Gartley is right about the standard procedure, then the helicopter was probably dispatched by some little j.g., or a petty officer, who wasn't in on anything. This was all on the radio, you know. All kinds of people might've wondered about it. So whoever is behind this, they probably had the jet pilots lined up in advance anyway, as an ace in the hole. The jets left long after the helicopter, you know. There was plenty of time to get orders to them.''

Smith shook his head. "Jesus, you people have sure built up a fantasy," he said.

Gartley took it more seriously. After all, it was his troops that were threatening to mutiny. But I could tell he thought we were full of shit too.

"What would be the point?" he wanted to know. "Why would someone on the staff of NISO or the Agency or MACV want to eliminate you?"

"Not us, necessarily. The agents. We didn't go into Hanoi, after all. Maybe it was something they found out while they were there, or something somebody thought they might find out, and he was trying to cover his ass. Maybe it was for money. Or maybe . . . maybe it was that Vuyen fellow they were trying to get." The thought had just occurred to me. "Maybe whoever was doing this was a double agent, and Vuyen could finger him."

"Maybe, maybe, maybe! I've never heard such a crock of shit!" Smith barked. "You people screwed up. You fucked up and let the North Vietnamese see your patrol, and now you're trying to blame someone else. You've built a case in your imaginations for a double agent in the headquarters staff somewhere, but I'll tell you right now to forget it. It's a house of cards, and we're not going to take it seriously." He turned to Captain Gartley. "Captain, I'll have to insist you get better control over the debriefing. I still have to conference with my agents tonight. Let's move on and get this over with. I suggest we start at the beginning, and that you keep Mr. Tyler on the subject of the insertion and extraction, and put an end to his stupid accusations.''

Things were strained after that. We went over the bare facts and gave clipped, short answers to their questions. After a while they saw they weren't going to get much more out of us and sent us off to rest.

The next day wasn't a lot better. Their questions were more detailed, but our answers were still short. They wouldn't discuss what we really wanted to talk about, and we gave them a minimum of anything else. Gartley's aides really got pissed off, but we didn't give a shit.

I'd had a few hours to think it over. I took Tony and Bob aside and said, "Look, I ain't going back up there for that damned Smith. No more jobs for that fucker. And I recommend you don't either. But if you decide to go on another one up north, don't think I'll be pissed off if either of you wants to lead it. I just ain't going to go.''

Bob said, "Oh, hell . . . ya will too. You'll go. You like this shit.''

"Not if the Agency has anything to do with it, I ain't,'' I insisted.

I surprised them. The next time Captain Gartley started talking about a mission up north I asked him if the damned CIA was involved with it, and especially that fucker Smith. He wouldn't tell me whether it was the Agency or DIA or just NISO, but he did tell me Smith wasn't involved. We went back up there not just once but several times in the next couple of months, and none of the missions were as hairy as that first one.

In all that time, there wasn't one letter for me from my wife. I finally started worrying about it. I went in to Special Forces headquarters and told Captain Gartley what the problem was. He let me use the telephone in his office to call home.

The phone rang about eight times before a man answered.

I didn't say anything for a minute because I was confused.

He said, "Hello, damn it! Who is this?"

"Well, who is *this*, damn it?" I said.

"Who did you want?"

"Well, I didn't want you! I was callin' my wife."

"You got the wrong number, motherfucker!" he said, and hung up, but in the background, just before the phone clicked down, I heard a woman's voice saying, "Who is it, honey?"

Her voice.

I sat there for a few minutes, thinking of every possible answer except the obvious one, but I couldn't deny it forever. Eventually I had to admit she was shacked up with some guy. Then I got mad, really pissed, and slammed out of Gartley's office and went to get a beer.

After three or four beers, my temper had cooled down, but I was feeling hurt and sorry for myself. If only there had been someone to talk to about it. Bob would only wise off, and I couldn't discuss anything that personal with the others. If only Billy was still around! Then I thought of my partner in my Shore Patrol days, and the first thing I knew, I was calling him up. He was still there. He said he'd go by and check on her and get back to me.

We were on a recon patrol west of Hue in the A Shau Valley. We'd been out about four days when

CINCPAC broke radio silence and told us to abort our mission and return to the LZ for a pickup.

I called in when we were still a little way out and told them we were getting close. Once we got there, I broke radio silence again and called for a pickup. "Delta One Five, Delta One Five: the Eagle has landed."

"Roger, Eagle. ETA two five. Repeat: Echo Tango Alfa two five." He was obviously on his way, to be only twenty-five minutes out.

It wasn't long until we heard the *whop! whop! whop!* of the rotor blades, and the radio crackled with a transmission.

"Eagle One, Delta One Five. How's traffic down there?"

We came back with, "Delta One Five, you have a green light."

The chopper flew low overhead and past us, then made a quick turn and came down to hover just off the ground. Within a minute we were on board.

At 1103 we touched down at the base. The guys grabbed their gear and jumped off. There was an LTJG waiting for us, holding on to his hat to keep it from being blown off by the rotor blast. "Tyler?" he asked.

I nodded yes as I walked toward him. The helicopter pilot chose that instant to hit the throttles and lift off, so I knew he couldn't have heard me if I yelled.

When the chopper was a couple of hundred yards away and the roar had died down a little, he said, "I have two jeeps here, waiting to take you to HQ."

"What's going down, Lieutenant?" I asked.

"I don't really know," he said, "but the commanding general of MACV is here, and I'm sure he does. Hop in." In less than a minute we were in the jeeps and on our way to the harbor.

"Do you suppose the Navy could wait long enough for us to clean our asses and get something to eat?" I asked, leaning forward.

"Yeah. They've made provisions down at the harbor. You'll be able to chow down, shower, and check your weapons," he replied.

When we reached the harbor, the lieutenant stopped the jeep in front of a two-story building and led the way inside to the first room on the right of a long hall. There he turned us over to an Army sergeant behind a counter. The counter had a strong steel screen from floor to ceiling, with a couple of sliding steel-screen openings to pass gear through. We checked our weapons with the sergeant. It reminded me of checking athletic equipment with a coach.

"Sergeant Long will take it from here," the lieutenant said.

The sarge told us we would be issued new weapons later, and that until further notice we would bunk aboard the U.S.S. *Eldorado*. Our gear had been transferred there from the barracks. I asked him what was going on, and he said the base was closing down. All U.S. personnel, except a few advisors, were going to be gone by the end of the month.

The *Eldorado* was the flagship of the Seventh Fleet, and carried the fleet commander, Admiral Jameson. When we walked aboard, they had Marine guards posted and a lieutenant commander was OOD. Sergeant Long told him who we were, and he called a first class petty officer to escort us to our quarters, one deck up.

I noticed as we went down the passageway that everyone we met was giving us hard looks. Could it have been because we hadn't showered or changed clothes in four hot, hard days?

It had been a long time since I had been on board a ship. The billet was small and would only hold two people. Bob and I bunked together. I went in and flopped down on one of the bunks. Our gear wasn't there, and the petty officer went looking for it. Bob started looking through the lockers to see if he could find something someone had left behind. Finally he sat down and leaned against the bulkhead.

"You need a bath, Jay. You know that?" he said, rubbing his face with his hands and looking at the little threads of oily dirt on his palms. I didn't answer him. There wasn't any use bathing until our seabags and fresh uniforms caught up with us. I just sat on the edge of the bunk and rubbed my cheeks and looked down at the floor. I hated sitting around waiting. It was nothing but time to worry or get horny, and there was nothing you could do about either one.

Of course, Bob always had a way to break your train of thought.

"When the war ends, we're fucked. You know what I mean, Jay? What kind of work are we going to do? All we know is search and destroy, and there ain't much future in that. Boy, are our families in for a surprise!" He was feeling down.

"Well, hell, it's good training for a revenooer!" I joshed him.

He put his head back against the bulkhead and said, "Shit! By the time we get back, all the moonshiners'll be growin' maryjuany anyway."

I shrugged and said, "Same-same. Maybe you can get a job as a private eye. All these sneak-'n'-peek patrols oughta be good training for that. You can sneak around peekin' in people's windows to see who's running around on their wives or husbands."

He snorted. ''Nobody's gonna give a shit by then, with all this sleepin' around and wife swappin'.''

''Well, you can always dive. Work on an offshore oil rig—they use divers, don't they? I can't even do that.''

He didn't bother to answer.

''Look,'' I said, ''at least we won't have to put up with each other's bullshit every day.''

He turned his head to look at me, and I could see a greasy spot on the bulkhead behind him. ''You tellin' me you won't miss that?''

He was right. I would miss him—and the other guys on the team. I would miss being part of a special group with a purpose. When the war ended we'd see each other for a while around San Diego while we waited for our enlistments to end, but then we'd all go our own ways. We might even run into each other at times, but it would be different.

The knock on the door broke us out of our down moods. It was the petty officer. He had our gear and we could start getting cleaned up.

We showered, chowed down, then went back to our rooms to get some sleep. About 1800 they woke us and took us to meet the brass. Everyone was quiet walking down the long halls of officers' country.

When the door to the conference room opened, the first face I saw was Admiral Jameson's. He introduced us to an Army general who turned out to be the commanding general of the armed forces in Vietnam, General Creighton Abrams.

''Pull up a chair, men, and we'll get started,'' the general said after the introductions. He didn't sit back. He picked up a folder, pulled out a photograph, and passed it around to us. It was a picture of an NVA officer. The General scratched his forehead with his left index finger before continuing. ''The picture you have in front of you is Colonel Minh Tho of the North Vietnamese Army. He was one of the NVA commanders who planned and organized the overrunning of Hue two years ago, and he is also one of the main advisors to the NVA Chief of Staff, Senior General Van Tien Dung. The information we have from our intelligence work is that his advice influences where and how NVA troops make their strikes and raids, as well as where their main supply dumps and routes are located in Laos, Cambodia, and North and South Vietnam.

''As you are probably aware, one of the hazards of being a general is that you are often, if not always, accused of fighting the last war instead of the one you're involved in, insofar as tactics and strategy are concerned. We've been aware for some time that General Giap, the Commander-in-Chief of the North Vietnamese Army, has been attempting to repeat his victory over the French at Dien Bien Phu, and that the results have been disastrous. He may be a hero to the hippies and peace freaks in Berkeley, but he's in disfavor with the North Vietnamese Politburo. It's hard to get rid of a hero, though, even in North Vietnam, so he is hanging on to his position. Frankly, we want to keep him there.

''General Dung is more innovative and flexible, and less predictable. Especially with Minh Tho advising him. If Dung replaces Giap, we could find ourselves in hot water fast. By the end of this year, we plan to have Vietnamization largely completed, and less than half the forces in-country that we had at the end of 1970. Our chief concern is that Dung will attack us as we withdraw, hitting the weaker stay-behind garrisons, cleanup crews, and the truck convoys to discourage us from ever reentering the war. A sort of kick in the ass for the retreating troops.

"Then they will build their strength and invade South Vietnam, confident we won't return to stop them.

"Colonel Tho will have a major role in planning and organizing the attacks. Our sources in North Vietnam tell us he has already been sent down to a camp just outside of Lang Mo—right here, about twenty miles southwest of Dong Hoi, and about twenty-five miles north of the DMZ. We think he's there to organize and amass forces for a major attack here at Quang Tri. If such an attack were to increase the pressure from Congress and the protesters to speed up withdrawal, it could topple President Thieu and lead to the fall of the Republic of Vietnam.

"For every man we send home, the Communist forces are relatively one man stronger. Sooner or later, they'll smell victory, and they'll come swarming over the DMZ with everything they've got, whether all our people are withdrawn or not. As you know, we're talking to them right now in Paris, trying to reach an agreement that they will hold off with their attack until we have all of our troops withdrawn. However, they haven't always kept their agreements.

"If we knew where their troop depots were, and their supply dumps and supply routes, we could attack them from the air to disperse their troops and destroy the supplies and equipment. That's where you come in. We want you to snatch Colonel Tho and bring him back here to us."

CHAPTER 14

I couldn't believe what I was hearing. It was bad enough reconnoitering south of the DMZ, with all the troops the NVA was slipping across the line. Up north, they were thicker than flies around a latrine. To go up for a sneak-and-peek job was dreadful; to go up and grab this asshole who was probably the second or third most guarded gook in the North—and try to get back with him—was damned near suicide.

I had to speak up.

"Just how well has Intelligence done their homework on this? I mean, you're asking an awful lot from seven people, General."

"You're Tyler?" he asked.

"Yes, sir."

"We know where the camp is located and approximately how many men are with him. We also know in which building he's staying. I understand your concern about the quality of our intelligence, but I assure you, we have been watching him closely for the last ten weeks, and on a less intense basis for several years. It will not be a wild-goose chase. I can also assure you we're not going off half-cocked on this. The man has information that will be very beneficial to the U.S. and to South Vietnam.''

"How do we go in?'' Bob wanted to know. "That's a long way to hike.''

"We'll have you dropped in about halfway. If we tried to get you any closer, we might get into their triple-A zone. They have SAMs up there now, and light and heavy AA guns. It's getting almost as bad as the Hanoi area. That's another reason we believe they're building up for a major attack: they've really built up their AA defenses.

"We don't have a layout of the building we think he's in, just the location. It will be up to you to determine how it is configured inside, and the best way to get in and get him out.''

"How long do we have?'' I wanted to know. "And what kind of support can we have to get it done?''

"You can have anything you need. Just let Lieutenant Burke, here, know what it is.'' He waved his hand toward a slender Army lieutenant who had been standing quietly to one side. "He'll see that you get it. But time is critical. We needed him yesterday . . . last week, even. We'll take him as soon as you can get him. It'll take a while to get the information from him, and we probably don't have very long.''

Somehow, I knew that would be the case.

"We'll need to beef up a little," I said. "Right off

the top of my head, I don't believe seven can handle it. There are some South Viets we've worked with in the past, some LDNNs—part of a South Vietnamese SEAL team we've been training. If it takes a lot of paperwork to get them attached to us, someone had better start it right away.''

"No problem," he replied.

"Do you have somebody that can identify this joker?" Casburn asked. "All these damned dinks look alike to me."

I made a mental note. Casburn would not be in on the actual snatch, if he couldn't tell them apart.

"Some of our agents in North Vietnam would be able to," the General said, "but I don't know if we have anyone in the South who could. I'll have it checked out."

The big brass left then, probably to go hoist a few in the Admiral's stateroom. They shook hands with us before they left. Frankly, I was impressed. I'd never been briefed by COMUSMACV before.

It took two days' planning to get everything worked out. The maps and air photos they had were helpful as far as getting in and out, but I was skeptical about the building they had picked out. It was out near the edge of the camp, and I figured they would have him staying in the middle of it.

We wouldn't know exactly how we could get him until we had gotten to the camp, and then we would have to do at least a two-day recon, watching for who entered and left the building, how many guards were posted, and if there was a set routine for changing and standing guard. The LDNNs would play a critical part because they could translate anything we managed to overhear. It was conceivable that they could learn what room Tho was in. The General hadn't been able to come up with anyone in South Vietnam who could positively identify him, so we would have to memorize his picture, we were told. Once we were in the building, it wouldn't be easy to pick his face out of a crowd, but the way I had it figured, the building housed only officers, so there wouldn't be very many staying there.

Not much bullshitting went on during those two days, and not much of anything else except the work of planning the mission. We were confined to the ship until we left on the mission. The four LDNNs were also brought aboard and detained. They helped with the preparations.

We requisitioned some booby traps and C-3 and C-4 explosives, plus some silenced AK-47s and two hundred rounds of ammo each. We also got radios and two starlight scopes. We might need a sniper, so we decided on Joe Magoun, who was a crack shot. He was issued a sniper rifle with a telescopic sight and a silencer that looked like a length of two-inch pipe. Two of the Viets took crossbows as well as their AK-47s. We were pretty heavily loaded. We figured it would take two days going in and two days of watching the camp before we were ready to move. We were planning on a quick extraction, though.

We would be paradropped from a helicopter about thirty miles northwest of Quang Tri, just above the DMZ and about twenty-seven miles southeast of Lang Mo. The camp was about five miles northwest of Lang Mo, which was a major assembly point for troops and supplies heading south.

Extraction would be by helicopter operating out of

Laos. One of those big black birds again. They'd pick us up at an LZ just south of the Ho Chi Minh Trail. A chopper would be kept on station for the length of the mission so it could reach us in a matter of minutes when we called.

The day before the mission we had mail call at about 1500, right after we finished the planning session. There was a letter for me from Bill, my old partner in the Shore Patrol.

I didn't open the damned thing for half an hour or so. I just let it lie there on my bed while I fiddled around and wondered what it said. I *knew* what it was going to say, that's why I didn't want to open it. Finally, just before we had to go pick up our weapons for the mission, I gave up and tore into the son of a bitch.

It was short and to the point. "Dear Jay, I went by and checked on your old lady like you said, and you were right. She's shacked up with a guy. This big black buck come to the door with just his shorts on. Write her ass off, Jay, she ain't no good. Bill."

Even if I was expecting it, the confirmation hit me like a punch in the stomach. Or a kick in the balls. I sat down on the bed and took a long, deep breath, trying to get control of myself. I was goddamned mad. The bitch had only been after my GI life insurance. She figured to fuck me for a few weeks and then play the grieving widow all the way to the bank. Her damned boyfriend probably moved in the day I left for 'Nam.

I dug down in my seabag and found the envelope with the form in it changing my life insurance beneficiary. I'd signed the damned thing but never sent it in. I tore it into little pieces and shit-canned it.

"Honey, I promise I'll take care of you when I get back from this little trip," I said to myself, and then put her out of my mind.

The night before the mission started we went to bed around 2100. They were to wake us at 0200 to get ready.

I didn't dream that last night, but I did think about what was going down. I guess everybody did. Just how good were we? We all had experience in sneaking into enemy camps and setting explosives and cutting throats, but not in kidnapping. The way we normally took prisoners was to blow away everybody around them, splash them with blood and brains, let them hear the bullets snap by their heads, and then yell at them to surrender. I didn't worry about the men doing their jobs right, but I did worry about how we would get back. If we got him without their knowing it, it would only be two hours or less until all hell broke loose when they checked on him and found him missing. If we fucked up, our families wouldn't even get a body back to sing and cry over at the funeral. This little bit of Arkansas clay would become part of the Vietnamese soil.

Getting back, that's where the real test would be.

In the middle of the night there was a soft knock on the door by an apologetic sailor. I hadn't slept a fucking wink, and apparently, Bob hadn't either. I hadn't heard him snore, and he got up immediately, red-eyed. He rubbed his face with his hands and used his favorite words a few times to get his mouth warmed up. "Shit, shit, shit, fuck, fuck, fuck, god-damn."

"Doin' yer mornin' exercises?" I asked. "Get the makeup . . . I'll meet you in the shitter."

The other guys were just coming out of their billets and going toward the head as I stepped out into the passageway. There was a muttered exchange of good-mornings, and I could tell from their glum faces they hadn't slept much either.

"Let's go get 'em, Jay," Tony said, putting his hand on my shoulder. *He* was cheerful, as usual.

"Fuckin' A," I replied. I went over to the stainless steel sink and turned on the warm water.

Bob came in and took the sink beside me. He handed me the camouflage paint, then started working on his own face. After a few minutes he backed off and admired his work in the mirror.

"Eat yer heart out, Twiggy," he said, turning his head this way and that.

I had to laugh. "Bob, if you was a model, they'd call you Stumpy."

He stopped admiring himself long enough to shoot me a finger. The guys laughed, and the mood lightened quite a bit.

"You hungry, Jay?" Bob asked.

Food was the last thing on my mind, but I didn't want my growling stomach giving my position away to the gooks, so I went to eat with the rest of the guys.

It was about 0245 and time to go. The twelve of us gathered on the foredeck of the *Eldorado* and a chief petty officer showed us to a truck that took us to the airstrip. When we unloaded beside the helicopter, I got everyone together and told the team to muster after we landed so we could regroup and get our bearings. I also told them to make damned sure they knew where each of the others was at all times when we got on the ground, and to stay within sight of one another so we could see hand signals. And they were to look behind them when they moved, not just for gooks, but so they would be seeing the terrain as they were going to see it coming back out, and would know the trail. Nobody said much when we boarded the chopper. Everyone was taking it damned serious, and they had good reason to.

The helicopter was one of Big Bird's sisters, big and black, with miniguns on sponsons and detachable fuel tanks for long-range work.

The rotors sped up and the pilot pulled back on the joystick, and we were airborne. As soon as we had leveled off I put my parachute on and started checking the rigging. Everyone else took their cue from me and did the same. Then we sat back down and waited. We wouldn't hook up to the anchor line cable this time. We were making a free fall.

Still no one said a word. We just looked around at each other, knowing that if one screwed up it could cost all of us our lives. The silence was broken by the pilot's voice.

"Stand by."

I looked down at my watch and it said 0330. Before I opened the door I had everyone synchronize their watches. I looked around at the men and reminded them, "Don't forget: fifteen minutes and muster. If you get caught up in a tree, hang tight. We'll find you. But try to stay close going down."

"Two minutes," the pilot said.

I unlatched the door and stood ready.

"Go!"

I went out, and quickly took the spread-eagle position. Once I was stabilized I glanced over at the altimeter on my left wrist. I had marked the critical altitude on the dial with a grease pencil, and hoped that I'd remembered to allow for lag in the instrument. I always avoided counting to myself, one thousand and one, one thousand and two, and so on, because once I started down I'd speed up—the sight of that ground coming up just naturally made you count faster. I avoided looking at the ground, too, because it would always fool you into popping your chute at the wrong altitude. On a dark night it appeared too far away until too late, and on a bright night it seemed too close, and in any case, without man-made objects to judge size by, visual estimates of altitude were undependable. One mistake and you were dead meat. When the altimeter needle was about to cut the mark, I pulled the ripcord.

As soon as the chute was open, I took a quick look around for the others. The first man out is usually at a disadvantage when it comes to looking for those following him, because he has to look up, past the open chute. When you free-fall to a given altitude, all the other chutes should pop at about that same altitude. Some pop early, of course, and some a little later, especially if they're keying on your chute instead of their altimeter. I spotted the chutes nearest me as they blossomed, but the treetops started coming up around me, and I had to concentrate on landing.

When we hit the ground I released my chute and gathered it up. Then I started looking and listening for the others. Someone had hit the ground about sixty feet from me. It turned out to be Tony. I headed toward him. When Tony had finished rolling his chute up, he went with me to the next man, and so on, until we had the whole group together.

"Okay, let's move out about a hundred yards and wait until daybreak. We'll bury the chutes. Bob, you and Tony take the far flanks. Quinn, you cover the rear, and I'll get the point. The rest of you fill in between." They signed that they understood. "Okay, let's do it," I said. I raised my rifle and headed out to take the point.

I wanted to wait and see if Charlie had heard the chopper when we flew over, or if there was a patrol in the area that might have seen our chutes or heard us land. You could never be sure where Charlie was. Sometimes he would pop out of nowhere. I also wanted to move during the daytime going up so we could study the terrain. That would make moving at night on the way back out a lot easier. We would have a better idea of where we were going.

We buried our chutes in a shallow hole with an M-5 pressure-release booby trap underneath. If Charlie found them, he'd get a hell of a surprise.

I looked up at the moon and saw that it was half full. It couldn't seem to make up its mind whose side it was on. I hoped that when things came to a pinch, it would be on ours.

It started getting light about 0545, and I motioned for them to move out. Charlie hadn't shown up, so we appeared to be safe for the moment.

None of us had worked in this area before, so we had to move slower than normal and with more caution. The brush was thicker than it was south of the DMZ, where big areas had been defoliated. The sun was almost up, and already I could tell it was going to be a hot day. There was a light mist rising from the ground that reminded me of the old vampire movies I used to watch back home. God! Were *they* ever spooky! God! Was *this* ever spooky! This was what you'd call a bad trip.

I had Magoun watch the treelines on the left and Casburn watch those on the right. I was sure the closer we got to the camp, the greater the odds that we'd see a patrol. We weren't to take anybody out or draw any attention in any way going in, and we couldn't leave any signs of our presence.

We didn't go straight toward the enemy camp but worked our way to it in a zigzag fashion, checking out the terrain about half a mile on either side of us as we went. I wanted to have the best route back to our LZ figured out, and to have an alternate route in case Charlie blocked the best one. It never hurt to be on the safe side.

The camp was about thirty-two miles from the LZ. We had gone almost six miles when I came upon a trail. I signed to Casburn and Magoun to halt. They relayed the message to the others, and I went forward to check it out. There had been some traffic along it, but just how long ago and how many I couldn't tell. I wished the Chief were here. The old Indian could've told me that, plus what they were carrying and what they'd had for breakfast. I didn't cross it. I followed it awhile to see which way it went. After a bit I could tell we would have to cross it sooner or later. It ran diagonally across our path. It wasn't very wide, so we could step across and not leave footprints. I went about four hundred yards to make sure it didn't turn toward Lang Mo before I turned back.

That was way too far, I knew. If a gook patrol

grabbed me that far away, and I didn't have a chance to shoot and warn them, the patrol could be ambushed. I would just have disappeared. I let an inexperienced man walk point once, and he just disappeared like that. He had only been forty yards or so ahead of us.

I went back to the men and signed for Casburn and Magoun to signal the men in. When they mustered up, I told them, "We have a trail up ahead, and we've got to cross it. I don't need to tell you not to leave any footprints on it. It's narrow enough that you can step from one side to the other, or hop across it, without stepping on it. Bob, you and Quinn set a booby trap, but don't arm it. We'll do that coming back out. When we come out, Charlie will take the trail if he's after us." It would be the fastest way to move through the bush, perhaps get ahead of us, and cut us off. "Mark it with that spray powder so you can find it at night. When we are across, take up your positions again and move on out."

By sundown we had only covered eighteen miles or so, as the bird flies, at least. That left another fourteen or fifteen to go. I decided to stop for the night, so when I spotted a good hidey-hole, I called them in, set four-hour watches, and posted two men with starlight scopes on opposite sides of the circle.

They spread out into the bush. Bob and I took up our positions, and he dug a roll of fishing line out of his pocket to tie our fingers together. He tied the end of the cord to his own finger and passed the roll to the next man. By the time it came around to me there was just enough to reach back to Bob. I put a loop around a twig because there were some things I needed to do before I settled down.

Looking at the map, I figured we were about five miles past Luat Son. We were also only ten to twelve miles from the Ho Chi Minh Trail network. *That* really made my asshole pucker. We infiltrated a lot of recon teams to watch traffic on the trail, and Charlie tried to keep them out, or discourage them at least, by setting booby traps along access routes to the trail. It was also heavily patrolled down this far, and the troops were hardcore. And if this Minh Tho was as important as the brass thought he was, the gooks would have their best watching him. I didn't want to tangle with them, but sooner or later we would have to.

I opened a can of C-ration peaches for "dinner." The juice helped quench my thirst and preserved the water in my canteen that I would've had to drink if I'd opened a can of beans and franks or lima beans and ham. Anyway, I wanted to avoid those, because they made me fart too much. The sound, not to mention the smell, could tip Charlie off if he came close. A slight breeze had sprung up as the sun set and the dusk grew into darkness, and it was blowing from Bob toward me. I sincerely hoped Bob would avoid the beans and franks too.

After I finished "dinner" I took a crap and buried the can in the same hole. Then I tied on to the fishing line and settled down to listen to the bush crack and pop as it cooled. I wasn't really sleepy, but I knew we would need all our strength later. I tried to get everything out of my mind so I could drift off, but I just kept coming back to thinking about the mission.

The moon rose to where I could see it through a clear space in the foliage overhead. It was half full. I guess that means we'll have a fifty-fifty chance, I thought. Wish you'd come down on my side on this one, Moon.

I was lying there thinking again about how we were going to cross the Ho Chi Minh Trail when I felt a tug on the string, followed quickly by two more. My watch already. My mind had been working so hard that time had just slipped away. It didn't mean a damn, though, because I was still bug-eyed. I rolled over to take my watch, and kept thinking about what lay ahead of us.

Even before the appearance of the faintest gray in the east, the night birds and insects stopped their quiet sounds, and the monkeys began to wake up. By the time dawn started to dispel the night gloom, they were screeching and chattering at each other, and the morning birds had begun to call. As it got lighter, the daytime insects started to sing. All this activity triggered a sense of unease, yet it was all normal. I thought back to yesterday's journey, and how a troop of monkeys just sat there in some trees almost within arm's reach and watched us walk by. It was unusual behavior.

The significance of it was now suddenly apparent. If the monkeys didn't run from us and alert the NVA that we were nearby, they wouldn't flee from the NVA patrols and alert us, either.

I tugged on the fishing line. Bob rolled toward me and half sat up, blinking the sleep out of his eyes. "What's wrong?" he asked, in a whisper.

"Bob, the damned monkeys—for the last three or four miles, yesterday, the monkeys just sat there and watched us go by."

"Oh, you noticed?" he interrupted, sarcastically.

"They're used to traffic in here. That's why they

didn't get scared off—they see people moving around all the time.''

He nodded as if he'd realized that all along. "You got it, bud." He looked at his watch. "Oh, well, 0530. Time to get up anyway."

I looked around at the growing light and agreed. "Wake 'em up. It's time to get moving."

Before we moved out I called the team together and reminded them of the monkeys and pointed out they weren't going to give us any warning of NVA patrols nearby. "That means we'll have to depend on our eyes more than our ears. Charlie will be doing the same, of course. But we're expecting Charlie, and with any luck, he ain't expecting us. So from now on, we're moving in close order, and each of you make damn sure you don't make any unnecessary noise. Keep your eyes open and check the rear."

The heat started to build almost as soon as the sun lifted above the horizon. We continued our zigzag movement just as we had the day before, but we expected Charlie to raise up out of every bush and blow someone away. Moving in the heat and constantly expecting an ambush put a mental and physical strain on us that wore us down quickly and slowed us considerably. I had hoped to cross the Ho Chi Minh Trail area in the early evening before we laagered up for the night, then press on to the camp in the early morning. It began to look as if that wouldn't be possible.

After covering six miles or so, the expected happened. I looked to my right, and Bingo! there he was, Charlie, moving slowly and scanning the area cautiously. I stopped and went down, signaling with my arm to halt, but never taking my eyes off him. Even though he was moving slowly he appeared to be at ease, so I figured he'd been this way before and was used to the area. I glanced to my left and saw nothing, but when the gook's head was turned, I looked back toward my men, and Thompson signaled there were three more out there. I decided we would be better off just to sit still and let them pass.

It took them about ten minutes to move on out of sight, but I waited five extra minutes before moving out.

Everything was pretty much routine for the next three miles or so. It was between 1300 and 1400 when I spotted another NVA. The bush was starting to thin out there, and I knew we were getting close to the Ho Chi Minh Trail. This one wasn't moving, he was sitting and looking around. He was almost directly in front of me and about twenty yards away. I spotted another one off to the right so I signaled for Bob, who was covering the right flank, to go check it out, and for Tony to get the left. When they returned they both signaled that there were two more on each flank. It looked like we had run right into the middle of an ambush but hadn't sprung it. Was it going to be another case like the return from Hanoi? Had the North Vietnamese been tipped off? Or had they just set the ambush as a routine precaution?

It was much too light for us to try to cross the ambush perimeter or even to move back, so we played the waiting game, where a minute became an hour, and an hour seemed to last all day. If your leg started to cramp you couldn't move it; if your asshole started to itch you couldn't scratch it. You had to sit absolutely still, unmoving, hardly breathing. I started worrying about the patrol that had passed us earlier. They might sweep back toward this ambush and catch us between them. They had to have a radio with them to report in now and again. If they didn't pull out, we would certainly have to take them out before we headed back out with Colonel Tho, because when they noticed he was missing they would contact all their patrols to be on the lookout. Somebody would have to come back and take out the ones with the radios just before we went in to get Tho. They could wait for us here. Bac Vo and Le Xuong had crossbows—they could do the job quietly.

Time dragged on, but eventually the sun set. As soon as it was dark enough to move, I went back to where the guys sat and called them together.

"How far do they spread?" I asked Bob and Tony. "How far would we have to go to get around them?" They just shook their heads. "All right, then we'll go between them. In pairs. They're spread out too far for night positions, and we can get through without being heard or seen. Bob, you and Thompson go first—Tony and I will bring up the rear. We'll regroup about fifty yards past them."

Bob and Thompson led the way, and we passed through without any problems. We regrouped just as planned, but a little closer to the ambush than I liked. I told Bob to *go* fifty yards the next time I *said* fifty yards. He probably shot me a dirty look and maybe even a finger, but I couldn't tell in the darkness. Not that I cared. I took one of the starlight scopes and had Bob take the other so he could see my hand signals. Then I took the point and left Bob with the main group.

The Ho Chi Minh Trail was about two miles in front of us now, and we had no idea what we might run into. I figured that once we were across it, we wouldn't see another patrol until we were within about a mile of the camp at Lang Mo. But there probably would be booby traps.

When I estimated we were within a quarter mile of the Trail I signaled Bob to bring the men up.

"Okay, watch your step, stay close, and keep checking the rear. We'll move in pairs, at thirty-second intervals, and we'll cross the Trail that way. Watch the pair ahead of you, and don't move on until they do. Go four hundred yards on the other side before we regroup. Look out for several trails . . . don't cross one and relax . . . there are three or four parallel trails in places."

Tony and I led the way. It was between 1930 and 2000 when we started across. Surprisingly, everything went smoothly. There was one trail at this point, really a narrow dirt road, and we crossed between columns of porters on bicycles after waiting for a dozen or so trucks to go past. The trucks were spread out and driving slowly with dim, hooded lights.

We regrouped as planned and headed toward the camp at Lang Mo. If we didn't run into any more trouble we would have a few hours to rest before sunup, and we all needed it. There wasn't a muscle in my body that hadn't been used on this trip.

Nobody had anything to say. They just listened and did what I asked. So far, I had been right in my decisions, and I hoped I could continue until we got back. They'd done well. I was damned proud of them. It isn't easy to move without making noise. It takes a lot of concentration and patience, and they are the two hardest things to maintain under pressure.

I just hoped that son of a bitch was worth what they were going through.

We passed Lang Mo, and it was 2205 when I saw a dim light over to the left. It could only be the camp, and I felt relief all over my body, like sinking down in a deep, cool pool on a hot day. It wasn't over half a mile away.

When the brush started to thin out I stopped and brought the guys on up. From there we could see the buildings and some soldiers moving around in the camp. Some were sentries they had posted. There were a few lights, like streetlights, but dim, and I was able to study the camp with binoculars.

Quinn put his hand on my shoulder and leaned close to whisper, ''Think they've got a cold beer in there, Jay?''

''I'm willing to bet my ass on it,'' I told him. My dry lips cracked when I grinned.

''Fuck the beer. I wonder if they got any pussy,'' Bob said.

I just looked at him and shook my head. Then I noticed the LDNNs, staring at me as if they wanted to take a look. I motioned them to come up and handed them the field glasses. Vo studied the camp for a few minutes and then passed the glasses to the next man.

''Well, what do you think, Vo?''

''You say piece of cake, I say piece of cake!'' he responded.

''Well, I say piece of cake, bro. Piece of cake.'' He liked that and so did the other three. They grinned and said something to each other in Vietnamese. About all I knew about them was that they had all lost their families in the war, and they had been fighting the communists since they were fourteen or fifteen. I judged them to be in their lower- to mid-twenties, except Le Xuong, who acted more like eighteen or nineteen. There was an air of pride about them as we lay there and watched the camp. They were proud to have gotten this far into the enemy's territory, proud to be members of South Vietnam's elite SEALs, proud to be trusted members of our team. And they were eager to get Tho. It would be an honor for them, and it would give them something to brag about to their kids and grandkids.

I told everyone else to stay put while four of us checked out the immediate area for security patrols. I didn't want to start the recon until the morning, so I told them we would just make sure there weren't any close by, then rest until morning. I took Bob, Tony, and Casburn. We found no one in the immediate area, but we found a dense clump of bush to hide in.

It was 2300 when I posted the first watch. I had the Viets take the first watch for three hours, Thompson, Quinn, Fitchew, and me the next three, and Tony, Magoun, and Bob the last watch because I wanted them rested especially well. They were the most experienced. Also, Magoun was our sniper, and I wanted his eyes rested in case we needed a long kill. We slept close together so that if anyone started to snore, someone could reach him to wake him. I made them all roll over on their sides or face down to go to sleep because they would be more likely to snore if they lay on their backs.

I was feeling much more relaxed now that we were here. I silently said good night to the moon peeping at us through the treetops and went right to sleep.

CHAPTER 15

When everybody was awake, I started assigning duties.

"Bob, you, Casburn, and Xuong check out the sentries on the right. Find out how many there are and how often they are relieved. See how close we can get to them. Also, how close together they are. Tony and I and Hu will do the same on the left. Thompson, Quinn, check out the area right in front of us here. Magoun, Vo, Bao—watch the buildings and movement in the camp. See if you can spot their generators and ammo dump. Be back here by 1700. Any questions?"

There weren't. We moved out. I had Tony take my left flank and Hu the right. We moved out to the left about four hundred yards and turned in toward the camp. We were about sixty feet apart and stayed where we could see one another. I was surprised how close we got before we saw the first sentry. Tony spotted him. I stopped and started looking for another one in my area, but didn't see any. I motioned for Hu to advance when I did, but we didn't go more than twenty feet before I spotted one. When I looked over to Hu, he was already signaling me that he had also spotted one. They were about the same distance apart as we were. They barely moved as they watched the bush in front of them. Every now and then they would look toward one another. Again we played the waiting game and time dragged on. I estimated we were about fifty yards from their kill zone. We still had fair cover and could maybe get another forty or fifty feet closer and be safe. I could hear faint voices coming from the camp.

At about 1000, I saw the gook looking back over his shoulder so I looked past him and saw another NVA walking toward him. It was his relief. If the time schedule was regular, they relieved sentries every four hours. The two sentries stood and talked for a few minutes before the one who had been relieved started back toward camp. The new sentry had a radio slung over his shoulder. I waited for him to settle in on his watch, then motioned for Tony and Hu to back off and move on farther to the left. We needed to see how many sentries there were down that way and, if we could, find where the patrols were going in and out.

We went another hundred yards and started forward again but didn't get very far before we spotted another sentry. We still hadn't seen a trail where their patrols were entering and leaving. A little after 1400 the sentries were relieved. So far, it appeared we would have at least four hours to get in, get Tho, and get out before they found the dead guards. I hoped Bob's group could report they had found where the NVA patrols were entering and leaving the camp. I motioned for Tony and Hu to head on back to where we'd split up from the others.

Bob reported that they'd spotted eight posted NVA about seventy feet apart and that they each stood a four-hour watch. He also thought we could get a little closer and be safe. Thompson said there were four buildings that had NVA troops going in and out constantly but the one closest to us seemed to have more officers entering and leaving. Bao said that, judging from the photos of the camp, that was the one we wanted, but to be sure, we would have to get a closer look. Also, it looked as if the NVA opened the doors and windows and left them open all day. There was a three-man jeep patrol that came around at irregular intervals, and the jeep was mounted with a heavy machine gun. That could be a real complicating factor.

My mind started to tick. If we could get in close enough to see inside the building when the doors and windows were open, we could figure out at least part of the layout. Our next step was to see if the sentries moved in closer at night and if they stood longer or shorter watches. I sent Bob, Casburn, and Magoun back out to the right when the sun had almost set, and Tony, Thompson, and Quinn back to the left. I took Vo and Bao to try to get in closer to the buildings for a closer look. If we found enough cover we could stay there all night and the next day. I would send one of the others back to let Bob know if we were going to stay over.

The two LDNNs and I moved out toward the camp. We ran into a sentry about two hundred feet from where we left the group. Slowly we moved forward, trying not to make any noise. We were almost within spitting distance when he turned and looked in my direction. I almost peed in my pants. I pointed my rifle at him and watched every move he made. I hadn't made any noise, but he might have seen my movement out of the corner of his eye. Something had caught his attention. He looked hard and long before he turned his head back and started his routine again. I moved on, and the two LDNNs followed. They were so quiet I had to look back to be sure they were there. The bush was getting a lot thinner, and I was looking for a place to hide. Over toward the suspect building the brush hadn't been thinned out so much as elsewhere.

I motioned for the LDNNs to move out in that direction. We were moving off to the right, staying low and checking the ground in front of us for booby traps. The bush I had spotted for cover hadn't been thinned at all. I guessed it was an emergency exit.

The sun wasn't up yet, but the sky was getting a little brighter. I couldn't see what was on the other side of the brushy patch, and I thought it would be a good idea to check it out before we entered. I told Vo to see how far back it ran and Bao to see how wide it was. I would check out the middle. If we were going to hide in there, I damned sure wanted good cover.

It was plenty thick enough to hide us, and from it we could get a good look at the south end of the building we were interested in. The front faced west. There was an exit on the south end. The building was about forty feet wide. By moving a little bit you could get a view of either the front or the rear. I heard a noise on my left. It was Bao, with Vo close behind. They reported that the area looked clear of booby traps or concertina wire and was about fifty meters wide. It went back about sixty meters, and it didn't seem to get any thinner. I mentally translated those distances to 150 by 200 feet so I could picture it in my mind. Vo also had spotted a sentry off to the left. I decided it was definitely an escape route. If there was an air strike or a raid, the officers could exit out the south door right into the bush. They probably had a slit trench or air raid shelter in there. It was getting near dawn and I had to make my mind up before it got too bright to be moving around. I sent Bao back to tell Bob we were staying.

We got in as close as we could, keeping bush between us and the building for cover. By looking around carefully as I moved in, I found their slit trench. It was well camouflaged and partly roofed over with sandbags. I moved toward the left edge of the brush so I could watch the front and south end. Vo went off to the right to watch the rear. I lay down on my stomach and laid my field glasses and weapon in front of me.

The sun was up and people began to stir. I hoped to get a look at Tho if he left the building. There were two sentries posted in front, and one at the south end who didn't seem to be paying much attention to the bush in front of him where I was lying.

Gooks came and went all day but not through the south door. At about 0915, a Russian-made jeep pulled up in front. A noncom stepped out and went inside. Twenty minutes later, he came out with Tho behind him. I had looked at pictures of his damned slope head so much that I couldn't mistake him. They got in the jeep, turned around, and headed north down the street. They were soon out of my sight.

Moments later the south door opened and two more noncoms came out. After they bullshitted a while with the sentry they went off to my left. Around 1000 the watch was changed. The new sentry was just as relaxed as the first one. The south door was left open, and I could see down the entire length of the hall. Looking through my field glasses, I could see there was a cross-hall about halfway down the other end of the hall, probably leading to the east and west entrances. At the north end was an office-type door; it was closed. Every now and then I would see a soldier walk across the end of the hall, so I could tell it made a T there. From where I was, I could only see three or maybe four doors on the right of the hall. The rooms might be offices, or billets for officers, or even billets for the sentries.

I was starting to get stiff and needed to move. I waited until the guard walked to the end of the building and leaned up against it. When he did I slowly moved to the right but not out of sight of the front. It felt good to move my legs and stretch.

The jeep patrol passed twice, at 1038 and 1302.

Around 1400, Tho returned, got out of the jeep, and went in the front door. The watch was changed a little late, at 1635. Everything was going smoothly for us so far.

Tho and two other officers came out and walked across to a building just across the street and went in.

As the sun was starting to set, I heard an engine start up. Soon lights started to appear in some of the buildings, so I knew I'd heard the generator. I couldn't tell just where it was, and I hoped Vo could tell. If things went badly we could knock out their generator and kill the lights. There was a light on a pole, just off to the corner of the building to my left, that lit up the front and south end of Tho's building, though it wasn't very bright. There was another near the north end. It seemed odd to leave lights on at night. They would make the place a very easy target to spot for bombing. Maybe they felt secure with all the SAM sites and AA guns they had around. Or maybe they realized the B-52s aimed their bombs with radar, and a blackout wouldn't help them much.

It was just after 1800 when Tho came back. About thirty minutes later two jeeps pulled up and three officers got out and went inside. With the light on, I wished I was on the east side so I could see in. After an hour had passed, a gook came out and said something to the drivers of the jeeps and they drove off. It was around 2000 and time to meet Vo and head back.

Vo told me he had seen a light come on about 1800 in a large room about midway down the length of the building. That could have been where Tho and the officers went. Vo had heard the generator too, but couldn't tell which building it was in.

Bob was waiting for us when we got back. He seemed a little anxious. "How did it go?" he wanted to know.

"Get 'em in here. It's time to rock 'n' roll," I said.

I didn't know if it would work, but I had a plan. It took about an hour for everyone to get in from their post positions. When they had mustered up I described the building and the layout of the camp to them and outlined the plan.

"Thompson, you and Hu take one of the starlight scopes and go back where the ambush was set, back by the Ho Chi Minh Trail. Get the gooks that have the radios, and any others you think you should get. Use the crossbow. Open a good-sized gap in their ambush line, then set a perimeter of claymores to keep them from closing it. Meet us back where we crossed the trail. Set some command-detonated claymores there to clear the trail about a hundred yards in either direction just in case there's traffic when we come back through and we're in a hurry. If we aren't there by 2200 tomorrow, you get the fuck out and go on back to the LZ. Take some claymores from the other guys here to be sure you have enough. You got it?"

Thompson repeated his instructions back to me, and I told him and Hu to take off.

"Quinn, Casburn, we're goin' to need about forty yards of area down to the right cleared of sentries, so yer goin' to have to take out at least three of them. Wait until they've been relieved, about 0200. That's when we're goin' in. Once you have them down, set claymores to take out anybody that comes running down the street from either direction, and then stand by there to cover our withdrawal.

"Bob, you and Tony and Xuong will go in with me. Make sure you've got the handcuffs and the tape and all the other shit we'll need. Fitchew, you keep the radio. You're rear security. Find us a place to hide about two hundred yards back out in the trees. There will probably be shooting, and I want to lay low with the asshole if the whole damned camp turns out to hunt us. So make damn sure it's a damned good place."

"We're not going to be moving at night?" he asked.

"If there's an alarm, this place is going to be crawling with gooks," Bob answered for me. "We can see them a hell of a lot better in the daylight, and make better time when we move." It was good to hear he agreed with me.

"If it gets really bad before we can get out of the camp, there's a slit trench in that bushy patch beside the building," I told them. "We'll try hiding in there. But only in an emergency.

"Joe, you get in position to take out the sentry in front of the building—and the one on the north side, too, if you can. Don't get too far away from Casburn and Quinn, though. I want to be able to pull out in a hurry."

To the others, I described what I had been able to make out of the hall in the officers' quarters.

"When we go in," I told them, "I want one man to post right away at the cross-hall, and one to go down to post at the T. The other two of us will check the rooms. Make sure you've got plenty of magazines and that your silencers are on your weapons. Use grenades only if the shit hits the fan and we have to get out under fire."

Bob and I would take out the sentries on the south and east sides. Then Vo and Bao would get into NVA uniforms and replace them.

"Any questions?" I asked when I'd finished. "Let's get going, then."

Quinn and Casburn moved off to the right. The rest moved out with me at the point. Before, time seemed to drag along, but now it began to pass more quickly. It wasn't long until we were back to the bush where

Vo and I had hidden. It was a little after 2400 when we arrived. The door to the building that Tho had come out of was open now. Raising the field glasses to my eyes, I could see a gook with a set of headphones sitting in a chair. I couldn't see what was in front of him, but I could tell the building was the commo shack. That radioman would have to be taken out.

"Magoun, come here and see if you can see this son of a bitch clear enough to get a clean shot," I said.

He moved over to where I was sitting and raised his rifle to his shoulder, sighting through the scope. "I can get 'im if he doesn't move much. Otherwise, I'll have to move back to the left and maybe shoot him through the windowpane."

"Okay, then. As soon as the guard is changed, take him out. Then stand by to take that front sentry out too, but don't shoot him unless he starts inside or we come out shooting." He was already screwing the big silencer onto his rifle barrel.

"Time?"

"It's 12:45, Jay," Bob answered.

As fast as time was passing now, from here on in we would be working against it.

"Tony, Bob, you'll go in with me. I'll enter first and start down the hall. Now, I don't know what's in the damned place or how many gooks are in there, but if even one shows his face, bust a cap in his ass and start for the door. I'm going to take a chance and say that Tho's billet will be at the end of the hall, on the right. If I'm wrong, we're fucked. Also, if we have to open up, Bob, you and Tony set a time delay to blow the place to hell. But only if we have to open fire.''

"Holy shit, I hope you're right," Bob said.

Pointing to Vo, I said, "You'll replace the sentry on the south end when I take him out. Cover me until I get him. Bob, you and Bao take out the sentry on the east side. No knives—I don't want blood all over the side of the building to alert somebody. Snap his neck.''

It was 0100 and we started moving into position. The light on the pole was on but it wasn't very bright. It lit up only about half of the south side of the building. The door was in shadow, and that would make it a lot easier to get in without being seen. The only problem was the amount of open ground we had to cross.

I took my boots off so I could move in more quietly. The others followed my example. We stuffed the boots in our packs and left the packs where we could grab them when we came out of the building.

The duty sentry seemed relaxed and didn't walk a set pattern, but I would have to watch his relief for a few minutes before I moved in. Bob would have to do the same.

Everything was quiet in the camp around 0130 when the door opened and a gook stepped out. The sentry turned to talk to him. The night was still and very quiet, and you could hear them talking plainly. I could see past them into the building. A glow was visible at the end of the hall, but I didn't see any light in the hall itself. The two gooks bullshitted for a while, then the other dude went back inside.

I looked over at Vo and asked him if he could make out what they were saying.

"He say he gots the shits but he come back, relieve the sentry soon as he get out of shitter. The sentry ask if the meeting over, and the other he say yes, they just talking now. You say 'bullshitting.' "

About fifteen minutes later the door opened again and the guy with the shits came out and relieved the sentry. Yawning, the former sentry waved goodbye and walked around the corner and on down the road. I waited until he had gone, then motioned Magoun to bust the fucker in the radio shack. I watched until I saw the man's body go limp. The shot was no louder than someone spitting forcefully. Then I turned my attention back to the sentry by the door. He'd noticed nothing.

It wasn't quite 0200. I watched him as he walked a regular beat back and forth in front of the door. When he turned around he would stop, look over at the other sentry, then step back with his left foot, turning as he did so. It was more casual than an about-face, but similar. He made a counter-clockwise turn at both ends of the beat, so when he was at the west end, he turned facing the bush, but when he was on the east end, he turned toward the building. A fatal habit. When he made his turn toward the building, I would make my move.

Of course, I had to coordinate with Bob. His sentry was walking a longer beat, so their turns didn't often coincide. We had to wait several turns until his man was turned and going back north and mine was just making his turn. In order to be within sight of one another but not be seen by the sentries, we had to be close together. That put us in a position where I'd have to cover twice as much ground as Bob.

When the sentry started back toward the east, I

slung the AK-47 over my back and made sure it was strapped down tight. I checked to make sure that my knife was handy, up by my left shoulder. I was ready to go. He was in a bad way, all right. He hadn't made it to the corner when he stopped and half turned toward the building, bending over from cramps in his belly. He put one hand on his gut and the other on his left knee. Bob's man had turned and started back. Bob moved, then hesitated. I moved. It was now or never.

I covered the ground between us at a sprint. I had to get to him before the cramps passed and he turned back toward the corner.

I got there just as he straightened a little. My left forearm slammed into the back of his tiny little neck and my hand clamped down on his right shoulder. The impact snapped his head up, and my right hand caught the front of his pith helmet and snapped it back. He didn't yell, and his neck was broken before he could even grab for my arm. His bowels emptied down his legs, loose and smelly.

Vo stepped right in and took over the sentry routine. I carried the body back to the bush. To drag it would have left marks. Of course, I got shit all over my arm. I laid him down where Magoun was crouching.

"If he moves, kill him," I said.

"Shit!" he said, with that gee-whiz grin of his.

"He did," I pointed out.

About five minutes later Bob showed up and stepped on the dead gook.

"What the hell?" he whispered. "Damn it, Tyler, why don't you put the son of a bitch in the way? I could've sprained an ankle."

"Bitch, bitch, bitch," I said. "Shut up and let's go."

We headed for the open door. Vo and Bao continued their sentry routines as if we didn't exist. In the dim light they were indistinguishable from the two they'd replaced. Vo even pretended to have a belly cramp at times.

We stopped for a second in the shadow of the entryway, until all four of us were there and ready to go in.

"Have to give them boys an Oscar," I whispered to Bob.

"I hope he don't overdo it," Bob whispered back. "They might relieve him and take him to the sick bay."

We switched our AK-47s to fully automatic. I opened the door slowly, just a crack, and looked down the hall. It was empty, and lit by only the dim glow I'd seen before. I opened the door wider and went in, with Bob and Tony right behind me.

The hall was dark, and I looked at the bottoms of the doors to see if there was any light showing through the cracks. We moved quickly but quietly. At the cross-hall, I signaled Tony to stay and cover all directions, and Xuong to go on down to the T. There was a door down on the right with a light shining through the crack at the bottom. I elbowed Bob and pointed to it. We had to check it out before we could start searching for Tho. Bob moved over to the other side of the door and put his hand on the knob, ready to push it open. I could hear voices coming from the other side.

I nodded and Bob pushed the door open. We went in fast, in a crouch. It was a big room laid out for a conference, with a long mahogany table opposite the door. There were six gooks in it, four sitting round one end of the table with a teapot and some teacups on the table in front of them. One man was sitting sideways on a chair between the table and the door. The sixth was standing near the head of the table, as if he'd been just about to leave and had stopped to bullshit for a minute more. Tho was the second man from the right end of the table. For the briefest instant we all froze, looking at one another. The image burned into my memory, and probably Tho's, as I looked right into his eyes and watched them widen with surprise.

The gook sitting sideways on the chair grabbed for something at his side and started to stand up. Bob had no choice. He opened up. When he fired, I did too. I shot the one standing at the end of the table and the one just to the right of Tho. Bob swung his gun to the right as I swung mine to the left. The gooks' bodies danced in the chairs and pieces of wood and teacups flew around the room. A chair fell over with a bang as the body in it slumped to the side. Ejected brass rattled onto the floor and rolled around underfoot. A piece of china flew up and nicked Tho's cheek, and he started to raise his hand to his face, then froze.

"That was the smartest move you ever made," I growled at him. I stuck my AK-47 in his face and then grabbed him by his shirt, lifting him to his feet and shoving his face against the wall. The scratch on his cheek left a smear of blood. "Don't move, don't make a fucking sound!" I told him. Bob quickly kicked the weapons away from the others, in case they were playing possum or came to, and then he stepped over and clapped the handcuffs on Tho. He taped over his mouth with a wide roll of green plastic tape, going around his head twice.

"We got 'im," I said to Bob. "Let's go!"

I pushed Tho ahead of me to the door. Bob got there first and checked both ways before stepping out into the hall. Tho stepped on some empty brass and it rolled under his foot, sending him to one knee. I grabbed him by the collar in the back and yanked him to his feet. As soon as Bob went out, I went and pushed Tho out in front of me. We rounded the corner and started for the south door, Bob ready for anything, and me holding Tho by his shirt collar and pushing him along, my AK in one hand.

The silencers really muffled our shots. All you heard was a sibilant stutter, but there was no way to muffle the drumming noise of the bullets hitting the table or the teacups smashing. Someone would be coming to see what all the racket was about very soon. I expected to see doors open and heads stick out all down the hall.

Tony waved at Xuong to come on, and was repeating in a loud whisper, "Let's go! Let's go! Let's go!"

One door opened as we went past, and a man stepped out, rubbing sleep from his eyes. He dropped his hands and stared when he saw me pushing Tho along. Tony shot him from close range. The man slipped to the floor without a sound.

Bob stopped to cover Tony and Xuong as they came down the hall, and I pushed past him with Tho. I stopped in the shadow of the entryway and looked over at Vo. He was still walking his sentry rounds. He stopped at the west end of the beat, looked at the sentry on his right, and started back. I knew then the sentry in front hadn't been alerted. Once outside I headed into the bush and held up there until the guys were all out of the building. Magoun and Vo were covering the front. Bao was covering the rear. None of the sentries outside had been alerted by the firing inside.

Once they were outside, they headed for the tree-line. They waved to Bao, and he came at a dead run. I took off too. I still had Tho by the shirt and was halfway dragging him. He knew better than to try to fight. He knew he was the one we'd been after and he wouldn't be hurt as long as he did what we wanted him to do. We must have frightened him, though. All of us were so damned much bigger than he was, and younger and stronger. Hell, sometimes I looked around at those green- and black-painted faces, with the intense eyes about the only thing you could see in the darkness, and they frightened *me*.

We grabbed our packs on the run and beat it on back to the treeline. We had gone about a hundred yards when we heard Casburn whistle from off to the left and headed in that direction.

"Did you get 'im?" he wanted to know. Then he saw our little prisoner and said, "Well, goddamn!"

"Get Quinn and Fitchew in here," I told him, and he left to round them up.

Those of us with our boots off hurried to put them on. The bottoms of my feet were tender, and my right heel was bruised from coming down on an ejected cartridge. Bob's foot was cut by a piece of broken teacup and bleeding a little. He took the time to apply a disinfectant before putting on his boot. Then we all shouldered our packs. We were ready when the other three showed up.

Bob and I took the point, and Bao and Xuong the flanks. Fitchew stayed behind with the radio. He would let us go about 150 yards before he followed us, to watch for any pursuit. I put Vo in charge of the prisoner, because he was the steadiest of the three Viets. We cuffed Tho's hands in front of him so he could keep his balance better and wouldn't slow us down so much. Just to make sure he didn't get away, we taped a grenade between his wrists and attached a wire to the pin. We ran the wire between his legs and tied it to the middle of a stick about three feet long. Hu carried the stick. If Tho tried to run away, even if Hu was shot and down, the stick would catch on the brush and pull the pin. And the grenade was right there in front of him, where he could see it and ponder on it.

All this hadn't taken long. It was just after 0200 when we went in, and it was about 0220 when we moved out.

We went about a mile from the camp before we stopped. I figured they would mount a really intense search right around the camp as soon as they found out we'd been there, and they'd find that out when one of the sentries on the west or north sides began to wonder why they weren't seeing those on the south and east sides anymore, and went to check on them. I expected the alarm was given about the time we moved out, but Fitchew didn't report any pursuit. Their next step would be to put out a cordon of patrols to try to cut us off. They'd have to estimate our rate of travel and try to put their patrols in ahead of us. By not moving for several hours, we might throw their timing off. They might have their patrols farther out. We'd get to them after they had searched several hours without success, and they would be starting to get discouraged and tired. And careless.

They'd also try to guess which way we would go. Straight south toward the DMZ was too obvious. West across the border into Laos would lead into the mountains. The route we were taking led right past the town of Lang Mo, and I thought it would seem to the North Vietnamese the least likely for us to take.

Casburn found a thick stand of brush for us to hide in. "It's heavy all back through here," he said.

"Okay. Spread out about thirty feet apart. We're going to play hide-and-seek." I retaped Tho's mouth, going all the way around his head with that wide plastic tape. He was breathing hard from exertion, and his breath whistled and bubbled through his nostrils, like his nose was stopped up. To Vo I said, "Tell this son of a bitch if he even breathes heavy we'll take one of his eyes out. And if he does, do it." Tho was supposed to speak English, but he looked a little dazed, and I wanted to be sure he understood. I left him with Vo and moved off to the right to cover myself with brush. It was time to play the waiting game again. It was around 0340 when we spread out to hide. Time would go slow until dawn.

It was close to 0500 when I heard movement in the bush coming from the direction of Lang Mo. I saw nothing but I knew he was out there. I switched my AK back to fully automatic and turned it in the direction the noise came from. Suddenly I heard a branch whip against something off to my right. There was more than one now, and probably more on the way. The noise was getting louder so I looked for a place to move to in case they decided to walk over my ass. I was looking hard into the bush in the hope of seeing where the son of a bitch was and which way he was moving.

"Come on, asshole, I just want to see your pointed little head," I thought. Bingo! there he was about twenty feet to my right. He was heading toward Bao and Tho. If he kept moving in the same direction he would pass between us. I turned back and looked to the left. Holy shit! I thought. I could see a gook's ass no more than ten feet from me, and I hadn't heard him at all. I froze. He was looking long and hard into the bush, turning his head slowly until he was looking in my direction. I didn't take my eyes off him, but I was aware that the other one was going on past. I dared not move. It was only seconds later that their footsteps faded away and I relaxed. They were heading back toward the camp.

Right before sunup, around 0530, I decided to scout ahead. We hadn't had much sleep, and my eyes felt scratchy every time I blinked. I moved back off to my left and back toward the Ho Chi Minh Trail and covered a hundred yards or so. Not seeing anybody I headed back toward the men. Bob spotted me and whistled softly. I went over to him.

"Anything?" he asked.

"No," I said. "How about you?"

"Not since that bunch that came through earlier. I think we ought to get our asses out of here, though."

I agreed, and signaled the men to regroup.

"How's the baby?" I asked Vo.

"He good," Vo said, grinning. "He good baby!" He prodded Tho, kneeling in front of him, with his rifle barrel.

"We're going to move on toward the LZ. Tony, you and Bob take the flanks. Casburn and Magoun cover the rear. I'll take the point. Keep each other in sight."

I headed out in front. We didn't have a lot of ground to cover to get to the rendezvous with Thompson and Hu, but it would be slow going. We had until 2200 to meet them, and I damned sure didn't want to miss our date.

The sun was all the way up, and even though the bush shaded us, it was still hot and humid. Our bodies were weak and wet with sweat but we kept pushing on. Every now and then the hot sweat would run down my forehead and into my eyes, causing them to blur and burn. My muscles were tight and sore from tension, and my right heel was bothering where it was bruised. But I knew better than to think about it. We had learned how to live with pain. It came with 'Nam, and I guess with any war.

We encountered the next patrol shortly after 1300, near the Song Dai Giang, south of Lang Mo. We had another two miles to go to the Ho Chi Minh Trail, and had to cross the river first. I had just stopped and was looking around for Bob and Tony when I heard a sound. I didn't know at first what it was, but it was definitely not natural. I was looking back to the right toward Tony at the time, and it seemed to come from in front of us. I began to curse my bad hearing in that left ear, and tried to keep my right ear turned in the right direction, but I couldn't do that and look for Tony. I finally spotted him, far out on the right and considerably behind me. I signed for him to hold up and halt the others. Then I turned to the left, to listen with my good ear and look for Bob at the same time.

I spotted Quinn, and signaled him to halt and pass the signal on. Then I squatted down to listen.

I didn't have long to listen before I heard it again, plainly, now that I had my good ear turned toward it: the frying sound of a radio receiver followed by the garbled murmur of someone talking. "Ambush!" was my first thought, but I could see no one. I even got out the binoculars, but they didn't help. I kept looking back at Tony and Quinn, but they signaled that they couldn't see anything either. We didn't dare move until we could figure out where they were, though I was sweating from worry that we'd been spotted and a patrol was on its way.

We waited until 1400, trying to spot them through the leaves and moving v-e-r-y slowly to improve our angle of vision, all without success. Then the radio crackled and someone spoke again, and four NVA got up from a tangle of undergrowth about thirty feet in front of me and sauntered off to the right, apparently unaware of us.

We let them go, but now I had a new worry. The listening post had been called in. Why? Had Thompson and Hu been caught?

We lucked out by not having to give our position away. I knew we were close to the Trail and that it would be patrolled heavily. I waited until 1900 before attempting the river crossing. We couldn't afford to wait until it was pitch dark, but I wanted it as dark as could be. First we patrolled up and down both riverbanks to see if they were clear, and repeatedly checked the other bank with binoculars. Then we crossed, one at a time. Bob carried Tho across, with five of us on the east bank and four on the west, covering him.

It was 2000 when we mustered on the east bank and headed for our rendezvous with Thompson and Hu at the Trail. We had two miles to go, and two hours to do it in, in the dark. We were going to be cutting it close.

We didn't run into any more patrols before we got to the Trail, but when we got there the area didn't look familiar. We worked back to the left first, then to the right, trying to locate our crossing. Time was getting tight, and I hoped they would give us a few extra minutes before they pulled out. Then Bob located a mark he'd made with fluorescent paint, and we knew we were close. I took a chance and broke squelch on my handset: two short pops, two longs, two shorts. A question mark. To my relief, there was a reply: one long. A "T." It was followed by a pause and then two short blips. All clear.

I called him up, then, and asked how it looked.

"The traffic is intermittent, either heavy or none at all, and it seems to be clear now," he said.

"Do you know why the chickens cross the road?" I asked him.

"To get to the other side, I guess," he replied. "I hope the chickens look both ways."

Damn, it was good to hear him. Bob and I went over to him when we got everyone across.

"How did it go?" he asked.

"We got him. How did it go with you?" Bob wanted to know.

"They moved their damned ambush," he told us. We were all sitting with our faces inches apart, talking in low tones. "We waited—we didn't want to hit them too soon—and the fuckers moved to a spot about a half mile from the Trail and right across our route again. They set up their ambush again there, but they're still spread wide apart. We took out three, including the radioman. We set the claymores to cover the sides of the gap, then beat it back over here. We got here twenty minutes before you did.''

"Been any increase in activity this morning?'' I asked.

"Shit, they know you've got him, and they're looking down this way. They've had a chopper fly over the area and set down not far from here, and there's been some traffic on the Trail. Trucks in the daylight, full of troops, jeep patrols, that kind. I'd say they've dropped off troops farther south and are working their way back north looking for us.''

"No shit! You should be squad leader, bud,'' I said jokingly. Bob gave me a dirty look and Thompson grinned. I went on, "What do you think is the best course of action?''

"Let's get the fuck out of here,'' he said.

"I'll buy that,'' Bob said.

"Collect your claymores,'' I told him.

We moved out cautiously and approached the ambush very carefully. Hu had done his job well with the crossbow. The other gooks hadn't noticed the dead ones were missing. We passed easily through the gap, and once we were on the other side, we picked up the pace. We'd gone half a mile beyond the ambush when we heard one of Thompson's claymores go off. Some gook had gone to check on his buddy. After that, we moved faster. We didn't run, but damned near it. The pace was so fast for so long that Colonel Tho began to have problems breathing through his snotty nose, and we had to slow down to let him get his breath. I didn't really feel sorry for the bastard, it was just that if he passed out, someone would have to carry his ass.

At about 0430, we were nearly to the LZ, and I called in for a pickup. We stayed about thirty-five to forty yards back, and I sent six of the men out to check and make sure that Charlie wasn't lurking somewhere nearby. When I heard the helicopter coming, I called them back in. By 0500 we were loading onto a big green and black chopper that was hovering right above the grass.

There were a couple of agents on that helicopter, in paramilitary uniforms without any identifying devices. They flashed badges at us and took over Tho. They put leg irons on him that were attached to the tie-downs of the chopper, and they left his hands cuffed and his mouth taped.

It was a forty-five-minute flight back to Quang Tri.

When we got there they took him away, and we were debriefed. I sat there in the debriefing and thought, "Not one casualty. Not one fucking casualty." I felt pretty damned proud of myself, and of them. But my feet hurt.

CHAPTER 16

After the business with Minh Tho, Captain Gartley thought we needed some R-and-R, and no one was going to argue with him. The last few weeks had been hard ones, and we had a break coming. We talked it over among ourselves and decided we wanted to go to Australia. Of course, the Navy arranged for us to go to Hong Kong, but we told them we didn't want to see any more Orientals, or strip joints, or brothels, that all we were interested in was round-eyed women and sunny beaches. Gartley fussed a little about the inconvenience of having to change the arrangements, but several of us said we'd as soon not go, and the next day, we were on our way to Sydney.

Sydney was everything I expected it to be. I had heard other GIs talk about how beautiful the beaches were, and that the women outnumbered the men five to one. When I saw it, I got butterflies in my stomach. How would the people who lived there react to us? Would they accept us? Here we were, saying, "We want to relax and enjoy your beaches and flirt with your women, and be accepted by you ordinary people who've never killed anybody in your lives. Just forget we're a band of killers and kidnappers and treat us like normal young men, like kids on a holiday." It had to be something like going home. I suddenly felt I needed another bath, that the stench of death and jungle rot still clung to me.

We arrived at the airport at about 0730 and were soon on our way to the motel on the beach. It seemed strange to be around so many round-eyed people. Bob, Tony, Quinn, and I shared a cab, and the other guys split a second. We all stayed at the same motel, but the rooms were on different floors. I wanted to be by myself, so Bob and Tony shared a room. We stopped on the way and got some beer and I bought a cheap little Styrofoam cooler to ice it down. Bob said, "Get me one, too, would ye, Tyler?" so I picked up a second one and held them out to him to choose which one he wanted. He picked the one in my right hand, goddamn it.

We got to our rooms about 0830. I had my gear and the cooler in my hands, so I set the gear down to unlock the door. I propped the door open with my foot and picked up the cooler with one hand to set it inside the door, but before I could set it down, the damned handle pulled out and the side cracked about a fourth of the way down, spilling beer and ice on the floor.

"You son of a bitch!" I said, thinking a run of bad luck was beginning. I got the rest of my gear out of the hall and grabbed a beer off the floor before I started to unpack. Of course, it spewed all over my pants when I opened it.

It was a beachfront room, with a little balcony, and the view was beautiful. I contented myself with opening the curtain and looking down at the ladies lying out on the beach. They were wearing tiny bikinis of the sort that would start a riot in the Midwest.

Bob and Tony came down the hall laughing and joking. I guessed they had already changed and were heading for the beach. As they walked by, Bob knocked on the door and hollered, "Let's go, asshole! Time's a-wastin'!" Their footsteps continued on, so I didn't bother to answer.

I took time to shower, just because it felt good, and because I wanted to scrub the rest of the Vietnamese dirt and rot out of my pores with clean, non-Vietnamese water. It was great to have all the hot water I wanted and to be in an uncramped shower stall.

Afterward, I took my beer out on the balcony and looked down at the beach to see if I could spot the guys. I saw Bob and Tony talking to a couple of girls that were lying out. The others were sitting nearby drinking beer. It looked like everybody was doing okay without my help, so I went over and lay down on the bed, without even throwing back the spread. It was soft and felt really good, and of course it wasn't long before I dozed off.

I dreamed a little about home, and a lot about 'Nam and the guys I'd lost. The green kid I'd allowed to walk point who just disappeared without a trace. Billy, who had it all going for him and who should have gone home to enjoy it, but didn't because I tried to save his ass and send him for help. Yancey and "Chinese" Lee—I hardly even got to know them before one of them hit a trip-wire on an underwater mission. That's when my hearing was damaged. Olfson, in the booby trap on Hill 484. Lusk, who died on the way down. "John" and "Duc," the spooks—I really didn't feel as responsible for them, but they were there along with the others. In the dream, there was some kind of sinister plot behind all their deaths, but I couldn't figure out exactly who was behind it. They all seemed to think I was.

When I woke up I went to get a beer and found the damned cooler had finished cracking the rest of the way down the side. I dug some green duct tape out of my bag and taped it together.

It was about 1330, so I called room service and ordered a hamburger. I asked the guy who brought it up if he wanted to buy a good Styrofoam cooler, but he wasn't interested.

You'd think with all the servicemen staying here they would have learned to make a good hamburger. They hadn't. It filled my need for solid food, though.

After I finished the burger, I grabbed another beer and went down to the beach. My mind was still on 'Nam and the casualties. When the first water sloshed over my feet, I wasn't prepared for it to be so cool. A chill climbed my legs and ran up my spine like a big spider, but it felt good. It washed away the thoughts of Vietnam and the war. Somehow, "cool" and "Vietnam" were two concepts I couldn't keep in my mind at the same time, and the cool waves kept slapping at my feet and ankles.

I must have walked about half a mile when I spotted Tony and Bob walking down the beach toward me. I didn't want to listen to their bullshit, so I thought I'd go back up the beach, but I didn't make it. Tony saw me and waved me over.

Bob had his arm around some chick and was really laying it on to her. Whatever he was saying, they were all laughing, except one, a brown-haired girl in a white bikini. She had a half grin on her face, as if she was just being tolerant.

When I got close enough that he didn't have to yell, Bob said, "Welcome to the land of the living, Tyler. Want a beer?" He was carrying his cooler in one hand, and I noticed his wasn't broken. It made me about half mad: Bob always had all the luck, the bastard. The girl he was wrapped around was good-looking, even if she was squealing like a little pig.

They were all pretty tight and seemed to be having a good time. Tony pressed a cold beer into my hand and introduced me to everyone, even Bob, and told them I was his team leader. There were seven women. They all lived about a hundred miles from Sydney and had come down for the week. The girl with the long brown hair and white bikini was named Rhonda. The others were plenty good-looking, but she caught my eye. I seemed to have caught hers, because she was looking me over too.

Bob had been running off at the mouth as usual, but I wasn't paying any attention. He tapped me on the leg with his cooler and said, "Thought you wanted to be alone, asshole. What are you doing down here on the beach?"

I looked down at the damned cooler and was tempted to kick the shit out of it, but didn't. He had a half-assed grin on his face that looked to me like a smirk.

"I do," I answered him, "but I thought ye was good for a beer if I stopped here to listen to ye brag about something ye haven't got." His girlfriend laughed shrilly. I walked off down the beach as the smirk turned into a snarl.

I turned and glanced back at them after I'd gone a few yards, mostly to get another look at Rhonda. They were going on down the beach, but she was looking over her shoulder at me. She smiled and framed the word "bye" with her lips. I smiled and waved with a little flip of my hand, and kept on walking, but I was thinking about her.

I thought about how she'd shaped her lips to say "bye," and how enticing they were. About the warmth of her big brown eyes. About the rhythmic bob of her breasts as she'd walked toward me. About her lithe body, a dark golden tan, looking as smooth as silk and soft as cotton.

I guess she fit the mental image I'd formed of Billy's wife, because thinking about her led me to thinking about Billy again, and 'Nam. It's not easy to live with the idea that you fucked up and got someone killed. Especially someone you liked and wanted to look out for. I fucked up on Hill 484, too, by not taking the radio up the hill, and by not aborting the mission when Olfson was killed. I should have anticipated there would be booby traps, too. Perhaps, if I'd warned him, he would have been looking out for a trap, and could have seen that one. When he got killed, I should have aborted the mission right there. Even when we spotted the camp, it wouldn't have been too late. If we'd just come back down the hill instead of hitting it, Lusk might still be alive. Coming back from Hanoi, if I'd waited at the clearing where there weren't any gooks until that smart-ass radio operator went off duty, we might have gotten out without losing John and Duc.

That was at least six fuck-ups. It might be better if I

just insisted they put somebody else in my place. Why they gave the patrol leader job to me I didn't know, but I had it and all the responsibility that came with it. What was so goddamned special about me? I guess I got to be patrol leader because I had the drive to survive. I didn't want to be the victim of anybody else's fuck-ups. For the same reason, I always walked point.

So why did I come back for another tour, and take up the pain and responsibility again?

I don't know.

"I'm thirsty," said a voice. It was mine, and, by God, it was right. It was time for another brew.

I turned and stood looking at the sea for a while, my hands in my pockets, so it would look as if I'd gone as far as I intended to go all along, and then drifted back down the beach toward the room.

I ran across Bob and his beach party before I got back to the motel. They were lying on the beach drinking beer. Bob was out splashing around in the water. I noticed his fucking cooler, all in one piece and full of beer, and thought about that piece of shit back in my room. I went over and dug a can out of the ice.

As I brushed the ice off the top of the can, I glanced around and there was Rhonda. She was a little off to one side, away from the others, lying on her belly with her legs crossed and her face pillowed in her hands. The pose accentuated her small waist and rounded ass and long, shapely legs. She had unfastened her top and pulled her long hair to one side, so the sun could tan her entire back and neck, and I could see the sides of her breasts. She was about five-foot-six and I guess she might have weighed 110, give or take five pounds. Quite a package.

The damned woman knew I was going to come

back. There was no way she could have seen me, with her hands in her face that way, yet she knew it was me getting the beer. "Bob said you were from Arkansas. Is it pretty there?" she asked.

It startled me a little that she knew it was me, but I recovered fast. "Yeah, kind of. Lots of oak woods and rolling hills, with a few mountains. I like it. It's home," I replied. I popped the top on the can and took a long drink, studying her body. She'd turned her head to the side and laid it on her crossed forearms, and was looking over at me now, but I was wearing my flight glasses, so she couldn't see my eyes hungrily scanning her body. "Did Bob tell you I was a backwards hillbilly?"

"Yes, it was something like that," she said with a smile. "I don't believe everything he says, though."

"You've got him figured out, then."

"You seem to have a strange friendship."

"He's a strange friend."

The conversation was interrupted when Old Motor Mouth himself and his girl came out of the water to get a beer. I turned toward them and knocked over Bob's cooler. I hoped it would break like mine, but the damned top didn't even come off. I set the damned thing upright again just as Bob walked up.

"Hand me a beer outa there, Tyler. That's a damned good little cooler, ain't it?"

I looked up and tossed him one, and said, "Yeah, boy!" Then I tossed another to his girl. She was about three sheets to the wind, but not too far gone to catch a beer can.

"You like my little cooler, baby?" Bob asked her, and she giggled like he'd said something nasty. That was probably the first sentence he'd spoken to her that didn't have "shit," "piss," or "fuck" in it. He just kept bullshitting her, his loud voice drowning out everyone else's, except hers when she squealed at some vulgarity. I glanced back at Rhonda and caught her studying me, but every time I opened my mouth to say something, Bob was talking or his girl was squealing.

Finally, I'd had about all I could take, and I got up and started back to the room. When I stood up, Bob looked up at me with a question in his eyes and shut up long enough so I could say, "Thanks for the beer. See you guys later."

There was a question in Rhonda's eyes too, as I walked past her toward the motel. She looked a little hurt, I thought. I wanted to stay and talk to her, and I thought she wanted me to, but I just couldn't handle being around Bob right then. I was a little afraid I'd have a flashback or something with Rhonda around. I felt a little awkward and shy around her. She wasn't some slope bargirl, after all.

It was about 1700 when I got back to the room, opened the door, and saw that damned cooler. The tape had come loose and dumped all my ice in the sink. The beer was lying on the ice. There were fourteen or fifteen left of the case I'd bought when we first got there. Bob must've finished a case himself by now. I retaped the damned cooler, going all the way around it this time, and put the ice and beer back into it—except for the coldest can, which I sat down on the bed to drink.

It was 1730 or so, and beginning to get dark out, when someone knocked on the door. I hadn't closed it all the way, so I said, "Come in." When I looked up, Rhonda had pushed the door open and was standing in the doorway, a silhouette backlighted by the lights in the hall. I hadn't turned the lights on when I came in because there was plenty of light with the curtain open then. Now the room had gotten dark, and I'm sure she wondered why I was sitting there in the shadows. "She probably thinks I'm brooding about something," I thought.

"Tony wanted to know if you needed any beer or anything. They're going to the liquor store to pick something up for tonight," she told me.

"Good old Tony," I said, disappointed she hadn't come up just to see me. I gave her some money and asked her to bring me back a couple of six-packs. Then I stood in the door and watched her walk down the hall and around the corner. When she was out of sight, I wandered over onto the balcony and looked down, thinking she might walk back down to the beach, but they weren't anywhere in sight. I guess she met them in the lobby. After a while, I gave up and went back inside. I turned on the television set, but the programs all seemed to be local talk shows except one feature on the Paris peace talks, and I didn't want to hear that.

When Rhonda came back she knocked again, even though the door was open.

"Come on in," I told her, "and turn on the light." It occurred to me then that she might not know what to expect when she did. I might be setting there bare-ass naked or something. But she flipped the light on and set the beer on the vanity. She put my change there beside it and looked at me for a minute. I was standing near the glass slider.

"Well," she said, and paused for a moment. "If you feel like it, you can come down. We'll be out on the beach."

"Okay, thanks," I said. She stood there a second or two and then turned toward the door to leave. "You can stay, if you . . . if you want to," I blurted out, before she could get to the door.

She stopped and looked back at me. She didn't smile, she just looked very seriously at me with those big brown eyes. I was sure she was going to say, "Why would I want to? You haven't been especially friendly," but she didn't. Instead she said, "I would like that," with a wisp of a smile. She helped herself to a beer, tilting the cooler to look at the tape I'd put around it and the water leaking from the crack in the side, and then walked around the bed to sit on the edge. I sat beside her.

Neither of us spoke for a minute or two. I lit a cigarette to cover the embarrassing silence, and offered one to her, but she lifted the can of beer to indicate that was all she wanted.

"Are you angry at them?" she finally asked.

"Who, the guys? Naw, I just needed to be away from them awhile."

"Perhaps you'd rather I went . . ."

"No . . . no. It's just that I'm around them all the time. I eat with 'em, sleep with 'em, bathe with 'em, and go to the bathroom with 'em. I like to be away from them some, that's all."

"Have you known them a long time?"

I reached over and took the beer from her hand and took a drink from it, then took a drag on my cigarette as I handed it back. "Bob and Tony I've known ever since BUDS," I told her. "That's what you'd call diver training, I guess. And Fitchew, Casburn, and Quinn. We all trained together. Bob and I made the bars together in San Diego, and we served together our first tour."

"How long is a tour?"

"That's a year, or it's supposed to be. I didn't make a full year. Just ten months. I was wounded."

She looked at me inquiringly. "Was it bad?"

What was she thinking? That I'd lost some useful parts? Or my mind maybe?

"No, not really bad, I guess," I replied. "I only lost part of the eardrum in my left ear. If you were sitting on my left side, I might not hear what you said sometimes. But two of the guys with me died."

"I'm sorry. Were they friends too?"

"They weren't enemies," I said, then decided that sounded a little harsh, so I explained, "I didn't know them all that well. They'd only been in my outfit a few weeks. But they were my responsibility."

"Bob is an unusual person," she said, steering the conversation off the war.

"Bob *is* an unusual person," I agreed.

She tipped up her beer and tossed the can at the wastebasket. I got up to get her another, and got one for me. I crammed another six into the ice while I was there.

"Did he tell you about himself?" I asked while I worked the beers into the ice.

"Oh, incessantly!" she replied, with a merry chortle.

I was serious when I handed her the beer. "I can depend on Bob," I told her. "I can depend on him to be vulgar, and rude, and filthy, but if I get my titty in a wringer, I can depend on him to be there to help." I stopped, realizing the indelicacy of what I'd just said, but I guess after what she'd heard from Bob all day, it sounded mild. Instead of being offended, she knitted her eyebrows and made a small "O" with her mouth, and moved one hand to her own breast as if she felt the pain. Then she giggled. I guess it was the first time she'd heard the expression.

"I think I understand," she said. "What about the others?"

I sat down beside her again. "They're good men, and most of 'em are easier to get along with, but I just can't depend on them like I can Bob. I know how Bob thinks—a lot like I do when it comes to a tight situation. Don't get me wrong: I learned my first tour if I was going to survive I had to count on nobody but myself. So I check and double-check everything Bob does, and double-check that he knows what I want him to do. But I know he'll hold up his end, or die trying."

I probably would have gone on some more, now that I had somebody to listen to me, but just then there was a loud *pop*. She jumped and looked around. I knew right away what it was.

"What was that?" she asked.

"My damn cooler. It was my damn cooler again."

I told her about the cooler and the bad luck I'd had with it, how I'd been trying so hard to save it, and how Bob had the same kind and had no problems with it. By the time I was through, we were both laughing like hell, lying back on the bed side by side. God! I hadn't laughed like that in a long time. I didn't want to stop.

After we ran out of things to laugh about, I looked over toward her. She was looking at me too, and smiling, and I thought I'd just about drown in those big brown eyes. I had the impulse to kiss her. If I'd stopped to think, I wouldn't have tried it, but impulse won out over caution. As I moved closer to her she moved her hand, and I thought for an instant she was going to hold me away, but her hand went to the back of my neck and pulled me nearer.

It wasn't a hot, passionate kiss, but it had a lot of feeling behind it. It was a very delicate kiss. Her lips were moist and softer than I had imagined, and her skin was like silk.

She pushed me back gently and sat up. I stood up and went to the door that led out on the balcony, to look out toward the beach and hide the erection that was making an embarrassing bulge in my pants. After a few seconds she joined me. We sat on the rail of the balcony and looked out at the sea and talked. We talked about everything under the sun. We talked about her home town, and mine. About raising pigs, and raïsing sheep. About her job, and about Vietnam. About everything but my wife. I couldn't bring that up.

About 2000 I finally thought about dinner and asked if she wanted me to call for room service. She said no, the others were going to have a picnic on the beach, and they should have plenty left over for us, if I didn't mind joining them. It sounded like a good idea to me now, so we went down and walked along the beach until we found them.

It was beautiful. The moon was almost full, and gleamed off the whitecaps out in the bay. Every star in the heavens was out. I looked up at the moon and silently thanked it for being on my side this time. The sand was cool to our bare feet, and the salty tang of the sea breeze was a sharp contrast to the smells of 'Nam. The sound of the waves was soothing, and you could just make out the pleasant tones of people talking and laughing together, and the murmur of traffic in the background.

"How different from 'Nam," I thought. When you heard the roar of the tide over there, you knew you were close to land and hell was just a short time coming. When you looked at the stars, you were usually trying to determine direction. The only sounds of civ-

ilization you heard were the roar of a boat engine or
a jet going over, or the *whop-whop-whop* of a helicopter rotor. The voices you heard were usually hurt or
frightened, listing casualties, or calling for help, for
artillery support or a dustoff, or both.

Rhonda slipped her arm around my waist as we
walked, and I thought no more about 'Nam.

All of the team was there with Rhonda's girlfriends,
sitting around a little fire, drinking beer, shooting the
shit, and taking an occasional dip in the water—all
except Bob and his girlfriend, Ginger. They were
making out like kids at a drive-in movie, fondling each
other all over and making all kinds of weird noises.
Everyone was watching them and laughing and egging
them on, but it didn't disturb them.

Rhonda and I prowled through the picnic supplies,
but there was hardly anything left.

"Bob was hungry," Tony explained.

"He must be pregnant!" the girl with Tony joked.
"He's eatin' for two!"

"We didn't eat dinner," I explained to Tony. "We
thought we'd mooch off you."

"Ow, wow!" his girl said loudly to the others, with
a wink and a leer. "They didn't have time for dinner!"

Tony jumped to his feet and pulled the girl up by the
hand. "I've been wanting a hot dog! Anybody want a
hot dog?" he asked. There were several takers, including Bob, who raised one hand and went right on
smooching Ginger. We finally decided to get a dozen
and give any left over to Bob. He would surely eat them.
I stood up to go with Tony, but he pushed me back.
"You and Rhonda stay here and watch the floor show,"
he said. "I've got all the help I need," he added, nod-

ding toward the girl. When I tried to give him some money he pushed that away too.

He came back with the food in just a few minutes, and the show was still going on. "Hey, Bob, here's your hot dog!" he said, but Bob never answered, so Tony finally shrugged and laid a couple of them down beside the couple on the blanket.

"All he's going to do tonight is sit on the edge of the bed and tell Ginger how good he's going to be tomorrow when he sobers up," I told Rhonda and the world in general. "The only thing about him that's going to be hard tonight is his toenails."

"Ginger won't remember," Rhonda told me. "I've never seen her this drunk before."

"He has a way of doing that to people," Tony told her.

"Oh, my God! You can see his crack!" wailed Tony's girl, and Rhonda fell against me laughing. It was true. Bob's trunks had pulled down in the back, exposing about half his ass.

"It's a little dandy, ain't it!" I said. Tony grabbed his camera and checked for film, but he'd already used it all.

Bob's hot dogs lay undisturbed on the blanket behind him.

"He ain't eating his hot dogs," I pointed out. "Maybe he needs some beer to go with 'em." I moved his damned cooler closer to him, so he'd roll over on it when he got up.

I got another beer and sat back down by Rhonda. A few minutes later it happened. I had just taken a drink when one of them farted—probably Bob, but I wasn't too sure. I laughed and spewed beer everywhere, and everyone else just roared and rolled on the sand.

The loud laughter finally got through to them, and they unlocked to see what was so damned funny. Bob rolled over onto his hot dogs and knocked his cooler over. He got up cussing, with mustard and sand and little pieces of potato chips all over his back. One of the wieners was stuck in the top of his swimming trunks, and a bun was flattened onto one of his cheeks where the trunks had pulled down. He started fumbling with the cooler, setting it upright. It wasn't broken. He picked up some of the beers that had fallen out and saw they were coated with sand, so he gathered up the lot and headed for the water to wash them off. When he turned around the wiener fell out of his trunks and left a smear of mustard right at the top of his crack. He stopped and looked at me. "What the hell are you laughing at?" he growled.

"Just your yellow ass, Bob."

"Piss on all of you, you sons of bitches!" he said, his legs wobbling around. He turned and staggered on down to the water to rinse the sand off his beer cans.

There was a burst of clapping. One of the girls yelled, "Looking good there, Ginger! Looking good!" She had raised up and was shaking the sand out of her hair, and one of her tits was hanging out. She saw it and started to put it back in, then stopped. She stuck two fingers into the other cup, and sand cascaded out, so she just took the whole damned top off and started dumping the sand. We just rolled on the ground and laughed. Ginger was too drunk to be embarrassed. She got up and wobbled down to the water to wash off, then she helped Bob wash the food off his back. When they came back, she had her top on.

After a while, when the fire had burned down to coals, and the beer was low, couples started wandering off up and down the beach. Bob and Ginger were lying in one another's arms looking at the moon. Rhonda looked up at me and said, "Let's go home."

The next couple of days went about the same way. We drank a lot of beer, and lay around the beach. We took the girls out to dinner and dancing and raised some hell in town, but Rhonda and I spent a lot of the time alone together. She was sensitive and compassionate, and she taught me how good it can feel to have someone who cares for you, and someone to care for. When I was with her I forgot 'Nam, and home, and my mind was at peace. I began to have some thoughts about coming back to Australia after I mustered out of the Navy, but I knew it would never work out.

We never could fix that damned cooler. Like a lot of other things, once fucked up, it couldn't be put back together.

Then the time came for us to leave. I kissed Rhonda goodbye at the airport and walked away, telling the guys, "Okay, let's get moving. Hell's a-waitin', let's don't miss our plane!"

I waved at her from the window as long as I could. I knew I would never see her again.

Intermission was over, and it was time to get back to the main feature.

CHAPTER 17

When we got back from our R-and-R, things had changed significantly. The Navy had pulled back from their base at Quang Tri and turned it over to the South Vietnamese. NISO was running all their operations out of Saigon. A lot to have taken place in three days, but that wasn't all.

Minh Tho had been under interrogation, and he hadn't held much back. Whatever he'd told the Intelligence people had them all in a tizzy. Of course, they wouldn't tell us what it was, but they were obviously excited. And worried.

They sent us up to a camp in Quang Tri Province and we operated out of there for about six weeks, running recon missions. We usually took the LDNNs with us, or some of the other Vietnamese Special

Forces, to get them experience in our way of doing things. To keep the units small, there were usually only two or three Americans and two or three South Viets. Sometimes we had four patrols in the field at one time.

We were on one of those recon missions when we got an urgent message to return to camp for airlift to Saigon. We weren't in a good mood. We needed a good blowout, especially Bob: he was always in heat and thirsty. We had been out in the bush for four days, and we were pretty tired and sore. But that wasn't all that was bothering us. There had been some shitty missions lately, and a couple of guys had caught a few rounds. On top of that, every time we asked for air support it had been denied. We weren't happy with the way things had been going. When the call came down urgent, I figured we were going to get the shaft again.

When we got to camp, Tacron was waiting to fly us back down to Saigon right away.

It was hot, and I sat close to the door so I could feel the breeze. My eyelids felt heavy, and it appeared everyone else felt the same way: their heads were nodding. It wasn't long until they dozed off. It was a long way to Saigon, and I thought I might as well catch some Z's too, so I propped my head up against the bulkhead to go to sleep, but as always, I'd taken Dexedrine for the mission, and now I couldn't lose consciousness.

I lit a smoke and sat up a little straighter. The pilot glanced back at me, but didn't say anything. I took a deep drag off my Marlboro and blew it out as I looked over at the men.

They were a great bunch of guys, and we had come

a long way together. They were good about doing whatever I asked, no matter what it was. We bull-shitted a lot and joked around, but when it came down to business, no one was more dead serious than they were. They all knew what they were doing. There weren't any fuck-ups or goof-offs among them, and that took some of the pressure off me in tight spots, but it still wasn't easy having the responsibility of seeing that they made it back safely. The last thing I wanted to do was let them down. I didn't want to be responsible for someone's death, any more than I wanted to be killed myself. I worried about that a lot. When we would lose a man they would look at me with what I thought was doubt. Many a night I would lie in my rack and think about it.

I must have been really deep into my thoughts, be-cause I said out loud without thinking, "God, will I ever get the taste of blood out of my mouth?"

That woke Fitchew up. "What did you say, Ty-ler?"

"Nothing, bud. Just thinking out loud." I must have been talking really loud for him to hear me over the noise of the engine and props.

It wasn't long until the pilot said, "Welcome to Saigon, boys. You made it back where you started." What he didn't know was that we would only be here for a short stay. Right before we got off the chopper he went on to say, "Hey, you want to know where you can get a good screwing?"

I looked at him and said, "No, thanks. We've been getting one for several weeks now, and we've prob-ably got another one already waiting for us."

He looked at me as if he wanted to say, "You smartass!" and shook his head.

When we started toward the field house, an officer dressed in khakis came out to meet us.

Bob said, "What in the hell is that?"

"A set of khakis, Bob," I told him. It seemed like a long time since we had seen anyone in anything except greens or black pajamas.

He was a skinny little shit with flight glasses, and he had the bill of his cap pushed forward so it was touching the rims. He lifted his arm straight from the shoulder, pointed his finger at us, and said, "You the SEALs from up north?"

"Yessir!" Bob said loudly.

"Sir?" Was this really Bob talking? I looked over at him and he told me in low tones, "I just couldn't help it, Jay: them khakis made me do it!"

"Shit!" I said with a grin.

The officer waved us toward three jeeps with officers in them. I began to feel apprehensive right away. If they were sending officers to pick us up in jeeps, instead of one officer and some enlisted drivers, some kind of deep shit was going down. We started toward them, and I asked the officer who met us, "What's going down?"

He only replied, "You'll be briefed later. Right now, let's get you a place to bunk."

We threw our gear in the jeeps and got in. Bob and I got in the same one.

Bob asked the dude driving where he could get laid, but the guy just shook his head, grinned, and drove on.

"Is there any place we could get a couple of six-packs?" I asked.

"There's an EM club where you're going," he said.

"How far is it?"

"Just a little ways down the beach."

"Any women?" Bob asked.

Again the guy just smiled and shook his head. He wasn't one to talk much. All he seemed to want to do was smile and shake his head.

I tapped him on the shoulder and told him, "What the man means is a human being with long hair, big breasts, a round butt, and a small hole between its legs. You ever seen anything like that walking around? Sir." Again he did the same little bullshit: shake and grin.

All the way to the barracks we tried to get him to talk to us, but he wouldn't talk.

We arrived at the barrack where he was to drop us off, and we got out and unloaded our gear.

"You're a couple of crazy sons of bitches," he said. Then he did his little shake and grin again.

There were two guards at the door, and a big dude with a high-pitched voice who was in charge of the barracks. When he spoke, I just about burst out laughing.

"Follow me, and I'll show you where you can bunk."

As we started down the hall I said to Bob in a low voice, "Looks like you might get that piece of ass after all."

"Piss on you, Tyler."

Fitchew was right behind us. "Bob, you could pretend he was female—he could talk to you while you were doing it," he said.

"Blow it out your ass, Fitchew."

The big guy looked over his shoulder and gave us a hard look. I just smiled at him and kept on walking.

Every one of us was in a shitty mood, and no one gave a damn if he wanted to start trouble.

He showed us where to bunk and told us someone would be by later to get us. As he started back down the hall I stopped him.

"Hey, man, you know where we can get a cold one?"

"Club's right across the street in the back of that building," he said.

The other men in the barrack were mostly communications personnel. I knew something big was coming up, or they would have put us in with other combat troops instead of hiding us. I had a sick feeling that this was going to be something like the Minh Tho mission, only worse. I had no idea, though, that it was going to be the kind of James Bond bullshit that it turned out to be.

Every once in a while someone would walk by and look into our room. I began to feel like a rare animal that no one had ever seen before. We had our black berets on, so everyone knew we were SEALs, and they were all wondering what the hell we were doing there.

It wasn't long before a kid knocked on our door.

"Which one of you is Tyler?"

I turned to look at him. "I am."

"They'll pick you up in an hour out front. Not much time, but you can grab a beer over at the EM club."

"Do you know where we're going?" I asked him.

He shook his head. "They don't tell me shit, except what to do," he said.

Bob stretched and arched his back. "Let's go get a beer. I'm thirsty."

It wasn't a bad little club, small, with a jukebox and a dozen tables. There were only four people at the bar and half a dozen at the tables. The bartender was talking to a dude in the middle of the bar when we walked in.

"Beer?" the bartender said. He gave everybody a round, and we pulled two tables together and sat down. I downed about half of mine, then lit up a Marlboro. Damn, it felt good going down my throat, and the smoke felt good filling my lungs. It had been a long time since I'd sat down, smoked a cigarette, and relaxed over a beer. From the looks on the other guys' faces, they'd relaxed too. It wasn't long until we were ready for another round, and then another.

Then a Marine sergeant showed up and told us it was time to go.

"Where are we headed, Sarge?" I asked.

"To NISO headquarters. Vice Admiral Jameson sent for you."

"You drive for the Admiral?"

"Hell, I drive for all the big shits. Wherever they want to go, I take 'em. Even bring their women to them. Sometimes I get what's left over. Sometimes I knock off a little before I get 'em there—those pricks don't know the difference."

Bob leaned forward. "Women? What did you say about women?"

"I said, the officers buy the good stuff. Not the three-dollar darlin's you're used to."

"You couldn't fix us up with some of it, could you?" Bob asked.

"You bet . . . if we had time." The sergeant was cool, not like that asshole driver we had before. We talked until we arrived at the NISO headquarters.

There were two Marine guards dressed in greens posted outside the door. They looked real nice standing there at parade rest. The sergeant led us into the building and down the corridor until we came to a cross-corridor where we turned left. There was a door at the end with two more Marine guards posted on either side. The sergeant knocked on the door and a Navy lieutenant, j.g., opened it.

"Yeah?" he grunted.

"The SEALS from Quang Tri are here, sir."

"Send them on in."

When we walked into the room, Vice Admiral Jameson, Captain Gartley, and several other officers sitting at a table all turned to look at us.

"Welcome, gentlemen," the Admiral said as he rose to his feet. He walked toward us with his right hand out, and spoke to Bob and me. "It's good to see you two again."

"You're looking good, Admiral," I answered.

"You're full of shit, Tyler. Look at this beer gut!" He patted his belly, which was bulging a little. His smile was genuine as he shook my hand, then Bob's. "Brewster, are you doing all right?"

"Never done nothin' right in my life, sir. You know that," Bob replied.

The Admiral chuckled and turned to the other officers. "I had the honor of pinning Silver Stars on these two young fellows."

He didn't tell them he also had the honor of bailing our asses out of trouble for slugging a Navy officer.

He shook hands with the other guys, and when he finished, he turned to the officers and introduced them to us. "Gentlemen, this is General Ames with MACV, and Captain Trueblood and Captain Knapp, both with NISO.'' We didn't shake hands with them but just nodded. Then we sat down.

"What we have is a high risk mission," the Admiral said. "We think you men are the best team to take it on, but it is *very* high risk. It is a type of mission that we very seldom undertake, and then very reluctantly. I regret that you men have to be involved in it, but I have the highest confidence in your ability to carry it out, and I know that there is not a security risk among you."

I looked at him closely. He really did look as if he regretted involving us. In fact, he looked like an old maid schoolteacher that had just stepped in a pile of dog droppings.

The Admiral looked at us one by one. "We can end this briefing right now, along with your involvement in the mission, if you are reluctant to take it on."

I had to speak up. "Just how high is the risk, Admiral? You make it sound like a suicide mission."

"There is a very high risk of failure, Mr. Tyler, but the nature of the mission is such that you're likely to survive even if the mission fails. The type of risk that's involved is not the sort that is usual for your assignments. There is a danger that you might be shot if seen, and since you will not be armed, you couldn't defend yourselves, and if you are captured while carrying out the mission, a lot of people besides yourselves could be in deep shit. Very likely, failure would mean you men would spend some time in the stockade at Long Binh, and the officers in this room might just be in there with you."

I raised an eyebrow and glanced over at Bob. His forehead was creased between his eyebrows, and he was frowning. Just what sort of a crazy mission was this, anyway?

"If the press finds out about your mission, there'll be hell to pay for sure. Ripples could spread so far, they might even reach the President."

Now I had both eyebrows raised and was grinning at Bob. I couldn't help myself, the grin was a nervous reaction. Bob had folded his arms across his chest and slumped down in his chair. He looked as if he didn't believe all this bullshit but was resigned to having to listen to it anyway.

"Do you wish to hear any more, gentlemen? Now is the time to speak up, if you want to refuse the mission. This is all I can tell you without some commitment on your part. You'll have opportunities to back out later, after you've learned more details, but if you do so then, you'll be held incommunicado until someone does complete the mission."

"What do you mean, incommunicado?" someone asked. Tony, I think.

"You would be kept under guard in Long Binh."

No one said anything. He had my curiosity aroused, and what the hell, I sure wouldn't mind sitting out a few days or even weeks of the war to find out what this crazy mission was. I had visions of kidnapping Hanoi's negotiating team in Paris, or something equally crazy.

The Admiral smiled and went on, "I didn't think you'd let me down. Captain Gartley, you may begin the briefing."

Captain Gartley stood up. He nodded to the Admiral and began. He didn't call us gentlemen.

"If you undertake this mission and are caught or killed, the United States Navy will deny any involvement. Our official position will be that you are acting on your own, probably for criminal purposes. You may face court-martial and internment.'' He paused and looked around.

No one was impressed. We'd heard worse before. I just waved my hand: cut the crap and get on with it.

''The mission involves entering and locating a subject in a closely guarded intelligence facility and terminating his command, either by extracting him or by eliminating him in such a manner that it appears he died accidentally or of natural causes. Successful completion of this mission could have adverse effects on your emotional and mental states and your morale.''

Now it was beginning to get interesting. Out of the corner of my eye I saw Bob sit upright in his chair. Tony leaned forward and rested his elbow on his knee, his fingers over his mouth as if he was afraid he'd say something he shouldn't. My mind was racing already, wondering why it would affect our morale, and trying to figure out why they wanted it to look accidental. Another part of my mind said, ''be patient: they'll tell you if you need to know, and if they don't, you can make a better guess when you know more about the guy.''

''We have reason to believe that this individual has been passing sensitive military information to the North Vietnamese. We want the flow of information halted. If you accept this mission, the choice of methods for completing it will be yours. Our preference is that he be extracted for interrogation. If this is impossible, we want him eliminated. However, his elimination must be handled in such a way that it appears that he died of natural causes or by accident.''

"If you want to question him, why don't you just send the MPs around to pick him up?" Quinn asked. It sounded logical to me, too.

"We don't want to tip off his contacts and accomplices. We're sure the facility is watched, just as a matter of course, to pick up any information about our activities they can get that way. If he were escorted off by MPs, the Viet Cong and the North Vietnamese intelligence structure would know in minutes.''

"So why don't you pick him up when he's off duty?''

"For the same reasons, actually, and some others that will be apparent later.''

He paused again, nervously sorting through the papers on the table in front of him as if uncertain how to continue. I figured he must be talking about some South Vietnamese officer from an influential family. He had to be from an influential family or he would simply have disappeared into the tiger cages on Con Son Island. To grab a South Vietnamese and accuse him of treason would really strain relations between the two governments, unless there was an ironclad case against him. The only other alternative would be to assassinate him, and then it would be a political football unless, as the Captain had emphasized, it appeared natural or accidental. Or unless the VC could be blamed.

Captain Gartley seemed to have found what he was looking for: a manila envelope. He took a photograph out of it and pushed it across the table.

I picked it up and glanced at it. It was a picture of

an American Army officer, a colonel, in his late thir-
ties or early forties, to judge by the graying temples.

"Who is this?" I asked, thinking he must be some
sort of contact or finger man.

"That is the subject," Captain Gartley replied.

I dropped the photograph as if it were a hot potato.

"Jesus! He's an American!"

"Yes, I regret to inform you that he is an American, a colonel in Army intelligence. Evidence has
been accumulating over the past several months that
he has gone sour on us. Then our 'friend' Minh Tho
talked, and he indicated that North Vietnamese intelligence had a source of information on our staff. We
aren't one hundred percent certain yet that this is the
man, but we have enough evidence to make us willing
to eliminate him, if necessary, to stop the flow of
information. We also think he may not act alone, and
we need to get to him without his accomplices knowing he's in our hands, so they'll continue their activities. That's where you come in."

I thought it was my turn to speak up, so I put in
my two cents' worth. "Let me get this straight," I
said. "You want us to go in and get this guy and
bring him out alive for questioning. But if we say it
can't be done, you want us to assassinate him instead?"

"That's about the size of it."

"Since this guy is an American, the intelligence
facility you're talking about must be an American facility."

"That's right."

"So there are going to be American soldiers
around."

"There will be American servicemen around, and

they must not be harmed. I repeat: *they must not be harmed.* That's why it may be impossible to get him out alive. It will have to be done entirely by stealth.''

"Just what kind of a goddamned facility is this anyway?'' I had visions of MACV headquarters.

"It's the flagship, the USS *Eldorado,*'' Captain Gartley said. For some reason, that shook me up. It really wasn't all that unusual for an Army officer to be attached TDY to a Navy unit, or vice versa. That wasn't what surprised me. The *Eldorado* was Admiral Jameson's flagship, *my* headquarters, so to speak, and they wanted me to go kidnap some officer from on board. Anyway, the goddamned thing was guarded like Fort Knox.

"Why don't you just grab the son of a bitch when he comes ashore?'' someone asked.

"We only have two days before the ship sails, and he might not go ashore again. Anyway, with the sensitive job that he has, he would be under tight security when he went ashore, as a precaution against his getting taken or assassinated by the Viet Cong.''

It was quiet again while we thought that over.

Finally, I asked the Admiral, "I'd like to know why you pulled us out of the bush for this mission when you had personnel in the area who could do the job just as well or even better than we could.'' Were they setting us up for something again?

"There are no such personnel,'' he replied. "The Tacforce was organized for just this sort of operation, and you're experienced. You've snatched people from heavily guarded facilities in hostile territory.''

"But not our own people, Admiral! Hellfire, you're talking about Agent 007 bullshit!'' I said. After a moment, I asked, "How many people in his command structure know about this?"

"I can't answer that," Captain Gartley answered curtly.

"If we take this on, what are our chances of getting out?" Tony asked.

"I would say your odds are about fifty-fifty," Gartley replied.

"COMPHIBPAC is not going to jeopardize the lives of six men, whom the Navy has spent many thousands of dollars to train, for no good reason. This situation has ramifications far beyond the here and now," Admiral Jameson said, with a deadly serious look. It was an odd way to say it, for he *was* COMPHIBPAC, but I understood what he meant: he was speaking for the command, not just for himself personally. He'd consulted with his aides before making the decision. I trusted him. He was a hard old dude, but I knew him to be fair. He had kept me and Bob from being court-martialed for hitting an officer, and transferred the incompetent son of a bitch out of his command. Of course, he sent us back to active duty, which I thought was about the same as a death sentence.

I looked around at the guys and said, "What do you boys think?"

"What if you get him, and you were wrong about him?" Fitchew asked.

"If we're wrong, he'll be cautioned against ever revealing what happened, and he'll return to his duties," Captain Gartley answered.

"And if not?" I prompted.

"Then he'll be court-martialed."

"What if there isn't enough evidence to convict him, but too much to let him go?"

"If he beats the court-martial, he'll be transferred to a less sensitive job."

"Well, what if we had to kill him, and it turns out he was innocent?" Tony asked.

"We'll cover you, in that case. The incident will be blamed on the Viet Cong."

"Unless we're captured," I pointed out.

"Unless you're captured," the Admiral agreed.

General Ames finally awoke and spoke up. "We understand your concern, but what we're dealing with here goes all the way back to Stateside. We aren't sure just how many altogether are involved in it, or who is involved, but our resources are pretty damned reliable, and that's what we have to go on," he said. Watching him as he talked, I decided he looked kind of cocky.

Bob was relaxed, and looking a little bored. I knew what he'd say. The others were thinking hard on it. I studied Captain Gartley's face, then General Ames's and those of the other officers, wondering how much to believe them and if we could trust them. Were they leveling with us? Were they giving us all the facts, or just selected ones to get us to take the mission? Would they really try this guy if he was guilty, or just eliminate him? And if he was innocent, did they really think they could just slap the guy on the shoulder and say, "Sorry about that. No hard feelings, okay?" and send him back to his job, after he has been kidnapped, probably drugged, accused of being an enemy agent, and roughly interrogated for days at a time?

I knew what I would do in his shoes: I'd blow the

whistle on the whole fucking mess. Of course, proving it wouldn't be easy. They'd just say he'd been on a classified assignment, and those records couldn't be released. They'd see that there were no scars or marks on him, no drugs in his bloodstream, before they let him go back. If he took it to the press, could he convince them he was telling the truth? There'd always be some who wanted to believe him. They might be able to find someone who'd talk, no matter how little they knew—and from that, put pressure on someone else, until they got enough together to raise a stink about it, maybe even get a congressional investigation. They'd holler about civil rights and all that. As I thought it through, I could see the Admiral and the others were taking just as big a risk as we were.

If we had to kill him, we'd always wonder if he was innocent. It would always be there, in the backs of our minds, nagging at our consciences: did we kill an innocent man?

If we didn't take it on, someone else would, and they might fuck it up. For some reason, I thought about that green Army lieutenant getting his platoon shot up by four or five Viet Cong. He was an extreme case of incompetence, but incompetence was the norm in the military. And even a very competent team might screw this kind of problem up. The target might escape, or they might get caught. Then, if they talked, the Admiral's nuts would be in a vise despite all the denials he would make. Some congressman would get his chance to make a name for himself by ruining the Admiral's career. He'd saved my ass and Bob's . . . we owed him this much, that we'd take it on so someone else didn't screw it up.

I heard my own voice as though it were someone else speaking. "I say let's do it."

The others agreed, some by nodding, some by shrugging.

Suddenly I realized—or maybe I'd known all along—that as sure as shit runs downhill, when they had called us in, we were already in this thing. They had it headed our way, and they knew how to put it to us so that we wouldn't refuse it.

"Whatever equipment or assistance you need, I'll see that you get it," the Admiral said.

"Where is the ship?" I asked the Admiral.

"It's tied up to Pier Twelve."

"How long do we have?" I asked.

"We'll be in port only two days," the Admiral said. "I know that isn't much time. Do the best you can."

"We'll need deck plans for the ship, and we'll need to know how many men there are on watch. And where they are. And we'll need to know where this guy's stateroom is," I said.

Captain Gartley picked up a manila envelope from the table and walked over and handed it to me. Inside was the photo of the officer and a layout of the ship. Marked on the layout were the sentry posts. A stateroom on the second deck had been circled in red.

The *Eldorado* was well guarded, being a flagship and a communications and control center. It wasn't going to be easy to get on board, get the guy, and get him off without being seen. At least, the sentries weren't crewmen from the ship. When the ship was at sea or anchored in the harbor, the crew had the responsibility for guarding it, but when it tied up to the dock, the Marines took over that responsibility.

General Ames's men. The Marine sentries wouldn't be as familiar with the layout of the ship. But there was one thing . . .

"Do they have dogs?" I asked.

Captain Gartley answered. "There is an occasional sentry dog patrol along the dock," he said, "but they don't bring the dogs aboard ship."

"What about the sentries—what if they turn out to be trouble?" I needed to know. We weren't supposed to harm them.

"Knock them out. If they see you, you'll have to bring them with you. We'll take care of them after that," Captain Gartley said.

"I don't want any of my men killed," General Ames said, "any more than the Admiral wants anything to happen to you."

Bob had been studying the photograph. "What's this cocksucker's name, anyway?"

"You don't need to know," Captain Gartley told him. "You have his picture and the location of his stateroom. That's all you need."

I put the deck plans and photo back in the envelope. "We'll have to study these and go down to look the situation over. We'll work out a plan and let you know in the morning what we'll need in the way of equipment and support," I said, speaking as much to the Admiral as to Captain Gartley.

"Good luck," the Admiral called after us as we filed out the door.

"We're damned sure going to need it," I thought.

CHAPTER 18

It was a quiet ride back to the barracks, probably because all of us were thinking about the mission. Bob and I were. He turned to me once and said, "Do you believe 'em, Jay?"

I thought about it awhile, then had to shrug. "Partly. Mostly, I guess."

He picked his nose with his finger and then wiped it on his pants. "You think it's all that big a deal? That big a security leak, I mean?"

"I guess it depends on his job."

"What do you think they'll do to him?"

"Do you give a fuck?"

"Naw."

"Then don't worry about it. We'll never know."

"Yeah. Ain't no skin off my ass, anyway."

He brought it up again, though, after a couple of minutes. "D'ye think they'll have a court-martial, and publicity, and all that shit? The way I figger it, they can't afford to. It'd come out that we grabbed him off the ship so they could interrogate him, and their asses would be in trouble even if he was guilty."

I hadn't thought about it that way, but he was right. There'd sure as hell be a stink if the press ever got hold of the fact that the guy had been snatched off the *Eldorado* and secretly held and questioned, even if he was as guilty as sin, and to have a court-martial would guarantee that it would come out. I didn't say anything because I was pondering the situation, but Bob had already thought it out.

"Ye know how they'll do it, don't ye?" he asked. "He'll jist disappear, and his family'll get a telegram saying he's missing in action. There won't be no court-martial. If they think he's guilty, he's gone."

"Well, hell, maybe that's for the best. His family wouldn't suffer no embarrassment that way."

"But, Jay, what if the son of a bitch is innocent?"

"You heard 'em: they're ninety percent sure he's guilty right now. I don't think they'd risk having us grab 'im if they weren't."

"He's as good as dead, ain't he, Jay?"

"Yeah."

"Then I don't guess it matters much if we have to kill 'im."

"No. It's just that they want to question him about his contacts and accomplices."

After a while, he said, "You know, Jay, it's going to be a bad sichyation."

"How's that, Bob?"

"Them guards is going to have guns, and we won't."

"Oh. Well, I'll tell you Bob, I figger to carry my thirty-eight anyway."

"Yeah. Me too."

There was a room with a table in it at one end of the barracks, and we commandeered that for a conference room. The big dude with the squeaky voice helped me get an urn of coffee and had some chow sent over for us. We sat around and shot the bull and went to the head while we waited for the food; we didn't want the deck plans spread out or the photo visible when they brought it in. When it got there everybody really dug in. It was the best damn meal we'd had in days. There was roast beef and mashed potatoes and gravy and cold whole milk—not powdered. We all drank several glasses of it. It had been a long time since any of us had had real milk.

As I ate, I couldn't help but feel like a Death Row inmate having his last meal.

After we finished we stacked the trays outside the door and closed it. Then we got the plans out and sat around drinking coffee and studying them. No one talked very much. Occasionally someone would point out something he thought the others might have overlooked. Every now and then someone would suggest a course of action, and the others would pick it apart. We all knew it had to be done at night, and it had to be done tomorrow night. Beyond that, there was little agreement. Our subject was on the second deck above the main deck, so we had to go up two levels. The only companionway that gave access to that second deck was forward. We couldn't agree on a plan to get on board, get up the companionway, and get to the stateroom, much less get off with the subject.

Finally, I stood up and began putting the plans back

in the envelope. "Let's go take a look at that damned ship," I told the others.

"Good idea!" someone agreed.

We called the Admiral's office to get a couple of jeeps sent around. We had the drivers drop us off about a quarter mile from Pier 12 and walked the rest of the way.

The *Eldorado* was moored at the end of the dock, tied up, with her port side landward, by big mooring lines fore and aft. A smaller vessel was moored in the slip just in front of it, and the slips on the other side were empty. There was a lot of traffic going on and off the ship, and it was well guarded. The traffic would die out by late evening or early morning; the guards would still be there, though. It would be impossible just to walk aboard. The pier was well lighted by large floodlights, but the stern wasn't as well lighted as the bow. Of course, there would be more sentries there to compensate.

To me, it was obvious we'd have to go aboard by climbing the mooring line at the stern, work our way forward to the companionway, then up to the second deck, get the guy, and return along the same path.

The mooring line, Bob pointed out, had a huge rat guard. It looked like it had been made especially to keep big rats about our size off the ship, he said. It was a formidable obstacle, too big to climb over or reach around, but if you could attach a line just this side of it, you could swing up and grab the mooring line on the other side.

"It's too steep an angle. You'd never be able to swing high enough," Bob said.

"When the tide's out," Tony pointed out, "the line won't hang at such a steep angle."

"So how're you going to attach a line so it doesn't slip?" Bob asked. "Tie a knot?"

"We'll figure out some kind of a clamp."

We went back to the barracks to work the bugs out of the plan, and a pot of coffee later we had a scheme we all agreed on. The only problem was the clamp we needed to get around the rat guard.

The next morning we went down to NISO headquarters and told them we wanted to talk to the Admiral. They said he was busy, so we told them we'd like to talk to Captain Gartley. When Gartley heard we had a plan worked out, he said everybody involved would want to be briefed on it, and it would take until 1100 to get everyone together. So we drank coffee and went over our plans again for a couple of hours, and bullshitted, and played grab-ass until all the big shits got there.

General Ames was the last one to arrive. He came in and sat down with a brief apology to the Admiral. An LTJG poured him a cup of coffee and then left the room. Captain Gartley told us to begin.

I was the squad leader, so I was the spokesman, and I stood up and spread out the deck plan on the table where everyone could all look at them.

"We've worked out a plan to get your man off the *Eldorado* alive," I began, "provided you can supply us with the necessary equipment and backup."

First, I explained the layout of the ship and dock to them. The Admiral already knew it, but the General and some of the others might not. Then I got to the important part.

"We'll go aboard the stern and take advantage of the shadows on the water between the ship and the dock. We'll have to board by climbing up the mooring line. That's no big problem, except for the rat guard. It's too big for us to get around without some special equipment. We'll have to have a clamp fabricated that is the right size to fit onto the mooring line, and it must have a way to attach a smaller line to it.

"Once aboard, it'll be a matter of waiting until the guards pass or turn their backs. We'll work our way forward to the companionway—that's a stairway, General—located here, and go up to the second deck. We'll enter the area of the officers' wardrooms here, and move along this central corridor to the subject's billet. Once we have him, we will retrace our steps and exit the stern.

"In order to board the ship without being observed, we'll have to have a diversion to attract the sentries' attention. There's some activity on the dock even at night, so it'll have to be a real ruckus in order for it to work, but not enough of one to send the ship to General Quarters.

"There's an empty slip across the dock from the ship. Maybe a patrol boat could pull in there because of 'engine trouble.' That's common enough. They can have prisoners aboard, too, and call for someone to come pick them up while they work on their engines. That way, the prisoners can cause a little commotion. The disturbance should be enough to get the guards' attention so we can get aboard.

"After the prisoners are taken away or quieted down, the crewmen working on the engines can revv them up and kill them and start over, as if they're having trouble getting the problem straightened out. That will make enough noise to cover any sound we might make carrying the subject back to the stern, especially if we have to take out a sentry.

"We'll reach the dock by swimming underwater. A

patrol boat will drop us off near mid-channel, without stopping, and continue on upriver. River patrols move through the area all the time and wouldn't be noticed. We'll have to drop off the boat far enough out that we aren't observed by anyone onshore. By approaching the dock underwater, we can avoid the harbor patrols and we won't be seen by the sentries on the *Eldorado*. We'll wait under the end of the dock until the diversion begins. We'll cache our tanks and masks under the dock while we're on the ship, and take an extra set for the subject so we can extract him in the same manner: we'll swim out into the river with him, underwater, and surface well beyond the lighted area to rendezvous with the patrol boat as it makes a return run through the harbor.

"We'll need a way to knock the subject out quickly, so that he doesn't make noise and wake the other officers and alert the sentries. A drug of some kind. Something we can give him against his will, like sticking him with a needle or holding a cloth over his nose and mouth. Something that we could use on the sentries, too, if we have to.

"The patrol boat can take us any place we can turn the subject over to you without being seen.

"That's the plan. So, again, what we need from you is a boat for transportation in and out of the harbor area, a clamp for the mooring line, a diversion, and some way of knocking the subject unconscious. We believe we can take care of the rest."

Captain Gartley and the other two captains had been taking notes as I talked. Admiral Jameson and General Ames seemed satisfied with the plan, but the junior officers had to show off how much they knew and try to pick holes in it. Captain Trueblood started off.

"Underwater breathing apparatus must have developed remarkably in the last few years, Mr. Tyler," he said. "When I last had anything to do with it, you had to breathe through a mouthpiece. If you tried to breathe through your nose, you breathed water. How are you going to get an unconscious man to breathe through his mouth instead of his nose?"

"Put a clothespin on it," Bob growled. Trueblood shot him a dirty look. The Admiral smiled.

"Clamp it," I told him. "Like Bob said. We can use one of those little rubber gizmos that swimmers use when they race. Or we can stuff wax in it, or just mash it down and tape the shit out of it. If he can't breathe through it, he'll breathe through his mouth naturally."

The Admiral interrupted at this point. "Captain, we selected these men for this operation because they are experienced in this type of thing, and fully competent to handle the technical details. Leave those worries to them."

"Yes, sir."

"The clamp you need can be made up this afternoon," the Admiral went on. "We have artificers that make up special equipment for special operations, and they know not to ask too many questions about where or how it's going to be used. Captain Gartley will take you to see them, and see that the job is done top priority." It was an order to the Captain, and to us, too.

"I have an idea for the diversion, sir," Captain Knapp spoke up.

"Go ahead, Captain."

"I've been working with the LDNNs for the past several months, and there are several extremely tough characters in that outfit that could create quite a fuss as 'prisoners.' They'd do it knowing they would take a beating for it, and do it without asking why," the Captain said. "I could supply the boat and crew as well. Men who wouldn't know the LDNNs. We could give them some false reason for the row with the 'prisoners' . . . tell them the men are agents and we're trying to give them some credibility with the Viet Cong. Tell them the VC are watching the dock because the flagship is tied up there, and we want them to see these men resisting their captors because we're going to let them escape later."

Admiral Johnson nodded and looked at General Ames. "Sounds all right to me. What about you, George?"

The General, his dead cigar clenched between his teeth, nodded assent.

The Admiral didn't even look at Captain Trueblood or Captain Gartley. Since both ranking officers had approved the idea, neither of the captains was going to object to it anyway. He asked us if we had any objections, though.

I looked around at Bob and Darren and Tony and the others. They all shook their heads. "No, sir. It sounds fine to us," I told him.

"Then that just leaves the drug, or some other means of knocking out the subject," the Admiral went on.

"I've taken care of that, Admiral," Captain Trueblood said. "It was evident when we first considered our options in this situation that, should we decide to apprehend the subject in a surreptitious manner, some quick and quiet means of rendering him unconscious would be most advantageous. An injection of this"— he held up a syringe of colorless liquid—"will do the job in a matter of seconds. If injected in the neck, five seconds or less. It isn't lethal except in extremely large doses, and has no potentially fatal side effects. Fur-

thermore, it won't interfere with later use of scopola-
mine, and all traces of the drug disappear from the
bloodstream in a matter of hours.''

"How much can you supply?" I asked.

He squinted slightly when he looked at me, as if
suspicious of the reasons for my question.

"You need no more than two doses—two syringes
full—even if you're delayed getting him off the ship
and it starts to wear off.''

"I want a syringe for every man on the mission,"
I told him. He started to object, so I went on, "If
there's any trouble getting on board, one or two may
be lost. Or broken. Second, we have no way of knowing which of us will actually go into his room and get
him. That will depend on how things develop when
we get there. I'll try to be one of them, but I might
get involved with a sentry or something. I might drown
going in. Third, if it works that fast, it's better than
the butt end of a pistol for taking out a sentry. There's
too much chance we might hit the sentry too hard and
kill him. And any man in the group may have to take
out a sentry.''

Trueblood looked helplessly at the Admiral, who
nodded to him. We would get one syringe per man.

"For God's sake, don't drop one on the ship,"
Captain Gartley said.

"And if you have to inject it in a sentry, bring him
off the ship with you," Trueblood added. "The drug
stays in the bloodstream long enough that they might
detect it.''

I nodded.

The Admiral stood up. "I think that takes care of
it, then. You all know what to do. If there is nothing
else . . .'' He paused and looked around. No one said

anything. ". . . I think the General and I had better get back to work. Thank you, gentlemen. You've done a fine job of getting this thing rolling. Good luck." And he left, the General right behind him.

We gathered up the deck plans and followed Captain Gartley. He took us to a building down near the docks and introduced us to the artificer, a petty officer in his mid-thirties with thick glasses and a splotchy red face. There was some kind of white cream rubbed on the splotches, and after a minute I realized they were burn scars.

After we described what we needed, he said, "So you want something like a rope-climbing clamp?"

"I guess. How does that work?" We didn't climb ropes with clamps in training—we climbed them barehanded.

"It fits around the rope, and it has a couple of cams inside attached to the frame with pins up near the top side. When you slide it up the rope, the cams swing out of the way." He demonstrated with the knuckles of his forefingers. "But when you pull down, friction against the rope pulls the cams upward, and the way they're mounted makes them pivot inward so they clamp down tight on the rope." He pressed his knuckles together.

"And it don't slip?"

"It'll slip a little. Half an inch, maybe, before it gets tight. Is this line hemp, or nylon or some other synthetic fiber?" he asked.

"Synthetic, I imagine. It's pretty small, and it has to be pretty strong. Why?"

"Well, the synthetics are slicker. The cam has to be textured to hold right. You know . . . roughed up. How big is this line?"

"Well, let's see . . . maybe this big." I held up my hand, making a circle with my forefinger and thumb about four inches in diameter.

"He's asking about the line, not your asshole," Bob said. He held up his hand and made a circle about an inch in diameter. "It's more like this," he said.

"Bullshit, Bob," Darren spoke up. "It's more like this." He held up one finger curled into a circle so tight there was hardly any airspace in the middle.

"What, the line? Or his asshole?" Bob asked incredulously.

"Oh, I thought you was braggin' about your pecker."

"Hell, that's his IQ," Tony said, holding his finger in a circle.

"Shut the fuck up," Bob growled.

I looked at the artificer and shrugged. "Hell, we don't know for sure. Two, three, four inches in diameter. We ain't been that close, to measure it. Can you make one that'll fit anything that size, up to about four inches?"

He scratched one of the red splotches beside his nose and then held up one finger in a "wait one minute" gesture.

"You said you needed an eye on the bottom for another line?"

"Yeah."

"Is there going to be much weight on that line?"

"We're going to swing from it, one at a time. So a hundred and seventy-five pounds, for the lightest, to, oh, two-twenty for the heaviest of us."

"Okay, that'll help. I'll put the eye on the cam so your weight pulls it in harder against the line. And I'll hinge it at the top so it'll slip over anything up to about four inches in diameter. That way, it'll fit almost any size line. And I'll put one cam in it that pulls up against the heavy line when you pull down on the smaller one. That'll make up for the different diameters. Does it need to be made of anything special? Aluminum, to save weight, maybe? Or is steel okay?'' He was sketching on a piece of graph paper while he talked.

"Steel's okay."

"Good. It's easier to work with. I can have this ready to go by, say, 1600 this afternoon."

"Good enough. We'll be by to pick it up then."

. After leaving the artificer we went down to the divers' shed and told the diver in charge there what kind of tanks and breathing gear we'd need, and how many. He said he'd have it ready about 2200 for us to pick it up. We didn't want to take it back to the barracks because we didn't want anyone there to know what kind of an operation we were going on, in case someone started investigating later.

Then we went back to the barracks to kill the afternoon. Some of the guys went over to the bar. I didn't; I wanted my head clear. Bob Brewster lay down and went to sleep. The barracks was quiet enough in the middle of the day, and with the door closed, the airconditioning made enough noise to muffle any sounds of people moving around or talking or singing, like they do in a barracks. Good old nerveless Bob. I sat on the edge of my bed and smoked cigarette after cigarette while I went over our plan in my mind, trying to turn all the "what ifs" that kept popping into my head into "ain't likelies."

What if a guard spotted us, and we couldn't get to him to knock him out? We weren't supposed to kill or even hurt any of those guards, and anyway, who'd want to shoot an American? There wouldn't be any choice except surrender or go over the side and hope we could get back to the dock to get the breathing gear.

What if somebody was up going to the head or taking a smoke, and caught us in the corridor? He wasn't going to get close enough to let us grab him. There was enough light from those red bulbs they use on board so that he'd know something was wrong long before he got within arm's reach. We could take a chance on pulling a .38 on him and telling him not to make any noise, but what if he yelled anyway? Put down our guns and surrender? Make a run for it? Take him hostage and bluff our way out? Everything seemed like a losing proposition. If we got caught with the body over our shoulders, we'd just make a run for it and go over the side. If he drowned, too bad. At least we had a chance that way. But if we were surprised before we got to his room? Run for it. Try to keep from getting shot and go over the side.

What if someone saw us just as we went in the room? We'd leave a man or two outside, and if they couldn't get to him to shut him up, we'd be up shit creek. Once we went into that room, the son of a bitch would be warned. We couldn't leave the ship then without nailing his ass. And it would take thirty seconds at least, maybe a minute or more, to knock him out and secure him. By that time the guards would be on their way. There'd be no way to control the situation except shoot the goddamned guards.

It would be better, if the alarm went up after we went in the door, to shoot the son of a bitch in his bed and get the hell off the ship.

What if we were spotted swimming in to the dock, or back out again? If they thought we were North

Vietnamese or Viet Cong divers going in to blow up the flagship, the harbor patrols would go on alert and all hell would break loose. We'd be in deep shit then, too. They'd be out there looking for us, with depth charges and the Lord only knows what else. If they spotted us under the dock, at least we might have a chance to surrender.

What if . . . what if . . .

Bob's snoring began to get to me, so I left the room and went down to the little room down at the end of the barracks where they had the coffee. The coffee was old and full of grounds so I threw it out and brewed a fresh pot, then got me a cup and sat down at the table they had in there and smoked and drank coffee and thought about every step of our movements from the time we entered the water until they pulled us back out again.

After a while, I looked at my watch. It was 1610. Not time to start getting ready yet. It had sure been a long day.

Then I realized it was time to go get our clamp from the artificer. I hoped the fool wouldn't leave before I could get there, and close up for the night. Or maybe I hoped he would.

No such luck. He was working late that evening anyway, and he had the clamp all ready to go. It seemed to be just what we wanted. He even had some four-hundred-pound test nylon line threaded through the eye and lashed tight to itself. When I decided how long I wanted it, he cut it for me and heat-sealed the end so it wouldn't ravel. We were all set, as far as his contribution to the mission was concerned.

I stopped by NISO headquarters to check in with Captain Gartley to make sure the diversion was all set and our boat was arranged for. Everything was "go," so I went back to the barracks and stopped back by the bar to round up the guys. It was time to pour some coffee down them.

It was a long evening. There were no weapons to check except our .38s and knives. Each of us was issued a syringe and instructed on how to use it. It had a glass cap over the needle. The glass was scored at the base so you could snap it with your fingers or tap it against the wall to break it off. Then you jabbed it in him and pushed the plunger. For fastest action, you wanted to inject the drug as near the brain as you could, so the muscles in the side of the neck were the ideal location. You wanted to avoid the arteries, because you might cause a bubble in his bloodstream and kill him. The syringes had a cord attached to loop around our necks. They told us again, Don't drop them or leave them behind.

We put on our camo paint, and I went to each guy and reminded him, "No shoes. It's a steel deck, so no shoes, and no rubber stockings. They squeak. Bare feet only."

It was a nervous group of guys that went down to the divers' dock from the NISO office. We drew our tanks from the divers' shed and checked them over good. I got a small grappling hook and bent it on the end of the little rope on our clamp, lashing it tight with a small line. Then we got on the boat they had down there for us and headed off downriver.

CHAPTER 19

We timed our arrival to 0130. The PBR chugged through the harbor at low throttle, so when we dropped off we were close together and it didn't take long to form up. We were half a mile or so out in the river, in the shadows just a little upstream from Pier 12 and the *Eldorado*. We swam in until there was enough light that I began to worry that we might be visible. By then the current had carried us a little downstream of the dock, so I estimated how much farther we had to go and took a compass bearing on the *Eldorado*'s stern. Then we submerged and swam on in. In that dark and murky water, I trailed a cord behind me and they all held on to it, so that we arrived together.

As we got near the shore, I listened for the slap of

waves on the pilings. That would be my clue that we were close. There was so much other noise, though, that I couldn't make it out. Just before I thought we should be there, somebody gave three hard jerks on the cord. That was the signal to stop, so I let myself drift slowly toward the surface. The water got lighter as I drifted upward, and I knew I would surface in a lighted area. Light penetrated such a little way into that brown sewer that I wasn't ready when my head broke the surface. I was between the pier and the *Eldorado*! Quickly I submerged again and swam for the pier, my back muscles tense as I waited for a bullet from one of the sentries.

The water was noticeably darker in the shadows under the pier, so I knew when I got there. I held on to a spike driven into one of the pilings as the others swam in to join me, and thanked the Lord the sentries weren't alert.

We mustered and stashed the diving gear so no one would find it. Then we waited for the PBR to show up. We'd brought a radio with us, and we listened in on the radio traffic for the boat captain to report engine trouble.

We only had to wait about ten minutes. We heard the boat captain make his call and report that he was coming upriver with two Victor Charlie suspects he'd taken off a sampan, and that he was having engine trouble. We could hear them coming upriver long before they came into sight. We knew it was them because the engine was running ragged and backfiring. As they got closer to the *Eldorado*, he reported that his engine was getting worse, and that he was going to pull in to dock until they could fix it. They pulled into the slip opposite the *Eldorado* and sat there for a few minutes with one engine idling and farting and missing.

Then their headquarters called them and asked what their status was. "She's still cutting out on us," the boat captain told them. "We have two Victor Charlies here, and we have to repair this engine. How about sending us some assistance? Send somebody to take 'em off our hands, or we'll have to kill 'em."

"Hold one," they told him. Probably went somewhere to ask an officer. When they came back, they told him, "Help is on the way. We've sent four men down in a jeep to pick them up."

"You need to get another boat back up in that area," the boat captain came back. "That area needs to be patrolled heavy. It looks like Charlie is moving some shit in there by sampan. It may take us an hour or two to get this engine fixed up."

"You can't stay that long," HQ told him. "We're already getting shit from the harbormaster. They're afraid they might have some incoming traffic that needs that slip. They don't want any small craft tied up there. If you can't get it going in thirty minutes, we'll send you a tow."

"Well, you need to get the prisoners," the boat captain said. "One of them is so goddamned fucked up he doesn't know where he's at. We don't want any more trouble out of him. We'll get them off the boat and out on the pier, so they'll be ready for you."

That was our signal. It was time to start. We shinnied up the pilings of the pier to reach the mooring line. There were barnacles and slime all over the posts, and they were slicker than snot grease. You had to get your feet around the post and lock them. If you slipped, the barnacles cut. God, did they cut.

Fortunately, there were cross braces between the pilings, and the tide was partly in, so there wasn't too far to climb.

Darren Fitchew was to stay behind under the pier and keep watch. He pulled himself up to the edge and peered over, keeping his head in the shadows of the piling. Thompson and Magoun stayed in the water with the extra mask and tanks. They would delay fifteen minutes after we went on board, then swim over to the starboard side of the ship and tread water in the shadows by the rudder, hidden by the overhang of the hull, to catch the body and put the mask and tanks on him before he could drown.

We didn't move until we heard the commotion. First there was some yelling and cursing, both in English and Vietnamese, and what sounded like a scuffle on the boat.

"They're takin' 'em up on the pier," Fitchew whispered. We heard them yank the prisoners out of the boat and throw them down on the pier. "One of 'em is thrashin' around . . . his hands and feet are tied . . . they're kicking the shit out of him." The yelling and cursing started again.

I was sitting on a cross brace facing away from the ship, and had to lean out and look over my shoulder up toward the fantail of the ship. There was movement in the shadows, the flash of a face turned toward the light. The sentries were taking the bait. I started counting to sixty before I moved, but by the time I reached thirty I decided that anyone that hadn't already gone to see what the fuss was about was either deaf, asleep, or the damned most dedicated guard I'd ever seen.

I leaned out from the cross brace I was sitting on and reached for the mooring line. It was belayed to a piling right at the level of the pier, and was just within reach. There was no slack sagging down toward the water, because the tide was in, and the ship was sitting high above the pier. I got a good grip and let myself slip off the cross brace. The line moved and sagged noticeably when my weight came onto it. My feet swung away from the pier as they slipped off the brace, and when they swung back I pulled up and hooked my heels on the line. Then I started climbing.

I felt as if I were sticking out like a goddamned fire engine out there, as if I had lights and sirens all over me. If one of those sentries looked my way he couldn't fail to see me. Going up that damned line wasn't easy either. It was naturally slick, and my hands and legs were covered with slime. I was breathing hard, and my arms were tired when I finally got to the rat guard.

I had to cling there with one hand while I got the clamp out and fixed it to the mooring line. Then I uncoiled the rope and let it dangle. The grappling hook on the end gave just enough weight so that I could start it swinging like a pendulum, and swing it higher each time, but I had to make sure it didn't foul the line behind me before I could work it high enough to catch on the other side of the rat guard. Fortunately, it caught on the first try. I checked it to make sure it was secure, then swung on the smaller rope down under the rat guard, and climbed up on the other side.

I looked around again for sentries. There was one not twenty feet away, but he was looking forward toward the ruckus on the pier. Then another came out, and the one near me turned. I saw him start to move, and thought, "I'll just let go and get the hell out of here," but he turned away from me and out toward the river. If he had faced me, he would have seen me.

If I'd dropped into the river—if any one of us went

into the water, even if he slipped and fell—the others would have to come too, and the mission would be scrubbed because the splash would alert the sentries.

When he turned away, I went up through the hawse-hole and ducked down behind the cleat. I was damned tired from the exertion of the climb, and it was a fight to keep my breathing quiet and even. The two guards stood there talking a few feet away. Finally, the one who'd come out from inside took off on his rounds. He went across the fantail and stopped and hollered back at the first guy, then went on. The first guy stood there and looked forward again.

I went over to the stern anchor chain locker and slipped down behind it. Bob was right behind me. He had been hanging on the mooring line. Tony was the third man. He had to hang on down by the rat guard until we could move on. Finally, the other two made it up, and we all crouched there in the shadows and whispered about how it had been a near thing.

The noise from the pier had died down a little when we moved on. Fitchew said later that the guy doing the yelling had quieted down when the other prisoner got loose. The sailors had them tied but not cuffed, and one of them got his hands free. He untied his feet and stood up, and a couple of sailors jumped on him to wrestle him back down. That started a scuffle, with the Vietnamese and the sailors cursing and grunting and wrestling around on the pier. He never broke loose, and the two sailors stayed close to him so the sentries wouldn't shoot him.

We left Casburn on the fantail to watch, and the rest of us worked our way forward. We had to slip past the sentries there and down a short companionway to the main deck, then a third of the way forward to where the deck stepped up a full level. After going up a long companionway, we had to work our way forward again to somewhere just forward of midships, where an outside companionway led up to the second deck and on up to the bridge. Fortunately, there was a lot of clutter and shadows on the deck to keep us hidden. Not mess, just tangles of pipes, electrical conduits, a bunch of radio and radar antennas, and the usual ventilator standpipes, cleats, stanchions, and winches. We stayed in the shadows and moved as quietly as we could. Usually it was just a matter of hiding and waiting until a sentry went past on his rounds. All of them made it a point to go across the deck and see what was going on on the pier, so that made it considerably safer for us to move around on the other side.

Bob led the way up the first long companionway. At the top, he waited until I moved past him. The sentry there had a long, reasonably clear path to walk along the rail, underneath a sunshade awning. It cast a good shadow, but there was nothing to block the sentry's view along the rail in either direction. Thirty feet or so forward of the companionway was a hatch leading to a corridor; I ducked in through the hatch. It was lit inside by the red watch lights, but there was enough bulkhead around it so that I could hide if the sentry came back. There was no one in the corridor, so I waved to Bob to move on up. Tony took his place at the top of the companionway as Bob moved out. Quinn was posted in the shadows under the companionway, to wait until we came back with the body.

Bob had gone only halfway to the next companionway when a sentry opened a hatch in front of him and stepped out. The hatch opened inward, and that gave Bob enough warning so that he could drop over the rail.

He clung to one of the rail posts while the sentry made his round back to the companionway where Tony was crouching. If he had looked down for any reason, he would surely have seen Bob's hands, but he looked out toward the next dock, and whistled softly to himself, and scratched his ass. He had his rifle slung over his shoulder barrel up. If we had to take him out, he wouldn't be able to get a shot off in warning.

He came on toward the stern, past the open hatch where I was hiding, toward the aft companionway. Tony moved back down the companionway and into the shadows underneath. I pressed myself against the bulkhead next to the hatch and hoped he wouldn't come inside, or even glance inside as he went by.

He didn't. When he reached the break in the deck line he stopped for a while, and then surreptitiously lit a cigarette. He cupped it in his hands to keep the glow from being seen, but the smoke hung heavy around him in the still night air, and drifted over my way. I suddenly began to crave a smoke myself.

He shifted around, glancing furtively up and down the deck. He was keeping an eye out for the officer of the watch so he wouldn't be caught smoking. I quickly moved to the opposite bulkhead so he wouldn't catch a glimpse of me through the hatch.

His cigarette smoke began to tease my nostrils with the urge to sneeze. I clamped my lips shut and stifled three sneezes before the urge passed.

Bob's hands must have been about to give way. Any minute now, I would surely hear the splash as he dropped into the water. The sentry would hear it too, of course, and run to the rail to look over. When he did, I was going to knock the son of a bitch unconscious and make sure he had the lit cigarette on him before I went over the rail myself.

It seemed like hours before he tossed the butt over the rail and moved off toward the port side of the ship.

Bob came over the rail and massaged his arms and hands for a moment. Then he crept on forward to the next companionway. It went up two flights, one to each deck level, with a landing in between. He went up to the landing, checked to make sure the next deck was clear, and waved us forward.

At the top and a few feet forward was the hatch or door to the officers' wardrooms. There was a sentry on that deck, but he was apparently on the port side watching the scuffle on the pier. We didn't know if there would be a guard inside or not. It was just a chance we'd have to take.

The door opened easily and quietly. I opened it only a fraction of an inch at first, then slowly swung it wider until I could look through. There was no one in sight down the length of the corridor. It ran all the way across the width of the ship and opened to a deck and companionway on the port side. The door there was also closed. I posted Tony to watch both doors, and Bob and I went down the corridor to find the subject's room.

And, I suppose, that's how I came to be in this situation.

Once we got the door open, stopping it when it was about halfway open so that it wouldn't slam against the bulkhead, I was relieved to find there was enough light from the watch light over his door so that I could see his head was turned toward the stern of the ship. That made it easier. I didn't have to worry about grabbing the wrong end of him. He was lying partly on his back and partly on his right side, with his knees bent. I was across the room in three quick steps, clamping a hand over his mouth and pushing his head toward the wall so that the left side of his neck was exposed. His eyes popped open wide and white and I could feel him tense as he awoke. Bob was there an instant later, jamming the syringe into the neck muscles as if he was trying to stick it right through, and I worried that he might miss and hit the carotid artery.

Bob left the syringe in the man's neck and grabbed his feet just in time, just as he began to react. The guy grabbed at my wrists and tried to pull my hand off his mouth so he could yell for help, but I had the advantage of using my weight against his efforts. Next he tried to kick me, or the bulkhead to wake his neighbors, but Bob had him pinned there, too. He thrashed around for a bit, but his struggles lessened as the drug took effect, and very quickly he went limp. We hung on for a few seconds longer, to make sure he wasn't playing possum.

The needle fell out of the guy's neck while he was struggling and fell to the floor. It made a weak but audible click.

When we were sure he was out, I took a roll of plastic tape and taped his hands and feet together. Just to be on the safe side, I taped his mouth, too, and used another strip for a blindfold instead of Bob's olive drab scarf. We didn't have time to be tying knots.

While I was taping him, Bob quietly closed the door.

Then we got him out of his bunk and onto the floor, and made up his bunk.

He had been sleeping in his underwear, without a T-shirt. His uniform was hanging over the back of a chair. We took his uniform and shoes and stuffed them inside our wetsuits. We wanted our hands free. We even got him a clean T-shirt. We got the change and his billfold off his nightstand and stuffed that in, too. He had a little alarm clock there, and we made sure the alarm was off. I even made sure we took his tie, and I pushed his chair back under his desk. When I did, I saw the needle on the floor and picked it up.

Then Bob picked the guy up and threw him over his shoulder, and I went to the door. I opened it just a crack and peered down the corridor, then opened it wider and checked the other way. The coast was clear, and we went out with him. I had to pull hard to get the door closed.

Tony was down by the hatch. The hatch only opened inward, and that was a problem because it made it tough to watch the sentry, and unless you could see him, you couldn't know which direction he'd walked when he passed on his rounds. As we came down the corridor, I motioned for Tony to open the hatch, but he hesitated. I didn't know what he was waiting for, but I was worried that someone would come in the hatch on the opposite end of the corridor, or get up and go to the head or something. I signaled to him again, more forcibly, and went back to the corner to look down the other corridor and make sure no one had been disturbed back near our subject's room.

Tony opened the hatch just a crack so that it let in a little light, and we waited. There was just enough light from the street and buildings along the shoreline to be a little brighter than the watch lights inside. Tony would be able to see the sentry's shadow block out the light when he went by, and from that and the sound of his footfalls, judge which way he was going on his rounds.

He and Bob waited just inside the hatch, listening for the sentry's footsteps. I stayed down by the corner, watching the corridors and the hatch on the port side, expecting at any minute for someone to come in that way. I could hear the sentry's footsteps myself, very faintly, but well enough that I could tell he was getting closer to the hatch. The louder his footfalls got, the harder it got for me to breathe.

Finally, they began to recede. I motioned for Tony to go on. He shook his head and pointed. The sentry had passed going toward the stern. We had to crouch there in that lighted corridor while he completed his circuit toward the stern and went back forward.

Tony went out first, and he ran back aft to the companionway to see if anyone was there, and to check on the position of the sentries on the deck below. I went over to the hatch and watched the sentry that had just gone by. He was about fifty feet forward of us, looking over toward the pier. I could hear a little noise down that way, and I looked past him and saw jeeps. They'd come for the prisoners.

I looked back toward the companionway and saw Tony come up and signal for us to come on. I motioned for Bob to go, and he started off at a fast walk after he got through the hatch. He had to maneuver the guy's body out the hatch and along the deck so his head or feet didn't hit a bulkhead. When he went, I followed, backing along the deck and keeping watch on the sentry.

Tony was on the landing of the companionway when we got to it, and he motioned us to come on down. It was just in time, too, because the sentry I was watching started back. He wavered, taking a step or two toward us but looking back toward the pier, and stopped for a second. Just as I ducked below the level of the deck he turned and came back toward us.

I almost bumped into Bob. He'd stopped on the landing. Tony was coming up from the foot of the companionway and motioning us back up. Of course, we couldn't go up, because the sentry up there was heading toward us. I squeezed past Bob and Tony put his lips to my ear.

"Sentry coming!" he whispered, pointing toward the foot of the companionway.

I jerked a thumb over my shoulder and whispered, "Up there, too!" with my lips only half an inch from his ear.

I could hear the footfalls getting closer on the deck below, but I couldn't hear the sentry on the deck above yet. We crouched there, as much in the shadows as we could get, and waited while they approached us from above and below. I hoped neither of them would decide to change decks. They had us nicely sandwiched between them.

There was just enough of a gap in their timing that if the guy below spotted us, we might be able to make it over the rail on the upper deck before the sentry up there could shoot. If the guy below went by, but the one above spotted us, we could go over the rail on the lower deck, because the sentry down there would have his back turned. I whispered instructions to Tony and Bob for both circumstances. Then we waited.

The sentry on the lower deck wandered on by at a casual, strolling pace. The one above came on at a brisker, more purposeful walk. I hurried the first guy with my thoughts, without success. "Get out of here," I thought. "Get on down the deck so we can get off this landing before the other guy gets to the companionway.'' He continued to stroll along, but the guy on the deck above turned around when he got almost to the companionway, and hurried back forward to watch the scene on the pier.

When the guy on the lower deck had strolled far enough forward, Tony went down and watched him from the foot of the companionway, and Bob went on aft with the body. I followed him. Tony came after us, backing up and watching the sentry. Quinn joined us when we went down the companionway to the main deck.

When we got back to the fantail, the PBR crew had the engines running, and they were fussing with them. They'd rev them up and let them slow back down, and they'd pop and backfire. The sentry stationed on the fantail would stay on his post for a few minutes, staring out toward the river, then go over to see what was happening on the pier. When he was gone, we slipped up onto the fantail and hid behind a cargo hatch cover. He was chewing tobacco, and he would walk over to the rail occasionally and spit. I was a little bit afraid that one of those times he might see Phil Casburn peering over the edge of the dock, or the guys in the water, but I don't think he really looked. I think he was daydreaming. After we got into position behind the hatch cover, I was just waiting for the opportunity to throw the body over the side and go over with it. I wanted to time it so that the roar of the PBR's engines would drown out the splash. But the sentry started back to the starboard side again.

Casburn was crouched in the shadow of a winch and was nearer the sentry than we were. I signaled him with a thumb drawn across my neck to silence the sentry if he came any nearer. Just then, however, the starboard-side sentry came back onto the fantail, and that first guy turned and gave him a little nod.

"Did they ever get those damn slopes quiet?" he called over to the other guy.

"Yeah. They took them off in a couple of jeeps. If it had been me I would have just killed the sons of bitches."

"What are they doing now?"

"Fucking around with their engines."

"Damned river rats. They fuck around more than anybody I've ever seen. Running up and down the damned river all the time like a bunch of kids on a lake."

"Yeah. Hey, can you spare a chew? I'm all out."

"Sure, I got a fresh plug."

The other guy came across the deck then, to bite off a chew.

"Well, thanks. I reckon I'd better get back forward before they come looking for me." He started back toward the port side.

"Catch you later," the first guy said. He went on over to the starboard rail and spit a couple of times, then decided he'd been over on our side too long and walked over to port.

The PBR was revving up its engine about then, and I signaled Bob to go. He carried the dude over to the rail at damned near the center of the fantail and just heaved him over. I ran over there to help but he didn't give me a chance. I thought we'd hold him over away from the hull and drop him feet first. Bob stuck his feet over the rail and dumped him like he was a sack of fertilizer. At least, he pushed him a little out from the hull, or he would've hit the rudder on the way down.

The body hadn't even hit the water before Tony and Casburn were over the rail and on their way down. Bob and I went over together, and Quinn came right behind us. As I went over I saw that the PBR was pulling away from the dock and backing out into the river. They had stalled as long as they thought they could. I saw Fitchew kick off from the piling he was on and go into the water. Then I hit.

Thompson and Magoun got to the guy right away. They dived after him and brought him to the surface in the shadow of the hull. Then they ripped the tape off his mouth and stuck the mouthpiece in. They jammed the nose pincher over his nose, stuck their own mouthpieces in, and went under with him. I looked quickly up at the rail. There was no one looking down, so the noise of the PBR had been sufficient to cover the splashes as we hit. We'd gotten off just in time.

We swam underwater to the shadows under the pier. Fitchew was waiting for us there with our tanks and gear. We quickly slipped them on and dived.

It took us about fifteen minutes to get out to the pickup site because we had to tow the guy. We took turns towing him, one on each side. That way we moved a little faster. We didn't stay submerged all the way. We broke surface out where the light was really dim and towed the guy on his back with his face above the water, just in case water was getting in around his mouthpiece or through the nose pincher.

The PBR came slowly down the river and picked us up. It was a slow pickup because we couldn't hold the guy's dead weight and roll into the raft for a fast pickup. Two of us grabbed the raft and handed him to two sailors who were waiting there. They dragged him on board and then handed him up to two more guys in the PBR. Then the rest of us caught on to the raft and rolled aboard.

We untaped the guy, except for his hands and eyes. He was still out of it.

"How about this shit, guys!" Fitchew said. "We did it. We fuckin' did it."

"You didn't do it, asshole," Bob told him. "You just watched."

"We all did it, Bob," I told him. "We all had a part in it. Right or wrong."

The boat captain had some brandy, and we passed the bottle around and tried to relax. Our nerves were still taut. I sat down by the rail and lit a Marlboro in cupped hands—something I wouldn't do on patrol, because the glow might be seen by VC on shore, but I needed to relieve some of the tension. Just how tense I had been I hadn't realized: I could hardly light the cigarette I had the shakes so bad.

About twenty miles downriver we rendezvoused with another boat and handed the subject over to them. They headed back upriver toward Saigon. No one ever said shit about it.

We messed around downriver until about dawn, and then headed back up to Saigon. The *Eldorado* was getting steam up and getting ready to sail. We pulled into the diver's dock and turned in our diving gear just like it was a normal mission. Then they took us back up to the barracks. The other guys in the barracks still looked at us a little uncertainly, and the dude with the high-pitched voice was still pissed at us for laughing at him. We felt like we had guilt written all over our faces, but no one acted any different toward us.

Except the brass. They sure as hell didn't come around and thank us for the great job we did, getting him off without anybody the wiser and without anyone getting hurt. They just got us out of town, that same afternoon.

I lay down in the barracks and tried to sleep, but it wasn't easy. I kept wondering if we'd done the right thing. In my mind I went through every argument I could think of to justify it. I hadn't fucked up. I'd made sound decisions and nobody had gotten hurt. But some doubt remained. Maybe I'd fucked up in a different way. Maybe I should never have accepted the mission at all. I could only hope that the guy we snatched wasn't innocent. Or even if he wasn't, that they'd treat him as fairly as any other American. I didn't want another American life on my conscience.

They flew us out to Cam Ranh late that afternoon. Normally we would have sailed on the *Eldorado*, but they didn't want us near the ship when the officer was discovered to be missing. They put us up in a barracks ship at Cam Ranh.

By the end of the week I'd developed an infection in my injured ear, probably from swimming in filthy water, the docs said. "What other kind is there in 'Nam?" I asked. The infection got pretty bad before they got it under control, and I got a fever and a cough from it. They decided it would probably recur if I stayed in 'Nam, and that was the end of my second tour.

Bob came back at the end of his tour, went back to 'Nam for a third, and survived that one. Tony died in a booby trap, and Fitchew and Quinn disappeared on an underwater insertion. Casburn made it back to his girl in Texas, Magoun and Thompson to Norfolk.

I served out the rest of my tour in San Diego. I divorced my wife as soon as I got back, and out of spite she threw out all my photos of 'Nam and even the medals I got over there. At the time, I didn't give a shit.

The medals were being handed out like candy at a children's party, and I didn't need any pictures of that damned place. I carried enough pictures in my mind.

I had a few problems adjusting to the States, just as I'd had before. I'd only postponed the adjustment. It wasn't any easier. In training they break your personality down and rebuild it the way they want it to be. Then the war goes to work on what they've built, and starts tearing that down. After the war, you have to pick up the pieces yourself and start over. It takes a long time.

It was ten years before I heard anything more about the Army colonel. There was no court-martial and no publicity. But one night I was watching TV, and they had a story on about the MIAs, about how their families were trying to get the government to do more about getting information on them, or finding their bodies. Showed some pictures of them. They had a woman on there crying her head off, and her kids were blubbering—you know how reporters like to stick their camera right up in somebody's face at a time like that. Then they showed a picture of her husband, an Army officer. They'll never find out about him, not from the government. And they don't want to know, neither. I'm sure as hell sorry I know.

Like I said, picking up the pieces takes a long time. A very long time.